OASIS JOURNAL 2009

Stories

Poems

Essays

by New & Emerging Writers Over Fifty

Edited by Leila Joiner

Copyright © 2009 by Leila Joiner

All rights reserved. No part of this book may be reproduced or transmitted in any form or by any means, electronic or mechanical, including photocopying, recording, or by any information storage and retrieval system, without permission in writing from the publisher.

Published in the United States of America by:

Imago Press
3710 East Edison
Tucson AZ 85716

www.imagobooks.com

Names, characters, places, and incidents, unless otherwise specifically noted, are either the product of the author's imagination or are used fictitiously.

Cover Design and Book Design by Leila Joiner
Cover Photograph: Open for Business © Gina Smith

ISBN 978-1-935437-08-6
ISBN 1-935437-08-9

Printed in the United States of America on Acid-Free Paper

In fondest memory of

Jane Boruszewski
November 18, 1926 – August 1, 2009

who never stopped writing,

and never stopped sharing the story of her life,

so that we might all learn something from it.

a friend who urged me to send in my stories

MARY R DURFEE
449 KINSLEY ST
SHERRILL NY 13461-1349

ACKNOWLEDGMENTS

I want to thank the OASIS Institute, all the judges who have generously volunteered their time to select our contest winners and comment on the work of our authors, and all the writers over fifty who continue to contribute their work to *OASIS Journal* every year.

May we all have many successful years ahead of us.

LIST OF ILLUSTRATIONS

"Visons and Volcanos," photograph by Pum Rote, p. 20

"Bees," photograph by Helga Kollar, p. 44

"Prince," photograph courtesy of Ginger Galloway, p. 52

"Poonam and Her Father," photograph by Marge Smith, p. 84

"Poonam and Her Family," photograph by Marge Smith, p. 84

"Poonam and Her Village," photograph by Marge Smith, p. 88

"Children on Beach," photograph by Celia Glasgow, p. 106

"Houdini," photograph courtesy of Henriette Goldsmith, p. 114

"African Woman," photograph by Emil, p. 134

"King of the Roost," drawing by Mel McLain, p. 230

"Fortuneteller," photograph by Pete Saloutos, p. 256

"Rickinghall Village," photograph courtesy of Margaret Francis, p. 276

CONTENTS

EDITOR'S PREFACE	15
WINNER: BEST FICTION CONTEST VISIONS AND VOLCANOS *Elisa Drachenberg*	21
1ST RUNNER-UP: BEST POETRY CONTEST THE GIFT OF PEDERNAL MOUNTAIN *David Ray*	36
EXTRAORDINARY *Tillie Webb*	37
DARK FLOW *Will Inman*	39
WINNER: BEST POETRY CONTEST PIETA OF ABRUZZI *Anita Curran Guenin*	40
LETTER FOUND IN A CAVE *Seretta Martin*	41
WITCH CREEK (BEYOND THE FIRE) *Marilyn L. Kish Mason*	42
BEES IN MY BONNET *Helga Kollar*	45

LATE AUTUMN, EARLY WINTER *Joan T. Doran*	50
PRINCE OF THE NIGHT *Ginger Galloway*	51
WHITE EXULTATION *Helen Jones-Shepherd*	53
MOTHER'S ANGELS *Eleanor Little*	54
2ND RUNNER-UP: BEST NON-FICTION CONTEST PICTURES *Mary H. Ber*	55
LITTLE GIRLS *Anne McKenrick*	58
MEMORIA *Annabelle Deutscher*	60
1st RUNNER-UP: BEST NON-FICTION CONTEST THE SECRET VISIT *Annabelle Deutscher*	61
MENDING *Una Nichols Hynum*	66
BE WARY OF WHO SAYS WHAT REGARDING GENEALOGY *Kathleen Elliott Gilroy*	67
WINNER: BEST NON-FICTION CONTEST EVERYTHING MUST GO *Carole Ann Moleti*	71
AUTUMN MEDITATIONS *James L. Foy*	82
UNDER THE FULL MOON *Mary R. Durfee*	85
UNCLE CHARLIE AND ME *Ruth Weiss Hohberg*	89

YOU SHOULD HAVE *Kathleen A. O'Brien*	93
UNTIDY CACTUS *Mardy Stotsky*	94
HARVESTING THE CACTUS APPLE *Zola Stoltz*	95
IN HONOR OF MY MOTHER *Gloria Salas-Jennings*	99
MARKET PRICES *Helen Benson*	100
GRANDMOTHER IN A GRAY FLANNEL SUIT *Joanna Wanderman*	101
BACK PORCH CALLERS *Anna Mae Loebig*	103
PILES OF PLENTY, STACKS OF STUFF *Celia Glasgow*	104
CLUTTER: TOO MANY GOOD THINGS *Celia Glasgow*	105
IT RAINS *Irma Sheppard*	107
EXUBERANCE *Nancy Sandweiss*	108
HIS NAME SHOULD HAVE BEEN HOUDINI *Henriette Goldsmith*	109
BEACH TREASURE *Mardy Stotsky*	115
JUVENILE GOSHAWK *Mimi Moriarty*	116
1st RUNNER-UP: BEST FICTION CONTEST THE ROAD KILL CHRONICLE *Marymarc Armstrong*	117

THE SCARAB BEETLE'S PERSONA 128
    Ruth Moon Kempher

LEE ROY 129
    Jan Rider Newman

OH, THE LONGING 133
    Annette Stovall

LETTER TO RITA 135
    Kathryn Romey

LEAVING 136
    Margaret Susan McKerrow

2ND RUNNER-UP: BEST FICTION CONTEST 137
ALL THE WAY TO HEAVEN
    Phylis Warady

ONE NIGHT AND A QUARTER OF TOMORROW 139
    Susan Cummins Miller

A SONG FOR BILL 140
    Joanne Ellis

THE MAN WHO WOULD BE ME 142
    Tony Zurlo

GETTING OLDER 143
    Kay Lesh

MIDDAY'S SUNSET 146
    Lena V. Roach

THE PARTING 148
    Lolene McFall

THE UNGUARDED TRUTH 149
    Tina Weaver

THE OLD NUNS 152
    Anne Whitlock

OLD BROTHERS-IN-LAW VISIT 154
AFTER THEIR WIVES' DEATHS
   Seretta Martin

WHEN YOU BECOME A WIDOW 155
   Anita L. Clay

HE DIED. NOW WHAT? 159
   Vera Martignetti

A BEDTIME PRAYER 165
   Ron L. Porter

2ND RUNNER-UP: BEST POETRY CONTEST 167
   BEFORE THE KISS
   Steve Snyder

JANE PELCZYNSKI'S WEDDING GIFT 168
   Evelyn Buretta

TRUST IN MAGIC 170
   Lolene McFall

SPRING BREAK 171
   Constance Richardson

SEXED ON A KONA BALCONY 178
   Ellaraine Lockie

AFFAIR 179
   Betty Birkemark

THE PARTY 180
   Jan Rider Newman

SHIPS THAT PASS… 181
   Frank Frost

TWENTY NINE TIMES 184
   Janet Kreitz

THE BOX IN THE ATTIC 185
   Jack Campbell

NOMEN DUBIUM *Andrew J. Hogan*	191
DURING THE WAR: MEMORIES OF LIVES THROUGH FOOD *Kathy Hayduke*	204
MY FAVORITE GAME *Jane Boruszewski*	207
THE FINAL FLOURISH *Deni Compere*	216
OH JOY! *Esther Brudo*	218
SONG AND DANCE *Neal Wilgus*	220
DELETED SCENES *David Ray*	222
ATTITUDE ADJUSTMENT *Sherrie Valitus*	223
TOILET TALK *Nancy Sandweiss*	228
KING OF THE ROOST *Mel McLain*	229
RAFTING ON THE GOOD SHIP MUCKAWAY *Eleanor Whitney Nelson*	231
STARTLING TRUTH *Harleen Gross*	238
THERE WAS A CROOKED MAN *Judy Ray*	241
DANGER ON GROVE STREET *Lucille Gang Shulklapper*	245
THE IMPERFECT CHARACTER *Nik Grant*	247

THE MURAL *Natalie Gottlieb*	250
HIDING FROM THE ENEMY *Mike Ramsey*	251
SAFE *Natalie Gottlieb*	255
A SPECIAL HALLOWEEN *Manuel Torrez, Jr.*	257
THE BIRTHDAY SHOES *Jackie Grant*	268
THE SHOES *Kathy Hayduke*	271
REMINISCENCES OF AN ENGLISH VILLAGE GIRL *Margaret Francis*	273
A GRANDMOTHER'S TALE *Adrienne Rogers*	277
THE CARDINAL *Sarah Wellen*	280
DADDY-O: A FATHER'S MEMOIR *Michael Thal*	281
THE DAY AFTER MY FATHER DIED, I SAW ELVIS AT THE 7-ELEVEN *Sally Carper*	287
DEAR MR. COSBY *Frank Bolek*	289
A UNIVERSE OF STORIES *Albert J. Stumph*	291
MY IMAGINATION TAKES NO HOLIDAYS *Manuel Torrez, Jr.*	294
CHAINSAWS AND CHINESE FOOD *John Barbee*	295

THE COLMAN TOUCH *Richard O'Donnell*	297
ONLY IN WASHINGTON *Richard Lampl*	309
THE SIDEWALKS OF CEDAR FALLS *Bill Alewyn*	317
ALL MY COURTHOUSES HAVE BURNED *Anita Curran Guenin*	328
REBUILDING THE DIVIDED HOUSE *Joan T. Doran*	329
CONTRIBUTORS' NOTES	331
ORDER INFORMATION	351

Maryrose Durfee
93 yrs.

EDITOR'S PREFACE

In this eighth annual edition of OASIS Journal, I am pleased to present the work of 87 writers over fifty, at least one of whom is in her 90's and still writing wonderful stories. No special theme is ever assigned to any edition of OASIS Journal, but I always try to link the poems and stories in some way when I put the book together. This year, a number of pieces seemed to focus on chaos in nature—or what we humans think of as chaos, as we would prefer to think we have some control over our lives. So I chose this as a starting point, eventually ending up in, of all places, Washington, D. C., where we would certainly hope to see some kind of order established, but commonly find more chaos. I suppose you could say this whole book is about the struggle to bring order out of chaos, and there were times, I admit, when it felt that way to me.

I'm happy to say that our judges this year were very orderly in presenting their final choices for contest winners, although the poetry and non-fiction judges found so many good entries that they simply had to include here some honorable mentions. So you will want to check out all those mentioned below, not just the winners designated in the Table of Contents.

L. J.

FICTION: Judge, Meg Files, author of *Meridian 144*, a novel; *Home Is the Hunter*, a collection of stories; *Write From Life*, a book about using personal experience and taking risks in writing; *The Love Hunter and Other Poems*; and *Galapagos Triptych*. She edited *Lasting: Poems on Aging*. She was the James Thurber Writer-in-Residence at Ohio State University and was awarded a Bread Loaf fellowship. She teaches creative writing and directs the Pima Writers' Workshop at Pima College, Tucson, Arizona.

WINNER: "Visions and Volcanos" [Elisa Drachenberg]
This story's sure, authoritative writing gives the reader no choice but to accompany Leah, an ill, failed artist, and Jon, her mixed-up husband, on their journey to Costa Rica where they explore their past, their present, and, at last,

their future. The descriptions, the dialogue, and Jon's observations build the story's intensity until, along with the volcano, the tension must erupt. Early, Jon watches the sunlight and shadows on his wife's skin and thinks that "by transforming her into a piece of art, he achieved two things: he removed himself from her misery, and he let the reality no longer matter." At the story's redemptive end, he is still observing her, but now "every new splash kept altering Leah's image, tearing her apart and assembling her anew," and he understands that she is his human love.

First Runner-up: "The Road Kill Chronicle" [Marymarc Armstrong]
In this surprising, touching, risky story, a mother helps her daughters deal with their losses in a rather shocking way — by telling the life and death stories of roadkill and burying the carcasses. The wonderful (and gruesome) details and the effectively implied metaphors (the marriage like the roadkill "in the process of decomposition, generally starting out as distorted but recognizable creatures" until "they dissolved in layers to become shadows a little darker than the asphalt or grass") bring the characters vividly to life.

Second Runner-up: "All the Way to Heaven" [Phylis Warady]
In this compact story, where every word counts, the child of a stern preacher tries to understand the mystery of death. The point of view walks a pitch-perfect line between the little girl's perceptions and the writer's ability to give voice to what the child can't. The rich subtext — the emotions and the father/daughter relationship — makes the story especially poignant.

Non-fiction: Judge, Nancy Wall, author of *The Swiftness of Crows: Poems of Two Continents*, who has taught writing, literature, and theater at the University of Arizona and Pima Community College.

Choosing the top three essays was an incredibly difficult task. After an initial readthrough, I had put aside at least fifteen I felt deserved consideration and a second reading. I've read most of those three times, some four.

I have to say that there were many other wonderful essays, and I'd like to mention just a few (in random order) that made my choices so difficult: "Getting Older" [Kay Lesh]; "Rafting on the Good Ship Muckaway" [Eleanor Whitney Nelson]; "Grandmother in a Gray Flannel Suit" [Joanna Wanderman]; Uncle Charlie and Me" [Ruth Weiss Hohberg]; "Lee Roy" [Jan Rider Newman]. And more.

Winner: "Everything Must Go" [Carole Ann Moleti]
This essay, through excellent use of detail, paints a remarkable picture of character, place, and time. The reader feels welcomed into a large Italian family much as the author was—even to smelling the meatballs cooking in the

kitchen—and is thus drawn into the emotional impact of loss and the relief of finally being able to let go.

First Runner-up: "The Secret Visit" [Annabelle Deutscher]
Skillfully evokes a child's mystifying experience through the lens of her adult self. The images are powerful, the details vivid, but softened by distance and an unmistakeable aura of the old South.

Second Runner-up: "Pictures" [Mary H. Ber]
Employs a few brief episodes to reveal a complex daughter-mother relationship near the end of the mother's life. The moments we see are powerful, stark, and emotionally charged.

Poetry: Judge, Barrie Ryan, author of *Creek Ceremony*, who has taught writing and (she hopes) love of literature at the University of Arizona, Pima Community College, and Green Fields School.

What a joy it's been to read these poems, so many of them excellent.

Winner: "Pieta of Abruzzi" [Anita Curran Guenin]
This poem has a beautiful and simply developed narrative with excellent word choice and stanza breaks. Its fine concluding stanza lifts the particular story into the larger frame of contemporary worldwide earthquakes and the uncertainty of our "node" on the dangerous, shifting plates of the earth. The title also contributes to the universality, as well as to the depth of feeling for suffering victims.

First Runner-up: "The Gift of Pedernal Mountain" [David Ray]
This poem is also simply and beautifully presented, leading to a surprise and fresh turn on an old derogative colloquial expression. The poem has a light tone, but is deeply thought-provoking.

Second Runner-up: "Before the Kiss" [Steve Snyder]
What a delightful moment to catch! Interesting and unusual imagery, leading us to that wonderful ending.

Special Mention: Also fine and memorable poems

"Memoria" [Annabelle Deutscher]
"Juvenile Goshawk" [Mimi Moriarty]
"The Scarab Beetle's Persona" [Ruth Moon Kempher]
"Late Autumn, Early Winter" [Joan T. Doran]
"A Song for Bill" [Joanne Ellis]

OASIS JOURNAL
2009

Stories

Poems

Essays

Winner: Best Fiction Contest

Visions and Volcanos

Elisa Drachenberg

After her haircut she looked even more vulnerable, and though he was not the kind of man who would have said, "I told you so," he would at least have liked to tell her she looked neither "cute" nor "sassy," regardless of what the women in her read-a-book-a-month group claimed. But that, too, was out of the question. With everything she was going through, she needed more than his support; she needed white lies and colorful surroundings.

"How about Mount Arenal?" he asked, holding up the paper's travel section. "They rave about the fire-spitting volcano."

She did not seem to understand, which happened so often lately that he had learned to rephrase his sentences. "Just look at this." He pointed to a picture of horses grazing on a lush green meadow below a dramatic-looking mountain. The photo could have been taken in Switzerland had it not been for the dark clouds emerging from the mountain's top. "Doesn't this look absolutely fabulous?"

Only half a year ago, she would have tossed her hair—her stunning fire-ant-red curls—and laughed at his "absolutely fabulous," an expression he had picked up from one of her book club friends. Today, the corners of her mouth stayed in place. He could tell she was still uncertain about what he had in mind.

"Horseback riding?" she ventured, unable to see through his flimsy Mount Arenal excuse. This woman whose mind so often had been too quick for his slower-working brain now needed explanations for the most basic things.

He smiled, immediately knowing his smile would be perceived as condescending, which, in a way, it was. He had always hated to be on the receiving end of that kind of smile. For almost two decades, she had been the alert one, the one quick to grasp every detail long before he figured out the gist of things. Now the roles were reversed, even though he realized he was merely the one-eyed king leading the blind. The temporarily blind, at that. To compensate for the effect his smile had on her, he put his hand on her shoulder and was not surprised when she shrugged it off. She might be slower now, but her instincts had not failed her. She could still detect his insincerities long before he would admit them to himself. Her head slightly tilted, she looked up at him, waiting, eyes clouding.

"I think we should get away. A trip would do us good…long walks, relax at a lake…a welcome change." He had clearly said "we" and "us," but she picked up on "change."

"I'm sorry you feel burdened by this…by whatever is happening to me." She walked away from him toward the stairs that led to the bedroom. "I'll do some sketches, and then I'll probably take a nap."

By the time she had reached the top of the landing, he heard her wheeze and, without a second thought, he raced up the ten steps. With his arms clasped around her bony shoulders, he murmured into her hair, "They have a spa in this hotel near Mount Arenal. Just imagine how much you would like that, lazing in water heated by a volcano." This time, she could not accuse him of ulterior motives. She was well aware that "thermal baths" were not his kind of fun. When he felt her body relax against his, he believed that to mean they would be going.

"All right. I'll call Sam," she promised, as if understanding his earlier hint now.

He did not dare sigh, afraid she would pick up on his relief. He needed her to go. He needed her to do something more than lie in bed and work on sketches and pastels that were always abandoned before they were finished, dismissed as "another piece of garbage." He was not the man who could convince her otherwise. And, precisely because he knew his limitations, knew he could not coax her into believing that her paintings were still good, he needed her to see Sam. He was well aware how much this wish revealed the degree of his helplessness. His feelings about her former psychiatrist had always been ambivalent, at best. This, however, was not the time for wounded egos. The past was the past, and whatever had happened then, he had to admit: Sam had been able to help her before.

Dr. Sam Green, the expatriate, who had somehow struck it rich in Costa Rica, no longer practiced direct soul-saving á la Freud. Now, in the Artists'

Colony he had created, he cheered the Muses and their healing powers. Perhaps, in that colony, her self-confidence would return. Perhaps there she could create what she envisioned. And, even more important, perhaps she would get well. He dared think no further.

But she broke her promise. She did not call Sam. Spring came and summer lingered. He pasted the picture of Mount Arenal on the refrigerator and never mentioned the volcano again. Then, in September, Sam called them out of the blue, his voice anxious.

"A composer canceled on me; suddenly he's afraid of flying. Sometimes I wonder why I bother with all those prima donnas. Anyway, that leaves the new bungalow up on the hill available for next month. It's large enough for both of you. Leah could paint, and you, Jon...well, I guess you could take pictures of birds or butterflies or something." Sam laughed.

Sam's complete dismissal of his photography had always stung him, but now he chose to ignore those remarks. He listened to Sam's latest accomplishments: five new artist studios built on the hill, classical concerts every Sunday at the main residence, an extension of the library.

"It would do us all good to see each other again," Sam shouted with rising eagerness. "And," he paused, as if wanting to take the urgency out of his voice, "of course, you'll get my bargain rate. It would be a damn waste to let the bungalow stay vacant."

Her hair was falling out even more now. One Sunday, he found her weeping silently in the bathroom, staring at something resembling a hairy, copper-red rodent in her palm.

"It's getting much thinner, too," she whispered, eyes wide.

"It'll grow back," he said.

"How do you know?"

He thought for a moment, watching her in the mirror, afraid to look at her directly. "I don't. But it can't go on like this, can it? You have to get better, right?"

She stared at him as if he had insulted her and told him to spare her his crystal-ball predictions. She needed facts, not meaningless, if well-intended, prophecies. Only when she noticed how his shoulders slumped forward to steady himself against her verbal blows did she stop.

"Do you still love me?" Her voice was suddenly small and uncertain.

Yes, he still loved her. Even though she was changing into this elusive creature whose irritation was always aimed at him, whose body was rapidly becoming skin and bones, and whose vibrancy was almost gone. And, yes, her hair, her once dramatic red curls with which he had fallen in love long before she made him fall in love with the rest of her, presently drooped lifeless around her face. But he loved her now for other reasons, some of which he had come to realize. If before he had been enamored of her looks and her independent spirit, he had slowly come to love her for what she saw in him and for what he had become because of her. He would have been embarrassed to admit how much she had shaped him by kicking his ass, but he was not ashamed to admit how much he needed her.

She prepared for the trip by desperately forcing herself to walk up and down the thirty-seven steps of their house to make her muscles grow stronger. But, instead, she was getting weaker.

"The nurse called," she said, coming up the stairs for the third time, huffing and puffing like an old woman. "Dr. Wharton wants me to get some blood work done before we leave." She raised her head to look up at him while taking the next step. "I guess he's finally realizing that I *am* sick, which I tried to tell him months ago, but no, he thought *tranquilizers* would do the trick." Emphasizing her words seemed to consume the rest of her energy. But she was descending the stairs now and, with her breathing becoming less difficult, her anger deepened. "Damn quack. If he had said…if he had dared to imply that my symptoms…that it was all between my ears, I would have ripped his head off. I would have—" She coughed, her voice more hoarse than usual. He saw her grab the wrought iron railing to pull herself up. Her entire body was shaking. A vein in her throat pulsed with dangerous speed.

He had never allowed himself to see her like this. Not really. Up to this very moment, he had clung to a vision formed when they first met. Over the years, and in sporadic flashes, he had come to realize that this image of her needed adjustments, that she was not nearly as perfect as he led himself to believe, but somehow, and for reasons not clear to him, he went on imposing his imagination on reality. Now he saw her labor toward him and made an effort to look away, to no avail.

Her crimson face was covered with fine beads of sweat. Her entire body glistened as if it had been oiled. Despite the fact that she was only wearing panties—a habit she had developed that summer—she was complaining about the heat. She, who had always felt cold, suddenly seemed to inhabit a sauna. He noticed the wrinkles on her neck, where before curls had draped her shoulders. The close-cropped hair that now hugged her tiny head like an orange bathing cap further enhanced the redness of her face, forming a stark contrast to her bony body's whiteness. A matchstick, a walking matchstick.

Instead of further scrutinizing her stilted, almost mechanical movements, he forced himself to focus on the way the railing cast its slanting shadows over her skin, and then, when the sunlight caught in the crystal chandelier and projected specks of rainbow on her shoulder, he watched in fascination how those reflections danced around the shadowy lines. And thus, by transforming her into a piece of art, he achieved two things: he removed himself from her misery, and he let the reality no longer matter.

In what would turn out to be the wettest October in a century, they arrived at Juan Santamaria, San José's quaint airport. It took a moment to adjust their eyes to the sudden greenness that stood in stark contrast to the parched Arizona earth they had left behind. Shouting taxi drivers rushed toward them to claim their suitcases, but Leah gesticulated with shaky hands and told them something in Spanish, of which Jon only understood "nuestro amigo." And, at that moment, the man she had called their friend slid his long legs out of a surprisingly old Jeep, arranged his crotch with practiced hands, and flashed them his broadest smile.

"How was your flight?" Sam asked, his large hands picking Leah up by the waist. If he noticed she had lost more than twenty pounds since he'd last seen her, he did not say a word.

She hung like a fragile toy, suspended two feet above the ground. Jon watched for the briefest of moments—as Sam kissed her on the mouth with wet, full lips that smeared her lipstick—before he looked away, rolled the suitcases toward the back door of the beat-up Jeep, shook hands with the bleached-blond driver who had jumped out in tasseled loafers, observed him hoist the luggage into the trunk with strong, bronzed arms, admired his well-built body, fought a tidal wave of age that approached and washed over him while maintaining to himself that he was still a man in the prime of his life, feeling old nevertheless, turned down a stick of gum the blond kid offered him…and, still, Sam was holding Leah up in the air.

Sam's driver seemed oblivious to the bizarre couple standing close enough to throw their shadows over him: the man, tall and sturdy with thick, white hair that glistened like diamonds in the morning sun, and the balding redhead whose thin arms grasped his shirt like a sick hummingbird. Now, the blond driver introduced himself to Jon, warned him that it would be raining by one o'clock, felt equally competent to predict a good coffee harvest—based on his three-month experience as a coffee-bean picker before meeting Sam—confessed to simply *love* Costa Rica, *love* Ciudad Colón, *love* the Artists' Colony, especially his mentor, who helped him write poetry.

"I am *so* blessed. Sam…I mean, Dr. Green…has *saved my life*. It's a *dream come true.*"

Jon could not help smiling and noticed that his earlier feelings of inferiority, caused by his constant need to compare himself to younger, better-looking men, were rapidly making room for schadenfreude. Po-étry? How had Sam wound up with this dunce? You could say a lot of things about Sam, but you could not call him stupid. Not that his training as a psychoanalyst had allowed him to make fewer or lesser mistakes than his patients; Sam had made some truly foolish choices. But, despite these choices, Jon had to admit that Sam was unusually brilliant, well read and well informed. Actually, Sam's reason for establishing the Artists' Colony a few years ago sounded plausible: he simply craved "mental stimulation and vigorous intellectual intercourse."

Remembering those words now, Jon felt the uncontrollable grin broaden on his face and tried to direct it away from the blond kid. Strike "mental," strike "intellectual," he thought, suddenly feeling smug.

"*Pura vida!*" someone shouted. A taxi driver was raising his hands in protest as one of his colleagues tried to cut in front of the line.

"You speak Spanish?" the kid asked, apparently mistaking Jon's grin for a sign of amusement.

Jon shook his head. "I don't, but Leah's fluent."

Suddenly, as if the mention of her name had broken a spell, they both turned their heads and saw Sam, just then towering over Leah, trying hard to muss her unmussably short hair with his large hands.

"Whom are you calling a queer, Pixie?" Jon heard him ask. Leah reacted as if to an old inside joke. Jon enjoyed his wife's sudden cheerfulness and the ease of her smiles, but could not help feeling left out. At precisely that moment, Leah turned her head and saw him watching her. She looked happy, until she noticed the blond hunk.

VISIONS AND VOLCANOS

∽

The hunk guided Sam's old Jeep through the morning traffic as if he were a native. He wove the car from one lane to another, sped up and braked, closely watched other drivers, anticipated their moves, and never once honked his horn. Sam sat next to him, looking a bit shabby and much older than two years ago, when he had invited them down to celebrate his seventieth birthday. Then, high-ranking government officials had stopped by for imported drinks. The Minister of Sport and Culture had not only taken the time to highlight Sam's achievements, he'd also revealed to the eighty guests and twenty resident artists how much the community owed to "*el guru gringa.*" The *Tico Times* later raved about the success of the party, mentioning celebrities and their clothes, naming imported wines and foods and, most of all, praising the benevolence and generosity of the host, the refined proprietor of *la colonia de artistas*.

With the extravagance of that birthday party still vivid in his mind, Jon could not help notice the large patches of silver duct tape on the upholstery of the Jeep. "Declining attendance," Sam explained, without being asked. Jon guessed there were other reasons, but Sam never mentioned once that he had lost most of his money to a pyramid scheme that suddenly crumbled. He never mentioned the infamous Lobos brothers or the disastrous effect their ploys had on the existence of his Artists' Colony. Nor did he mention his unique manner of compensating for his financial losses.

If Sam kept mum about his changed economic present and his threatened future, he tried his best to conjure up the past. "For Leah, I would have given it all up," he claimed with a grandiose gesture of his arm that indicated the immensity of this "allness." But, by bringing up his affair with Leah, Sam actually demonstrated the opposite: Sam never gave up anything or anybody. And—this thought disturbed Jon even more—to judge from the youth of Sam's newest acquisition, he not only wanted it all, he apparently got away with having it all.

Bewildered by the array of emotions that suddenly took hold of him, Jon made a conscious effort to restrain his hand from slapping Sam. Twenty years ago—actually, nineteen years and seven months ago, when she was still his patient—Sam had introduced Leah to various other uses of his couch.

"I was flattered that such an erudite and accomplished man chose me," she'd explained. Flattery deafens and blinds. Jon understood. But soon

Leah's unfailingly accurate ear had picked up on discrepancies, and her uncompromising eye spotted Sam's conflicting traits: what Sam gave in therapy, Sam took away in life; the analyst who had vowed to heal souls could not help himself from inflicting harm. One could have full faith in Sam, the shrink, but not trust Sam, the man. Leah, having no delusions about herself or her capabilities, never believed she could change Sam, the quintessential equal-opportunity lover.

Jon glanced at Leah, surprised to find her this silent. She had not said anything since they left the airport. Sam, on the other hand, grew more talkative the closer they got to Ciudad Colón.

"I'm only as old as the men I feel," Sam bragged, adapting an old Groucho Marx joke. Leah showed no sign of having heard Sam's remark. "My Michelangelo here drives like a Tico," Sam said, as if the kid's driving skills were somehow his accomplishment. He rubbed the driver's neck and squeezed his arm. The kid kept his eyes on the road.

"Where is Carlos?" Leah suddenly asked, a question she would have considered tactless, downright rude, a year ago. Her illness had made her blunt, sometimes even cruel, but poor health was not the reason for this question. Jon watched Sam's jaws move in a chewing motion. When he turned around, the wrinkles of his face were frozen into a smile.

"Carlos? Why Carlos is where he always is: home. Taking care of the place." Sam could match Leah's cruelty anytime.

It was no secret that Leah liked Carlos, had always liked Carlos, ever since meeting him at Sam's birthday party two years earlier. Carlos, Costa Rica's first tennis pro with undeniable talent. Carlos, Sam's strapping Adonis. Carlos, Leah's patient model. Soft-spoken, strong-muscled Carlos, the reason why they had never gotten around to visiting any of the sights in Costa Rica. Leah had spent the entire week painting him, fussing about "catching his essence," all the while marveling at the perfection of his profile, the magnetism of his smile, and the soft tint of gold in his eyes.

Jon clearly remembered how much Sam had admired the finished portrait, and how long it had taken him to find the perfect spot in the living room to hang it, where the morning sun would light up Carlos's eyes. But now Leah's open display of sympathy for Carlos seemed to irritate Sam. He patted her knee, as if aiming to annoy her, and switched to his Carolina drawl. "We've gotta fatten you up, honey. When we get home, I'll tell your

Carlos to fix you some grits with lots of butter, sausages, eggs, and fry some of those nice plump tomatoes we now grow on the tennis court."

"He's not *my* Carlos, and you know I don't touch that stuff. Besides, whatever I have can't be fixed with food." Leah peeled Sam's hand off her knee. "Talking about tennis—" she began and stopped. She looked at Jon with her fix-it expression, but he had no idea what she expected of him, what she wanted him to say. Her recent bouts of forgetfulness frightened him. Yet, once again, he ventured into the unknown wilderness, every time surprised anew if he actually guessed her needs correctly.

"I brought my racket," Jon tried.

Leah waved her hand impatiently, indicating that he'd failed to read her mind.

"No more tournaments after he broke his ankle. Then he stopped playing altogether. Carlos's getting chubby," Sam said matter-of-factly.

Instantly, Leah's hand stopped waving and returned to her lap.

"I bought him a massage table. Voila. In-house, home-schooled." Sam reached toward the glove compartment, took some coins from a worn wallet and handed them to the kid. "Let's take the toll-way," he said. "It's faster."

That night at Sam's house, Carlos served marinated calf tongue covered with toasted garlic, with mashed potatoes made especially for Sam, golden fried platanos, and rice and beans. The blond kid never appeared and was not mentioned. They talked and laughed and drank—mostly water to avoid having to drink Carlos's choice: a horribly sweet Costa Rican wine that tasted of artificial apricots and promised genuine headaches. They discussed politics: American, of which Sam seemed to know everything, and Costa Rican, of which Leah and Jon knew nothing. Sam urged them to visit the University for Peace and got into an argument with Carlos. "Of course, they can walk there," he insisted. "It's only five miles." But Carlos kept insisting they needed a taxi. Their argument, seemingly silly, was fought with somber seriousness.

During the entire dinner, the rain that started at noon—just as the blond had predicted—pounded on the corrugated steel roof. But when Carlos began serving coffee, the noise lessened. As suddenly as the rain had begun, it stopped. Large moths drifted inside; banana plants emptied their overflowing leaves in sudden gushes; mist hung lazily over the coffee plantations. Jon and Leah were used to monsoons in Arizona, but they had never experienced this much rain, this forceful, for this long. With each unexpected stroke of thunder, Jon saw Leah shudder, every time startled anew, until finally the thunderstorm disappeared, grumbling and hurling its last bright zigzags up and down the hills.

They decided to have their dessert on the terrace. The *orejas* that Carlos had bought at a little bakery in town were crunchy and sweet. There were papayas, bright orange and luscious, sprinkled with sweet-lemon juice. And the coffee was blacker and stronger and more delicious than anything Jon had ever tasted back home. All seemed well.

The sounds of the village rushed up at them: dogs barked endlessly, women and men laughed or shouted, children's screams mingled with Latin music from a dance hall, the church clock struck every fifteen minutes, reminding them of the rapid passing of time, roosters crowed feverishly as if needing to announce dawn. Yet, somehow, between all that ruckus, they could make out the melancholic hoot of an owl.

"It's not like before. Things are changing." Sam arranged his sandaled feet on the glass table and, without another word, lit a cigar. All four stared silently into the starless night.

When Carlos began clearing off the dishes, Leah helped him carry everything inside. For a while, Jon stayed on the terrace, listening to their chatter, inhaling secondhand smoke, and fighting off mosquitoes. Since the darkness held no promise for him, he eventually went to join them in the kitchen. But off they went toward a room in the back, where Carlos's portrait now hung. Jon was stacking dishes into a brand-new dishwasher when they returned.

"He need disswasser now," Carlos whispered, bending down to place the last cup in the rack, his head almost touching Jon's. And Jon gathered from the sadness in Carlos's eyes that there had to be much more meaning to these words than he could understand. It was not until later that he did.

Leah was ready to leave, but Carlos, like a child trying to stretch out the time before having to go to bed, suddenly wanted to show them his massage table, and even offered to loosen the knots in their shoulders. Leah pleaded exhaustion. "You go," she told Jon.

"Jus' take off your eh-ssirt," Carlos said, when Jon, in an attempt to show his appreciation for something that was absolutely meaningless to him, sat down on the black bench and patted the soft leather. If Carlos had not added, "I no live in house now. Sam no want much massage, no more," Jon would have enjoyed getting the tenseness worked out of his shoulders. But the misery in Carlos's words and the desolation in his look complicated matters, made it impossible to accept. Suddenly, Jon could not bear to subject his skin to Carlos's lonely fingertips.

"I'm too drunk," Jon said, realizing immediately that this lie would only increase Carlos's feelings of rejection, since they both knew Jon had barely touched the wine. "Some other time," he added, getting up from the table. He hoped Carlos would not take him up on this promise.

As Jon reached the doorway, he hesitated. He was tucking in his shirt when he caught a glimpse of Sam, ambling in from the dark terrace. Standing behind Leah, Sam placed his huge hands on her hips. Leah bit her lip, but went on wiping the countertop even faster. Jon saw Sam's lips move and strained to hear.

"And it seemed as though, in a little while, the solution would be found."

Jon heard the pathos in Sam's voice. But before Sam could go on with what sounded to Jon like a quoted line, Leah spun around and interrupted him. "Yes, yes, your favorite passage from Chekhov; I remember it only too well. *Then a new and splendid life will begin.*" She waved the dishtowel at him. "He is not your Pomeranian, Sam. You cannot do this to him."

"He's doing it to himself, and the correct quote is, 'And it seemed as though in a little while the solution would be found, and then a new and splendid life *would* begin.' Not at all certain, is it?"

A series of Leah's angry karate-chops hit his upper arm, catching him by surprise, despite their lack of force.

"Why do you keep him around?"

Sam shrugged. "I guess he loves me, and I guess I still love—"

"You love *him*?" Leah shook her head, incredulous.

"Dear, you are putting words in my mouth. I still love his *cooking*."

Jon wanted to believe that his body had somehow succeeded in blocking the entire conversation from reaching Carlos's ears. Seeking for something appropriate to say, he turned his head. "Thank you again, Carlos, for the delicious meal."

∽

They settled into a routine of work. Sam had lied to them; their "bungalow" turned out to be a one-room cabin, neither big enough nor private enough for both of them. Leah claimed a small corner of their living quarters as her work area, where she installed her easel, arranged her colors, and prepared the drawing paper with layers of rancid-smelling linseed oil. Every morning at dawn, Jon cut up a papaya or pineapple, broke off a small branch from a bush next to their cabin, arranged its white, lavender, and purple flowers around the edge of the plate as talismans for inspiration and reminders of his love, placed everything in the refrigerator to protect her breakfast from the myriad tiny ants that roamed the place, and left. He knew the flowers—the Ticos called them *yesterday-today-and-tomorrow*—would still look fresh when Leah finally woke up.

By then, he had been wandering the village for hours, his mind clear, anticipating nothing, alert and open to everything that presented itself to his camera by mere chance. He took purely ordinary pictures, or so he thought, but somehow they looked strangely decontextualized. He was not a photographer of birds and butterflies; in his uncertain, often bewildered state of mind, he felt safest when he could aim his lens at surreal details or distorting reflections. But no matter how much he tried to incorporate the diffuse light of Costa Rica's rainy season, he failed to achieve the brilliant quality of his Arizona photos. Unlike Leah, though, Jon did not complain.

Leah suffered. She worked her oil sticks over the paper. She mixed colors, scraped shapes, blended, masked, exposed, accented as fast as her trembling hands would work. But when Jon returned around lunchtime, carrying anis-scented rolls or rum-soaked cakes, she pointed angrily to her work. "This doesn't look like anything I meant to create. My fingers have forgotten to translate."

He tried to comfort her with his food, not knowing how to react to the uninspired paintings she turned out day after day. "You worked so hard," he said, and immediately regretted his words, knowing what she would say.

"It doesn't matter how hard I worked. Only *result* counts. Effort going in doesn't mean art comes out. This picture is proof of that." She sighed. "Art doesn't reward us for mere trying."

This trip, Jon understood, was a disaster. If he had hoped Sam's usual poise would rub off on Leah, he had been mistaken; if he had expected her health to show signs of improvement, he had been wrong; and he had truly been foolish to assume that the beauty of the new surroundings would miraculously return her gift.

"I've lost my touch, my craft, and surely my art," she maintained with steadfast rage.

"If that's what you think, why don't you give it a rest?" he said.

"But Jon, if I waver, I am lost."

She hardly slept at night and was on edge during the day. Still, she worked doggedly, trying to coax epiphany to come. It did not. She lamented the time and effort that disappeared into works that she dismissed as "painting by numbers done by a zero." With each new day, more oil-stick shavings covered the tiles; with every jittery step she took, she spread the multitude of colors. Vibrant patches appeared around her easel, spread and grew into organic shapes. "This," she claimed, after Jon had taken photos of the floor, "this accident is far superior to what I produce intentionally." And, in the way he was slow to respond, she found confirmation of her basic worthlessness.

After seeing her struggle like this for more than two weeks, feeling incapable of providing the necessary illusion that would give her hope to go on, Jon suggested they take their trip up north earlier than planned.

"Oh, right, your volcano." She told him she could not figure out why he wanted to see something he already had directly under his nose. Hadn't he noticed how she felt hot and bothered, ready to erupt any moment? But this time Jon insisted. They would go.

It was Carlos who knocked on their door the next afternoon, waving a fax from her doctor in Phoenix. It was Carlos who arranged an appointment with the endocrinologist at the Clinica Biblica in San José. It was Carlos who got the medicine to slow her pulse. And, finally, it was Carlos who made their hotel arrangements and insisted on driving them both up to the resort.

Physically, Leah felt no better when they left for the hot springs, nor was she expected to feel any better until her thyroid gland was removed. Yet her mood had improved dramatically. Now that her sickness had a name, and she understood that something called Graves' disease was responsible for nearly everything that ailed her, she allowed herself to stop fighting. Her heart still raced, but her mind calmed.

"Who would have thought a little gland could wreak such havoc?" Jon shouted from the backseat in an effort to have his voice heard above the rattling air-conditioning. The Jeep was swaying from side to side over a rock-strewn road filled with potholes and deep grooves. Brown dust rose and clung to the car, making any rear view impossible.

"Eh-ssorry?" Carlos swerved around the fallen branches that last night's thunderstorm had flung onto this secret, only Tico-known shortcut.

"Leah's little gland…" Jon shouted and leaned closer to Carlos's ear. "Hey, isn't that a nursery rhyme?" He focused on Leah's profile and began singing, "Leah had a little gland, little gland, little gland—"

"Yup, shaped like a butterfly, stings like a bee." Leah turned around in her front seat and, when her eyes met Jon's, both burst out laughing.

"Eh-ssorry?" Carlos said again, and they kept laughing in a way they had not laughed for almost a year. Afterwards, when their laughter had died down, they struggled to explain their hilarity to Carlos, but failed.

"It's a cultural thing," Jon finally said, and for no good reason he and Leah began laughing again. This time, Carlos joined in. And only because Jon could not bear seeing the lightness of this moment slip away did he raise his thumb and then one finger after another while reading from the hospital report he had pulled from his shirt pocket. In the keyed up voice of a sports announcer whose story gathers momentum, he bellowed, "And here is Leah, this little woman who has it all: anxiety, depression, hair loss, insomnia, irritability, and, of course, muscle weakness, palpitations, shortness of breath, sweating, tremors, not to forget weight loss—"

"You can stop anytime." The moment had passed.

"Marvelous," Leah kept repeating, as she strolled through the lush park of the resort at the foot of the volcano, gripping Carlos's arm, pointing out details as if she needed him to see everything through her eyes. Small signs identified every plant, bush, and tree and indicated the temperature of every different pool or connecting stream; vigilant gardeners removed each withering flower before it could die; uniformed servants picked up discarded straws and empty glasses; maids provided stacks of thick bath towels; benches and lounge chairs and tables nestled in secluded corners to which tireless waiters brought drinks or snacks; steam rose from the hot water pools and wafted like mystic tufts of tulle over vegetation and people alike.

Jon trailed them, overjoyed to see her so animated. Perhaps these images would find their way into her interior landscape and emerge as the epiphanies that, lately, had eluded her. He hoped they would.

"Twenty-twenty vision means nothing, if you ain't got eyes to see," he overheard one fat tourist say to another as they positioned themselves for photos under waterfalls and palm trees. Jon was still wondering if he had just overheard a profound truth or the greatest banality, when Leah called, "How about a picture of us on this bridge?"

"You know I take terrible snapshots," Jon complained, but removed his camera from its case. He waited, lens aimed. Leah's red hair reflected in the smooth surface of the pool like a smoldering sun. And then, for the first time since they'd arrived, the volcano rumbled. It was a forceful sound, a hissing roar that made the earth tremble under their feet. A sound much lower and louder than thunder. A reverberation that forged memories.

"Sam say, isse like eh-steam locomotive." Mount Arenal's growl failed to mask the desolation in Carlos's voice.

Leah heard it, too. She threw her arms around Carlos, but managed to give Jon one of her intent looks that could mean anything. "Forget about Sam!" she said.

"*Pero*—"

"No 'but'," she said, with such passion that Carlos looked away.

Rain clouds formed and gathered with remarkable haste. Mount Arenal belched a series of black fumes into the darkening sky, and then, with another incensed roar, spewed molten rock into the air. When the first heavy raindrops began hitting the mirroring pool, Jon shifted his focus away from the volcanic fireworks. He watched, mesmerized, as Leah's face melted, and her body twisted into uncanny forms. Lines broke, became fluid, shifted and danced around blotches of color. He saw how every new splash kept altering Leah's image, tearing her apart and assembling her anew.

Leah released Carlos from her embrace. With the crook of her arm she wiped the rain from her face, but seemed in no rush. "Let's forget about Sam," she repeated, her voice much softer, yet more insistent than the first time.

"Let's," Jon murmured.

All three turned and ran for cover. Behind them, the mountain overflowed with burning lava, but they did not look back.

First Runner-up: Best Poetry Contest

The Gift of Pedernal Mountain

David Ray

> *Indian Giver:*
> Colloquial term for ritual tradition of giving, then taking back

Near Ghost Ranch, New Mexico,
where Georgia O'Keeffe lived
there is a mountain—or volcano—

called Pedernal, and Georgia said
of it that she had painted that mountain
so many times that God was going

to give it to her, but a young Navajo
said with some indignation
that God could not give it to Georgia

because he had already given it
to the Native Americans for eternity,
and that God is never a White Giver.

That's what this young brave said
as I pondered the wonders of language,
how it is never too late to unfork a tongue.

Extraordinary

Tillie Webb

Margarita was astounded, as she and her companion sat in front of the travel agent, to learn that, with all of her supposed knowledge of geography, she had never heard of the natural wonder they were discussing. Natalie and the agent were waxing eloquent with enthusiasm and planning a side trip to see it. What to do? She did not want to appear an unseasoned traveler, so she nodded in what she hoped looked like knowing assent.

There was not much time to do any research on the area. Before she knew it, she was sitting in the comfortable cabin of the plane that soared above lakes, beaches, what looked like two different isthmuses, and some of the highest mountains she had ever seen. The long trip over, they were happy to be welcomed into the home of a friend. The following day, they hit the streets of the busy metropolis. They noticed the European-style architecture of many of the buildings, attended the ballet and a concert, visited a folk art fair in one of the many parks, and savored the bustling busy-ness of this former national capital.

The next scheduled stop brought even more excitement. In the city famed for its carnival celebration, Margarita noticed with an inward giggle that people seemed to dance, not just walk, on the sidewalks. Though not especially warm in May, the beginning of winter, the beaches were long and beautiful.

Finally, they were winging their way above the lush canopy of the tropical rain forest toward the much awaited side trip. The sweet soggy scent of the jungle flora and all-enveloping humidity at the small landing field was not the only sharp change they experienced. There was the constant noise, a low rumble interspersed with what sounded like rolling waves. It followed them to their rustic lodgings. It continued through the night. It was there when they awoke in the morning.

Their guide appeared and told them, in a mixture of three languages, to prepare to be assaulted by a great deal of water spray. They trudged down an overgrown series of paths until they were at the edge of an amazing cascade of water that went on forever.

Besides being two or three times as wide as Niagara, the cataract on the Iguazu river between Brazil and Argentina tosses some 450,000 cubic feet of water over its banks per second, they were told later. Communication at that point was impossible because of the deafening roar, but the grandeur alone was incredible. One grouping was aptly named the Devils' Throat because of its shape and the peculiar sight of clusters of circling black birds cavorting in the 100-foot cloud of spray. And, yes, by this time, Margarita and Natalie were completely drenched. But the best was yet to come.

They were clambering down some uneven stairs and along a narrow and not too stable catwalk when their guide indicated that they should leave the shadows and continue to the end of a pier-like structure. With the light at this time of day, he explained, a more complete view was to be had there. While holding onto the ropes and looking down, Margarita spied what looked like the polychrome hues of a rainbow begin to form between the slats of the little walkway. As they proceeded tentatively, she noticed the colors grow more extensive and brighter. Almost at the end, the colors began to join together on both sides of the two young women, until the sightseers were completely encircled by iridescent ribbons of light. They stood transfixed.

Later, Margarita confided to Natalie that they would never believe her back home if she told them she had been surrounded by a 360-degree rainbow. Natalie agreed, and added it was probably foolish even to attempt to describe this natural phenomenon, which, for them, was way beyond extraordinary.

DARK FLOW

Will Inman

teeth of the galaxy
chew dark matter until it glows
blue sky spirals green fern
birds alight on stem
darkness grows wings
i go so far and return
birds chase spirals down
who can fly so far so fast
i am here now sooner than when
dark matter cloaks my shoulders
this is as far as I can know
look with me into the light
and weep

Winner: Best Poetry Contest

Pieta of Abruzzi

Anita Curran Guenin

The man, near naked
is lifted from
his cavern of rubble.
Stunned by the light,
he collapses into his
liberator's arms, sobbing.

The saviour holds him,
kisses and kisses his head
like a child
who's fallen, been hurt
by the first
of many surprises.

On each side
men support his arms
on their shoulders,
lift his feet from the dust
while his legs move like fabric.

This man from rubble
reborn into a still
trembling Italian day,
finds his village a sea
of brittle mounds, his
history lost in broken strata.

What will he do now?
What will we do now,
riding our precarious
earthly plates,
surfboarding
on the magma inferno.

Letter Found in a Cave

Seretta Martin

When on a stroll, if you meet a galloping herd of feathered horses with copper mouths snapping open and shut, resist the urge to kneel before them offering sugar. I say this to protect you. I could say nothing, but I care for you more than you want. In the forest at night silver frogs make a blessed bellowing, deep and low, like a draft on open flames. I welcome the hollow sound of gunmetal sky. I add one further thought to you, a question rather. Does the water flow uphill in your country too? (I don't remember reading about it.) I'm writing to you from the end of the last day. Here, the stars burn a hole in the sky; space between them is narrowing beyond. No one knows why. There's little for us to focus on and we have lost sight of the wind. We've lost sight.

Witch Creek
(Beyond the Fire)

Marilyn L. Kish Mason

This dark Sabbath day
A Devil wind hurls fire
that weaves its way
from tree to tree
in a drunken dance
of stoked desire,
reeling toward the sea.

Scudding clouds
play unaware,
like selfish children
refuse to share
their gifts of rain
to quench the thirsty
tendrils of flame.

Nothing would save
the dying brush,
dying trees,
dying dreams of families.
Years of treasures
turned to dust,
pyres of grief
beyond measure.

A survivor stoops,
sifts through cinders,
and tenderly scoops
a ring here
a picture there
scarred reminders
of the sacrificial flare.

A vision burns
where hope abides.
A seed is planted
in soil and inside
the heart of those
who now desire
to seek new life
beyond the fire.

Bees in My Bonnet

Helga Kollar

Advancing carefully to avoid unnecessary noise, I approach the tree. Nothing is stirring. There is no sound, not a trace even of the familiar scent. What is wrong? Is this eerie silence due to the rain last night?

Cautiously, I move closer and peek discreetly into the dark hollow of the oak tree. The nest is totally empty! I stand and stare; this cannot be. To make sure I have observed correctly, I try to get a closer look and…wait… is there a sound, a humming in the air? I strain to hear. Nothing. Only the cheerful chirping of birds in the trees and gentle, rustling leaves.

I had strolled up the trail feeling glad, my heart open, raising my eyes to the tops of the local Santa Monica Mountains. Inhaling the fresh air and delighting in the glistening leaves—everything washed clean by last night's rain—I was happy to be alive. The bark of the oak trees, wet and darkened on one side only, indicated the direction from which the rain had come. The sun was warm on my face, and a gentle breeze tousled my hair. I stood still to admire a covey of quails that noisily skittered across the trail. How their colorful feather dresses sparkled! A small rabbit hurriedly popped into the brush after them.

"Hey, little bunny, I'm not going to eat you," I called after its bouncing fluff-tail.

A wave of warmth rose from the earth where I stood, intermingled with a multitude of fragrances—laurel, sweet anise, sage—and surged upward, as if to meet and greet the sunrays breaking through the clouds. A tiny bird, its plumage embellished with yellow stripes, was hopping from branch to branch, cautiously giving me the eye.

When I reached the oak tree, I was totally unprepared for the sight that awaited me. The uncharacteristic stillness was the first warning. The last time I had visited here was a month ago, and I had been delighted, as usual, by the purposeful bustling about. Humming and buzzing with eager, single-minded intention, the little creatures, hind-legs heavily laden with pollen, had landed on the rim of the cavernous hole and scrabbled into the interior to divest themselves of their sweet burdens. All around the tree, a palpable aura of steady buzzing and the characteristic sweet scent, as if woven into a shimmering, finely spun web, seemed to give notice that bees were seriously at work here.

My love affair with bees began when I was seven years old. In 1943, our worried grandmother hastily gathered my sister and me to flee from the heavy bombings over Berlin for the safety of a rural place near a lake. Neuwedell, as the little town was called, was situated in Pommern (Pomerania, today part of Poland). We got out just in time. Our new apartment, which we had never yet seen, let alone lived in, was leveled by bombs shortly after our departure, just like the previous one from which we had barely managed to escape. In 1943, Onkel Arthur, youngest brother of our paternal grandfather, was teaching school in Neuwedell, where he gently tended his younger sister, Ida, who was ill with breast cancer. His own stomach ailment had kept him home from war duty. He also cared for his small garden of vegetables, fruits, and flowers. Much of his attention and special care were devoted to the inhabitants of the lovely yellow bee house, home to about five or more hives. He would grab my hand and take me along whenever he had bee business, which, fortunately for me, was frequently. I loved being inside this little house. Equipment for bee keeping purposes was suspended in orderly fashion from one wall and included several gardening tools. Smaller items, such as spare honeycomb frames, apiary books filled with bee pictures and bee wisdom, an array of gloves and items for 'smoking' opened hives, were neatly arranged on shelves on the longer wall. With its warmth, sweet scent, and calming hypnotic hum, this little house seemed to me the safest place in the whole world.

Onkel Arthur had taught me to treat bees with respect and love. I can't remember ever having been stung, even though I would sometimes sit outside, right by the hive entrance, to watch their comings and goings or, with eyes closed, enjoy the soothing hum. My uncle was tireless in explaining the mysteries and complexities of the apiary world. His caring and knowledge were infectious, and I couldn't get enough. I was hooked for life. With increasing interest and fascination, I learned what a queen looks like, what a drone—a male bee that has no stinger—feels like when buzzing in my hand,

and what each creature's hive-duties were. With loving care and diligence, Onkel Arthur had coded the entrance to each bee colony with bright primary colors. "To make it easier for bees to find their way home," he explained.

I longed to be a bee, so I, too, could fly home to a beautiful and well-loved community. Watching spellbound through a glass placed on top of the honeycombs, I followed my uncle's finger as he pointed out which bees were announcing to their sisters where they had found good sources of nectar, pollen, and honey. They accurately communicated how much was available, what it looked like, and how far it was from the hive. The dancing was performed by the bee amid a circle of eager observers, and each twisting and wagging of the tail in various directions contained precise data for their orientation, to be acted upon by these intelligent little creatures. The fact that bees dance to transmit important details to other worker bees has long since been scientifically substantiated.

One hot Easter day, during a picnic in the desert area of California's Joshua Tree Park, I demonstrated the bees' communication skills to my children. Knowing how important water is to bees, I set the water-filled lid of a bottle on a boulder. Sure enough, after a short while, a scout bee had found it and was swooping down to have a drink. We watched as she slowly lifted up and, before taking off, spiraled several times above the water source, obviously taking notes of the location to pass along. Sure enough, after approximately five minutes, several bees arrived for a drink.

Many years later, I still remember the loud crackly sound of the whirring, flickering projectors in our biology class, when old black and white movies revealed to us the secret of bee communication. The worker with the information had been marked with a white dot on her back, so that the camera and the viewers, too, could follow her movements without losing her among look-alike sisters. An amazing variety of patterns was displayed by this swivel-dancing. To help the observer better appreciate the complexities of the dance movements, diagrams of simplified line drawings were presented in the film. I still remember how relieved many of us students were when we had not been called upon to reproduce these intricate designs from memory.

In springtime, bees will swarm out of the hive. Onkel Arthur and I would listen to and identify the location of the fine distinct signals emitted by young queens emerging from their hexagonal cells. Many times, we went in search of and brought home swarms that had escaped with their royal matriarch. Wearing only a hat with a net over his face for protection, Onkel Arthur would give a strong, sudden whack to the branch on which they were clustering, catching the bees by surprise. Dislodged, they plopped right into the box waiting beneath. Covered with a lid, we brought them straight to their home and installed the wayward swarm in an empty hive box. Of course, it was important that the queen was among them, or the bees would escape again to find and protect her.

In early 1945, my uncle was deployed to the eastern front to help stem the avalanche of bloodthirsty and rape-hungry Russians, who were already ransacking and pillaging in German territories. Even sick old men and fifteen-year-old boys—every last man, though some not quite yet 'man'—were rounded up and sacrificed needlessly in a desperate, last ditch effort for a cause already long lost. Shortly after Onkel Arthur's departure, his sister died. Grandmother had to find temporary refuge for us, away from the bombings of big cities. We never heard from Onkel Arthur again. My love for him and the bees has remained alive in my heart, and I consider these memories a highly treasured inheritance bequeathed by this gentlest of men.

Back at the oak tree, toward the shadowy recess in the empty bees' nest, now devoid of all activity, I can discern honeycombs, silent and pale, like bones bleaching in a graveyard. What a stark contrast from the warm, golden-fuzzy, eagerly bustling and productive life to this silence of a tomb. I am feeling sad and bereft, as if the melancholy scent of autumn has settled deep into my bones and is beginning to unmask a bottomless grief. Decades of loss, centuries of tears unshed by generations of women spring into blinding focus. Helplessly, I stare, transfixed, at the conjured faces and images of long-lost family and friends. I feel desolate and bent as if the pain of the world is pressing me down and into the ground. The senseless destruction of the bees' nest and realization of their homelessness is sending shock waves through my nervous system like ghostly echoes, howling ghoulish refrains from centuries past.

I shuffle and rustle my feet through drifts of wet oak and sycamore leaves, the musty odors wafting up to my nostrils. The colors and scents of autumn are in the air, though here in California seasonal changes are less dramatic. Suddenly, totally unexpected on this primarily sunny day, a gray cloud unzips its pregnant contents, and a brief drenching washes from my spirit the sorrow that, like grimy sludge, has choked my exuberance. Somewhere deep inside, I reconnect with a glow of hope—my indispensable guiding light, which encourages me to continue to trust that life is irrepressible. With a little bit of luck, maybe next spring a young colony will start a new cycle in that old oak tree. And I will be there to watch with unflagging fascination as another generation whirls and buzzes in the sweet dance of life.

Late Autumn, Early Winter
—Highland Ridge, New London, N.H.

Joan T. Doran

That sugar maple near our house
is returning to its roots, leaving behind
the modest consolation of its armature
ink-etched against encroaching dusk,

as near it, swamp trees disappear
into the background of the bog,
and birches fling their final
golden coins into the ditches where
lately asters showered purple stars—

Our maple in its frozen interlude may,
to my snow-blind eyes, seem fast asleep.
I know, though, even as the chilly winds
rattle ice-clad branches overhead like bones,
that out of sight small creatures drowse,
as do some human creatures,
held in that warm place near deep roots.

Prince of the Night

Ginger Galloway

I met my Prince on a cold, snowy Christmas Eve, during the ninth year of my life. Outside, the snow was swirling, darkness had embraced the farm, and we feared a blizzard was on the way. My daddy had gone to Ashland, Kentucky (bluegrass country), and we kids were all in wait of his arrival. The cows had been milked, the calves fed and tucked away in their beds of straw. We would open one present, soon as Daddy came home, soon as he finished dinner.

Sometime during that evening, in all the chaos, Daddy told me to grab an old blanket that we kept on the back porch and come with him. I never asked any questions as I walked beside him. I thought maybe one of the newborn calves was sick, or we needed to fix a broken water pipe. Why else would I need to carry a heavy old blanket?

When we arrived, Daddy opened one of the barn doors, and I stood there in the moonlight, speechless, like a frozen icicle. Before my eyes, lying on a clean bed of golden straw, was a very small creature…very young, red in color, four white socks, a white star in the middle of his forehead. The awesome sight literally took my breath away.

I slowly knelt down, looked into his precious little eyes and welcomed him to our farm. I put my arms around his neck, and it was only then that I felt the tears running down my cheeks.

The fur of this little creature was soft as velvet; he smelled like hay. My father took the blanket and gently covered up the both of us. He left a little bag of apple chunks so I could feed the pony when he got hungry. I remember being all alone with Prince (as I named him), eating apples with him, laughing, kissing him and hugging him, and incessantly talking to him for at least two hours.

I knew a lot about horses at the age of nine because I read all the horse books Ms. Martha had on her bookmobile. We did not yet have a library at our school out in the country. I read *National Velvet* three times, *The Black*

Stallion twice, *The Return of the Black Stallion*, *The Red Pony*…I read every book Ms. Martha had with a horse on the cover!

In second grade, the first story I wrote was about my dream horse. I guess you might say I dreamed my pony into existence! So that night in the barn, as I lay with my little charge, I taught Prince everything a horse needed to know, and he listened. He even whinnied a couple of times. We bonded for life, and we both dreamed of the adventures that lay before us, running fast across the pastures like a streak of lightning, my arms around his neck, my cheeks against his mane.

Sometime during that night, my daddy returned to the barn, covered Prince, picked me up, carried me back to the house, and tucked me into my own bed. I'm sure this thoughtful gesture was carried out under the watchful eyes of my mother, for it was a very cold night.

I remember waking up early the next morning, passing the Christmas tree and all of Santa's presents. I remember grabbing my coat in silence, pulling on my boots, and running out into the snow…back to the barn… back to check on my little charge…back to Prince! What a smile he brought to my face, what happy tears to my eyes! That was my favorite Christmas gift, and it is no wonder I still hold that memory very close to my heart.

White Exultation

Helen Jones-Shepherd

What is it that intrigues me about snow?
Is it the starkness of the white, so clean, so pure,
while untouched by footprints of children gamboling low?
Or how it glistens when the sun spreads its warming rays secure.

I feel the arctic chill when it snows and stings my cheeks,
and yet relish the flakes, even purposely trap them on my lips.
What a glorious phenomenon; I watch it intently as it drifts and
seeks places to rest, changing a garden statue into a ghostly apocalypse.

Giant redwoods covered with cotton lightness adorn the woodland,
altering its state, an ethereal place now; only the heavenly are permitted.
Venturing into this chalk-white setting, my pulse slows and I suspend
belief, in the pulchritude nature presents to me the lowly and committed.

Rain down on me, I cry; cover my woolen red striped hat
and suede jacket with white moistened flecks that cling and hold fast.
Then, let me join the trees in their serenity. My revelry ends; I desire to
make an angel, and excitedly throw myself to the ground, waving my arms.

For, incredulously, this moment becomes an odyssey into the mysterious
and fanciful world of blinding whiteness that engulfs us all every wintry day.

Mother's Angels

Eleanor Little

You loved angels—
they decorated your room all year.
One dressed in burgundy velvet,
flowers encircling her head,
ribbons of gold at her waist,
hung next to your bed.

Did you know
you had earth angels, too?
Sparks from you,
their Genesis;
two strong women who love you.

In a garden on top of a hill
angels tend roses and peonies,
trees dressed in flaming colors
rustle bright blouses,
a chill of white
melts into spring and summer.
You are home.

Second Runner-up: Best Non-fiction Contest

Pictures

Mary H. Ber

I have these pictures of her.

In one of them she is sitting on the edge of the examining table patting her gerontologist's pregnant belly. And her face is beatific. My mother's face, I mean—not the gerontologist's.

"You'll have an easy delivery," she tells her doctor. "Not like me."

I squirm, scrunched into the hard plastic chair of the examining room along with our two coats and two purses, my hands wound around her walker and her inhaler. I am the difficult delivery. I have never been permitted to forget it. But my mother's smile—part Raphael Madonna, part high school girlfriend! Maybe if I'd given birth to one of her grandchildren, she'd have blessed me with a smile like that.

As it is, my next picture is not nearly so pleasant.

The doctors have given my mother morphine during that third leg surgery. My sister, Judy, and I wrote down her allergy to morphine on the hospital intake form, but they must have forgotten to read it. And she goes bonkers again. Last time, she was only fearful. This time, she gets mean. "Judy, I will never forgive you for leaving me in that room by myself with the snakes and those wild jungle animals. And Mary Helen, the way you floated up to the ceiling and took off all your clothes in front of the doctors and nurses! I always knew the only thing you ever wanted was sex."

I gasp as if I have stubbed my toes rounding a familiar corner. How much do her hallucinations reflect her real feelings? Of course, Judy and I laugh about it later in the hospital coffee shop, but I can still feel her words like splinters under my skin.

I try to be a good daughter. I really do. I call her as often as I can, and I visit her at least once a week. But it's never enough. And I find it so hard just to talk. As soon as I walk through the doorway, she starts in. "It's about time you came to see me! The days are so long in this nursing home. I can put that call light on for hours before a nurse shows up. I hear them laughing and gossiping down the hall as if they had nothing else to do. They enjoy knowing I'm suffering."

One day, just to get her mind on something else, I tell her about a dream I had the night before. "There was some kind of battle going on, Ma. And I was one of the volunteers taking children down to an underground shelter—you know, like the London subway during World War II. I went up in this elevator to get the children, and then down again with them. Up and down. And one time, as I was riding along—it must have been up because I don't remember any children in the elevator—I was surprised to find you standing in the corner. See, I think about you so much, you're even in my dreams."

Then something beautiful happens. Right after I finish the story, she flashes me the sweetest smile—deep and quiet with some kind of secret knowledge. "I was taking you home," she says. And smiles again.

I live on that smile for a long time.

Things get a little better between us after that, partly because her memory wanders off a lot now. She's ninety-two, and I figure she's entitled to go where she wants—though all the experts say it's good to reorient old folks into reality as much as you can. Mostly, she wanders back to the old neighborhood and her old friends. But the other day, when I dropped in to see her, I didn't know where she was—in her dreams, maybe.

"Mary Helen, it's good you're here today. Somebody has to do something about those children."

"What children, Mama?" I speak gently, try to bring her slowly back to her own room in the nursing home.

She gets impatient. "The ones by the front door, when we came home earlier. Two little girls dressed kind of alike, so they must be sisters. But the one with such a bloody face. I can't get it out of my mind."

"There are no children here now, Mama."

"Oh, the blood was all around one eye—that poor little boy's eye. And I wanted to ask them their names and get some help, but I couldn't."

My breath catches in my throat. The little girl in that imaginary country has changed into a little boy. What are the rules of reality in such a land? I try to ease her off her obsession. "I don't think you need to worry about the children, Mama. Has Judy been here yet this week?"

And she does shift. "Did you come from home? Is Judy back from work yet?"

"No, Judy's still at work. It's only four o'clock. Would you like me to take you into the TV room before I leave?"

But she stiffens in her wheelchair and stares out the window at the bare autumn courtyard. "I want to go home. Take me home."

I am stunned at the passion in her voice, and how it manages to sound as if it comes from a place that is part dream and part memory, a place that still holds the deepest desire left in her. Then she is back with the children. "They were hurt, and they were crying. Tears coming out of that little bloody eye. I wish I could stop thinking about them."

I haven't seen her so upset in a long time, so I leave for a moment to check with the nurse. "Has she been like this for long?"

The nurse, a gentle-voiced Pakistani woman, doesn't seem worried. "A couple of hours. That's how it goes lately. The doctor took her off the anti-hallucinogens last week, after she fell. You remember. We called you about it."

I nod. "Please let me know if it continues."

I turn to leave, but the nurse halts me a second; the tips of her fingers brush my arm. I know from previous conversations that she has an aging mother too, and she understands.

"We will," she says. "I'll make a note to do that. And don't worry; we'll be updating the doctor, too."

My mother is staring into the twilight when I return to her room to say good-by.

"Shall I turn your light on, Mama?"

"Yes. The light. They were crying so hard—the children. And nobody cared. Where did you go?"

I stoop to kiss her cheek. "I just went to see the nurse for a moment."

There is expectation in my mother's eyes. Once again, I will probably not be able to fulfill it, but once again I will try.

I kiss her forehead. "The nurse said to tell you not to worry anymore. They took care of the children. The children are all okay now."

Little Girls

Anne McKenrick

Huddling in a little group, whispering, tee-heeing,
giggling until they can't stop. Shrieking, then gasping for breath,
they fall like rag dolls to the ground.

"Grandma, please give us some privacy," my little one asks.
I know little girls have their secrets
that require time and seclusion to discuss.

At ten years old, the chattering is about boys,
musical groups, hairstyles, nails and nail tattoos—
and OF COURSE, Hannah Montana!

They're learning to care for each other, give advice,
and listen with concern to their friends' problems,
checking to see if everyone is okay.

"Grandma, I have to change my clothes.
I'm wearing jeans, and my friends are wearing capris.
I have to change into capris."

Playing school is a favorite way to spend their time; soon
they're all singing and doing the latest dances they see on TV.
The next thing I know, they're running to get their dolls.

They are learning how to interact with each other;
is there a natural leader? Will the others follow
or will they want to be leader sometimes?

When three little girls get together, you can bet two will
"gang up" on one. Or if two have a disagreement,
the third one will be the peacemaker, carrying notes back and forth.

Complex little people they are: one minute, all-knowing,
telling me things I didn't know; the next, crying over a skinned knee
or elbow, needing to be comforted.

It's a paradox to see them walking down the street
with their arms around each other.
What cute little girls; yet, somehow, so grown up
and growing much faster than I would like to see.

Memoria
—for my sister on her 70th birthday

Annabelle Deutscher

There we were
trudging down
a country road
two small girls
tugged along by an
imposing old woman
whose purse swung
side to side
whose feet moved
steadfastly forward
as if to a
noble destination.
Fine silky dust
settled about us
and sunrise, bathing
the air with its
lush peach color
hushed our breath.

The house
we were led to
spilled with strangers—
long-limbed, black-eyed
full of voice—
who placed hands
upon our heads
spoke our names gently.
Who are they?
you implored with
your silent eyes
and now that they
are gone—
all of them gone—
the immutable answer
Family.

First Runner-up: Best Non-fiction Contest

The Secret Visit
—Purcell, Oklahoma, 1930

Annabelle Deutscher

I feel certain the trip began in twilight, the three of us wrapped in purplish, opalescent air and hurrying across brick-paved streets to reach the waiting bus. I was four years old, my sister Patricia not yet six, and our paternal grandmother, Bertie Rose, marched us forward with unalterable conviction. Her calloused hands gripped our small ones tightly, as if at any moment she feared some unknown person might appear and snatch us away.

"You girls mind me now," she murmured in her slurred Virginia speech. "Go to the very last row on the bus—to that real long seat?—take off your shoes and stretch out like you're going to sleep."

When my sister and I boarded the bus, we did as we were told. Grandmother followed and settled across from us, her hat pinned squarely on top of her silvery bun of hair, her voluminous purse anchored safely in her lap. As the bus moved away from its parking place, I could feel the anxious pressure of my sister's stockinged feet pushing against mine.

"Don't wiggle," Bertie Rose warned in a lowered voice. "You'll muss your dresses. Just close your eyes and, when you wake up, we'll be there."

My next recollection was of early morning, brilliant peach-colored clouds, a puzzlement of where we were and why. Half awake, we stumbled from a bus that seemed to have abandoned us in the silence of a dusty country road. Bertie Rose immediately began to whisk us into shape: a tugging of hair, a vigorous brushing of clothes, a licked handkerchief for sleepy eyes.

"This is Purcell," she announced matter-of-factly, although I saw no evidence of a town, "and you girls are going to meet your great-grandmother. It's her birthday."

I glanced at my sister expectantly. Where was the response, the preeminent knowledge that an older sibling should offer at a time like this? Was it true that our mother had said yes to this adventure, while our father declared no, absolutely not? And, if so, how had we managed to get here? Some secret scheme between Mother and Bertie Rose? As if burrowing into my mind, grandmother gripped my chin, twitched my head around to stare directly into my eyes. "Margaret," she began in her soft wheedling voice, "your daddy has gone away for two days and, when he gets home, don't tell him we came here. This is our secret. Will you do that for grandma? Will you?"

I nodded. To question an elder as imposing as Bertie Rose was unthinkable. Then, too, having an accomplice—an older sister at my side—offered security enough.

To describe that visit, even Purcell itself, I am limited to one specific dwelling and the road leading to it. A just-on-the-edge-of-town road sprinkled with squatty little houses. Genteel junk piled up in every side yard—rusty hand plows, rolls of chicken wire, sheds with sagging doors, rain barrels at every house corner. And porches—always the second or third step askew—lined with lawn chairs padded with homemade cretonne pillows. Warm cushiony chairs that I now realize comforted not only the body, but furnished some desperate need for continuity, for the familiar. The house of our destination was exactly like all the others on that road with one exception; on that particular day it filled with relatives—the Thompson clan, all brothers and sisters of my grandmother, Bertie Rose. It also filled with clattering dishes, baskets of food, the hum and pitch of male and female voices. The walls seemed to bulge, overflow with those tall, black-eyed people. Men in dark trousers, broad suspenders, white shirt sleeves rolled to just below the elbows. Men who slouched against a side wall, leaned lazily, propped one foot aside. The women, hovering about the rooms in a kind of fluid, perpetual motion, wore skirts, pale blouses bolted at the neck with gold bar pins. In varying degrees, all of them—men and women—seemed younger than my grandmother, but absolutely akin.

What, I now wonder, did my sister Patricia and I do with ourselves for that entire day—two small girls cast like immigrants into a flock of relatives so unknown to us that even the vowels and consonants of their names were unfamiliar? Jeffery, Sulie, Dell, Albertina, James, Rawl, all Thompsons, all

THE SECRET VISIT 63

siblings of our grandmother, Bertie Rose. And the mystical force of the gathering, the star, the one we'd been brought here to meet, Great-grandmother Beulah Thompson, whose every vague, wistful appearance activated a flurry of concern, of instruction—*pull down the window shade*—*you can light the stove now*—*stand back and let her have some air*—until finally, at last, our introduction by Bertie Rose.

"Mama, this is your great-granddaughter. She is four years old." I was led forward by Bertie Rose, who tilted her large frame over me and whispered against my ear, "Say something to Great-grandmother. Say your name."

"Margaret," I blurted out. "I'm Margaret."

Marooned in her padded Morris chair, the old woman before me lifted her head and squinted through milky eyes. "Margaret," she repeated in a gluey voice. Slowly, she raised her hand and touched my head. "Hair," she muttered. "Lots of it."

Like a shuffling of cards, I was tugged away, and my sister placed in front of me.

"And this is her older sister, Patricia Gypsy."

"Patricia Gypsy?" Again the lifting of head, the reaching of hand. "Slippery hair and not much of it." A wild burst of laughter erupted, then applause—certainly a signal that Patricia and I had performed our part successfully.

With those initial introductions over, my sister and I were ushered outside to play, and the Thompson's themselves, unable to fit together for long in that tiny house, soon drifted after us. In changing shifts they cranked the wooden ice-cream churn, lounged on quilts beneath two lone trees, a cherry and an apple, weeded the garden, talked continually. Their words invaded our small child ears, lulled us, and the hours of the day slid past in a blur—through lunch, through dinner (what was it we ate?), through singing a song for Great-grandmother (what was it we sang?) until at last it was early evening.

"Hurry now, little girls. Clean up. It's time for the party."

Once again, we were led into the crowded meeting place, the kitchen, and seated at a table next to Great-grandmother Beulah Thompson. I was astonished to see no birthday gifts, nothing but a large cake with one lone candle in the center. As the first slice was cut—a knife held in the unsteady grip of old Beulah herself—I squirmed self-consciously in my chair, trying not to stare at her aged, featureless face. But as soon as my plate was served, I could no longer resist. I looked at Beulah timidly and recall the strange impulse to turn away. Yet how quickly that impulse vanished when, with shocking agility, her hand shot forward and stabbed a fork into my cake. "Mar-gar-et," she coined my name slowly, deliberately. "The first bite will always be the best. And don't you forget. Ready?" I nodded, opened my mouth wide, and she shoved in the wedge of cake, leaving me convinced that I had just been bequeathed a mysterious gem of wisdom that I must never forget for the rest of my life.

After the cake celebration, Great-grandmother was guided to the porch, seated, made comfortable with pillows, and a soft rush of dialogue began. By then, late evening, a hazy light filtered through the house and yard. I have been told that, soon after this, my sister and I were put to bed on a straw mattress in the attic, that I wheezed allergically through the night while Patricia sat bolt upright and awake, anticipating our return home and fearful our father would chastise us for making this visit. I recall none of this. What I do remember clearly is early morning and, in that once-crowded kitchen, a breathless silence. The Thompson clan seemed to have vanished, and Bertie Rose was urging us to be quiet. "Very quiet," she whispered, "so as not to wake Great-grandmother. It will cause her to cry if she knows we are leaving, so let's just slip away." We did just that. Gathered our belongings, tiptoed from the house, trudged down the country road to the highway to meet the bus that would take us home.

Of that final puzzling event, a departure with no good-bys, I suspect it was Bertie Rose herself who would have wept. Certainly not old Beulah Thompson who—except for that one lucid action of stabbing my cake—had noticeably drifted into some protective recess of emotion. When she died soon afterwards, it seemed clear enough that the party in her honor had not been for her birthday at all. It was a farewell party. And, finally, the promise: my grandmother's wish to keep the trip to Purcell a secret. Long years later, I discerned that her unlikely request somehow involved my father's embarrassed disapproval of the Thompson clan—their humble beginnings, their provincial speech, their rag-tag ways.

What a pity, for I have at last discovered that family gatherings, whether chance or planned, often offer a rich endowment of spirit, a consummate tie to what most of us long for. Belonging. Now, many decades later, what most redeems that bewildering childhood visit to Purcell is this: the flickering images of those tall, angular bodies, the Thompsons, perched about on steps, leaning against porch posts, their stories flowing endlessly, their voices rising with laughter, dropping with regret, forever capturing time. Add to those images one other. Great-grandmother Beulah, who touched my head, spoke my name, and in one wily maneuver of fork and cake thrust herself forever into the warp of my memory.

Mending

Una Nichols Hynum

A big family is always one phone call away
from a really bad day—especially if it's collect.
Compared to the deluge of global warming,
terrorism and genocide, this is only a light rain.

But sometimes I'd like to see the rip
in the universe repaired without my help.
Sometimes I stand still and watch
the slow maneuver of its needle
pushing through the terrible fabric of life.

Be Wary of Who Says What Regarding Genealogy

Kathleen Elliott Gilroy

Here is a major error of secrecy. Being stoic, tight-lipped. Genealogy researchers may record misconstrued events. Link wrong events to one person or another. Damage or exalt lives lived by those now dead.

What if my father, or his brother—the closest one in age to him, not the other one we never met, nor the sister whom we heard of from idle gossip taken out of context—had decided to just sit down and lay facts on the table, as they say. Sit us down and make us listen. Like prayers before the food is eaten.

What if my father—or the brother closest in age to him—had ignored the way most lives were lived in their time; nothing said to children. They could have dismissed the adage of children being seen and never heard. Ingrain in them, instead, the need for truth. Lay it on the demarcation line, like people do on reality shows, or in intense discussions, in serious conversations. Then fabrication could be debated, wrung and twisted like a rag, hung on the line, thrown in a dryer. Tossed aside. Recognized as false fabric in the pieced quilt of life.

I say this because of my great-grandmother, Emma Dollar. This is the way the story went as it was told to me late in my own life:

She married a man named Bert Elliott, who is my actual lineage grandfather on the Elliott side. The myth reports she divorced Bert Elliott, married a sheriff, and took her two sons with her to live in South Dakota. There, so the story went, she had another son named Barney and a daughter named Icyella, who went by the name "Ercela." All of them with last names of Mitchell, including my father, Lester William, and his brother, V. William, nicknamed Bill.

More intensive research by me (entering late in the research effort), years of research by my eldest son, Rusty (Elliott) Gilroy and our lineage cousin, J. C. (Elliott) Shelby in Missouri have cleared up part of the myth and the mystery.

Emma Dollar actually married my great-grandfather, Joseph Elliott. They moved from Osceola, Missouri to Highland Park, California, where my grandfather, Bert X. Elliott, was born in the late 1800's. He was an only child. Emma died young and is buried in Highland Park, California. Joseph returned to Missouri and, over the years, he married two more times. He had several more children. But none of the records mention Bert as a further part of the family.

Bert eventually lived in Helena, Montana, though. There, my father was born, as was my Uncle Bill. None of our research has provided how my father—and his brother, Bill—came to have their names changed to Mitchell. We have located no information on who raised them. But it was in South Dakota.

The mystery of my father's family stayed in my mind over the years. It sometimes came up when I thought of the last name, Mitchell, and how it affected the family I was born into. During WWII, my Uncle Bill joined the Navy, leaving his wife and three young children so he could serve his country.

My father joined the Merchant Marines (Mariners) and was scheduled for officer training. Then he was told his legal name wasn't Mitchell. It was still Elliott. He and my mother were remarried, using the Elliott name. My older sister, Doreen Janet, was born July 28, 1934; my older brother, Sydney Boyd, November 8, 1935; I (Kathleen Mary), November 4, 1936; my younger brother, Dennis Frederic, September 10, 1939. All four of us, given the surname Mitchell at birth, had our birth certificates reissued with the surname Elliott and date of the change.

There ought to be a good midway point before we discover more, so this is the one I offer. The year that my father died (1952), we took our annual trip from Salt Lake City, Utah to Rawlins, Wyoming to visit my mother's older sister. What a surprise when Father stated, as if relating a mundane thing, "We're going to Casper, Wyoming, too. So I can see my father."

His father! A subject never mentioned before! And all those trips we had made to Wyoming, while a grandfather had been in the same state. We parked in front of his small bungalow and waited while Father went in. Then, miraculously, I was called to the door to enter in. Yet I had only the barest glimpse of him before we were gone. Never sitting down, never mentioning him again. I do not know why I was asked to come to the door. My sister had run away two years before. My brothers were silent as we drove

BE WARY OF WHO SAYS WHAT REGARDING GENEALOGY 69

away. We knew better than to ask what had happened here. Our father was a strict disciplinarian. We went to visit another family there in Casper, where children were told to go outside, and we did.

Years later, in 2002, I went to Casper, Wyoming again, to visit my eldest son, who had chosen Casper as his home, never knowing a great-grandfather had lived there, too. My son had begun genealogy research, and our search now was focused on learning about the grandfather I never knew.

Before I left, we found his death certificate and visited the cemetery where he was buried in 1958, six years after my father died in an industrial accident. Six years after my father's funeral, where the man who had fathered him, the man Father had visited just two months before he died, never sent even a card to my father's funeral.

During the years from then to now, thanks largely in part to my eldest son, I respect the grandfather I never knew. I have come to accept that I have no answers for decisions made before I was even conceived. Yet I feel strongly that my Elliott grandfather is important to me: he was a participant in the birth of my father, I carry his DNA, I am a link in a legacy he thought he needed to step away from. I do not know what happened to Grandfather Bert as a child whose mother had recently died. Where did he go? Who took him in? What happened when his father, Joseph, remarried? How did the surname Mitchell come in?

Now, it is 2009. I recently came back from a trip to Missouri with my eldest son and my only daughter, Erin Gilroy Thomas. We visited the farm where our genealogical history began. We met descendents of great-grandfather's siblings. We were accepted as family.

Back in Casper, Wyoming, before our nine-day venture would draw to a close, my son, my daughter, and I visited the cemetery again. We were guided to locate the burial sites of Bert and his long-lived marital partner, Labelle. Their flat bronze grave markers had long ago sunk into the burial sites. There was nothing to acknowledge the value of them to people they knew, much less the three of us. We agreed on new, concrete headstones, to be eventually placed on site. Both my son and daughter are artisans of laser stone art. They will eventually design and create the headstones that a bonded stonemaker will put in place.

As the cooperative employee pointed out to us, there is room on the grounds at their site for a memorial tree, which we can buy and have planted there. Looking around, we saw such a tree was needed. The section our family is in is sparse of trees. We decided, with a cemetery official's agreement, on what we would buy, and spent the rest of the day looking at trees for sale.

Two days later, after my daughter and I returned to San Diego, California, Rusty called to tell us he had purchased a red oak tree, taken it to the site, and it would soon be in the ground. In the meantime, he left a beautiful bouquet of flowers at the site.

Less than one week after the tree was delivered to the cemetery office, it has been planted. Rusty says it not only makes locating their gravesites easier when he stops by, but it adds beauty to what was a treeless section in an already serene, well cared for cemetery with many other trees that accent the surrounding Casper Mountains and tree-lined sections of this older part of the city.

I sense that particular tree will be an expansive, living monument of beauty, its canopy offering home to local wild songbirds that inhabit the area. It will belong to future generations of viewers who may never know any of our family history, or how the tree came to be there, but it will add to the serenity that comforts those who are grieving a loss.

I surmise that, for us, it is our healing tree, and the beginning of healing unresolved issues, a way of saying: "Here lies a good man, a grandfather and great-grandfather who never knew us. Here lies the woman he chose as his long-term wife. Here lie the remains of part of our family."

Winner: Best Non-fiction Contest

Everything Must Go

Carole Ann Moleti

> **Garage Sale**
> **Sunday, May 21**
> **9-3 pm**
> **Everything Must Go**

I'd driven by the house on my way to work almost every day for the last eighteen years. Until I saw the sign, it was easy to deny how much time had passed since I creaked open the gate and meandered past the immaculate garden, up the long driveway, through the back door, and into the cozy kitchen with pots simmering on the stove. I can still smell garlic in the meatballs and the bittersweet tang of stuffed cabbage and sauerkraut balls. The cat would brush against my ankles, while the dog's tail beat a welcome across my legs.

The dining room hosted Thanksgiving feasts of turkey, bread stuffing, candied sweet potatoes and peas—but only after the lasagna. On Christmas mornings, we crowded into the living room and plunked onto bulky chestnut colonial furniture upholstered in trendy orange and brown. A fire flickered. Stockings hung from the mantelpiece. Pale winter sunlight filtered through ivory lace curtains, glinting off the dark wood paneling and polished hardwood floors.

The tree was surrounded by more presents than one could ever imagine for three teenage children and their assorted boyfriends and girlfriends. The cat and dog ran rampant through discarded wrapping paper. There was always My-T-Fine chocolate pudding for dessert, with Saran wrap on top to prevent the skin from forming.

More love to go around than the average family, and you could feel it the minute you walked in the door to hugs, cries of welcome, and fights. Was it really over?

I married into the family in 1979, but was welcomed in many years before that. We met when Michael was a seventeen-year-old star shortstop, and I was a fourteen-year-old Little League groupie. Like most love struck teenagers, we vowed to stay together forever and went steady for eight years before finally getting married. He encouraged me while I pursued the career I so desperately wanted, and had faith that I was going to be the best nurse ever. I knew he would succeed in business and finance. We stayed married long enough to graduate college, land good jobs, and buy not just one house, but also a vacation getaway in Vermont.

Mike Sr., his dad, had a passion for finding treasure amongst the trash at the New York City Sanitation dump where he worked. "Put in your order," he'd say. Most of the time, within a few days, the request was filled. Some of the most memorable finds were cases of counterfeit bills (so bad even the FBI didn't want them) and Gucci bag knockoffs. We all paraded around The Bronx with three or four different Gucci's apiece. He brought home furniture, glassware, and other decorating items regularly. Some turned out to be valuable antiques.

Anything else, Michael's mother, Ellen, made. She hung wallpaper, painted, and could fix or refinish almost everything. She rarely bought anything for herself, but always splurged on gifts for her children.

My parents were very conservative financially. Pay cash; never overextend yourself. Ellen and Mike spent every penny. They wanted all their kids to go to college, and Ellen figured out how to pay for it.

I had two mothers. My own suggested what I should do, raising her eyebrows and saying "o-kay" when she didn't agree. I never appreciated her advice until I got older, and the realities of life caught me by surprise.

Ellen never hesitated to tell me what I should and shouldn't do, and I almost always did as she advised. She was a master gardener, who loved to sew, knit, quilt, and crochet. I was book smart, but Ellen educated me about the practical things in life. She ignored our pleas to quit smoking, though. "Please, it's the only vice I have. Let me enjoy it."

My dad is the most loving father any daughter could have. He took me fishing, skiing, and taught me to swim and sail.

Mike Sr. considered me his daughter, too. He yelled at me, teased me, hugged me, and brought me gifts. He never finished high school, but proudly described himself as the happiest garbage man there ever was. Once, when I was in graduate school studying environmental science, I made a field trip to the incinerator where he worked.

"See, even that there Columbia University sends students to pick through the junk. Who says there's no future in garbage?"

There were links amongst the families not unusual with immigrants who settled in The Bronx. Michael's great-grandfather delivered ice to mine from a horse-drawn cart. My great-grandmother, the midwife, delivered Mike Sr.

My great-grandfather was the local barber. Grandpa Al, who drove his mother to her midwifery calls in one of the first Model T Fords, had done a fine business as a mechanic in the neighborhood.

We considered ourselves Italian, but no one wanted to admit that both Ellen and my mom had some German in them. The stuffed cabbage and sauerkraut balls were only occasional specialties; meatballs ruled.

Mike Sr. and Grandpa Al spoke the same language.

"Fuggetaboudit!"

"Getowdahea!"

"He's Irish, ain't he?"

"Yeah, but he keeps his hair short."

"Did ya wrap the fig tree and put the bucket on top? Don't fuget the bucket!"

"Fuget that acid/base crap. Lime sweetens the soil; it's good for the tomatoes."

In that world, ethnicity defined you. Sure, it was bigotry, but "What are you?" was a question I can remember being asked many times. My best friend "was" Irish, and my mother, German. That dictated everything about your family—where you lived, the food you ate, and the way you celebrated holidays and family events.

The summer of '84 began like most in New York City. Hot, humid, and with tensions high as Local 1199 (the service wing of health care employees) walked off the job in early July.

A nurse-manager, I worked fourteen consecutive twelve-hour night shifts, hauling laundry bags and doing messenger, transport, and cleaning duties. I got two off, but Michael was away on a "business" trip. Then I worked the next fourteen days.

By the time we got to see each other, I sensed Michael's newfound interest in designer suits and ties was a bad sign. The strike continued until just before Labor Day. My nerves and my marriage were shredded. He moved out the day after my birthday that September.

A few months later, he moved back in and swore he was no longer seeing her, but slept in the guest room. Some nights, he wouldn't come home. I'd sit up, waiting to see the headlights in the driveway, usually falling asleep in the chair and waking up the next morning to one of the dogs kissing my face.

I went down hard, as Anna Quindlen once put it, on my "first slip on the cosmic banana peel." Lonesome, I went on a date a friend set up for me. It felt so nice to be complimented and treated like a princess. Sam took me out for elegant dinners and on weekend vacations. Who cared that I was still married? If Michael could get away with it, why not me?

I did things no self-respecting Catholic schoolgirl should, like commit adultery on Good Friday. I justified it at the time by not eating meat.

The relationship burned out when I found out about Sam's past arrests and drug use. He was a stockbroker, a fast talker, and this was the 1980's, when cocaine, yellow ties, and greed ruled the markets. I had enough self-esteem left to realize that my career and my life were on the line and stopped seeing him.

Ulcers and depression made me understand why people commit suicide, though it never got that bad. The families held out hope, but Michael and I were finished. Their disappointment made it feel even worse. It was hard to remember when we hadn't all spent holidays and special occasions together.

One night, I found a pair of panties in the laundry that didn't belong to me. When I confronted Michael, he tried to convince me they were mine. I threw them in his face, screamed that women know what their own goddamn underwear looks like, and told him to get the hell out. He just walked away but, later that night, when he saw all my bottles of medicine on the bathroom shelf, Michael said he realized the situation was killing me, and I had done nothing to deserve it. He promised to move out for good.

Two weeks later, he came into our bedroom early one morning and cuddled with me for the first time in over a year. There were no words exchanged, but we both understood this was the end. He kissed me on the cheek, said he was sorry, and left.

We weren't just a man and woman with two pretty houses, everything divided amicably, joint custody of the dogs, no alimony. The fabric of several lives was ripped to shreds. All those long, intertwined threads were sundered, leaving gaping holes.

I tried to remain friends with Michael's family, but it got to be too hard. One Christmas, I went to see them before Michael and his girlfriend got there. Ellen's last gift to me was a pair of tricolor earrings. Pink and green swirled through gold, complex, intertwined—like our relationship. I still marvel at the patina, and the way they glint through my hair and light up my face.

I stopped going, dreading the tension, the tight jaws, the awkward silences in a family that never had a shortage of things to say. The last time I visited, Mike Sr. was lying in bed, out of the garbage pits with a back injury. The look in his eyes, the tears welling up, and the tight grip on my hand said it all. I'd see Ellen in the neighborhood, shopping or bustling in her garden, always with a cigarette dangling from her mouth. I couldn't bear to see pain and conflict in her eyes, so I didn't call out to her. I knew how hard it was for Robin and Tracy, my sisters-in-law, and their fiancés, Jimmy and Kevin. We had been friends for so long.

I decided to spare them the need to side against their son and brother, and called Tracy and Jimmy just before their wedding to tell them I wasn't coming. "I don't want to ruin it for everyone. Yes, I know you want me there, and I want to be there, but the family can't take it."

I heard the disappointment in Tracy's voice, but she said she understood. I sent a gift and never heard from them again. I missed the births of their children. I never got invited to Robin and Kevin's wedding. Ellen and Mike Sr. never became the grandparents I had always envisioned them being to the children that Michael and I never had.

I finished graduate school, pouring all my energy and frustration into working full-time at night and going to classes during the day. When I quit my job and went to Boston to do a midwifery internship, Michael handed me a $3000 check for living expenses. He paid my mortgage for the entire time and took care of the house while I was away. Lack of generosity was never one of his faults.

I dreamed, over and over, that I was stuck in a paper bag, the light shining in from above, while I punched and clawed to get out. My therapist, friends, and family hauled me over the top. I started over in a new job, lonely, but peaceful and excited about beginning a new life and a new career at the same time.

During that same year, 1987, I answered a personal ad and met the man destined to be my new husband. It had to be mystical destiny. I never read the *Daily News*, but picked it up that day and sent a photo and short note to the SWCM, age 30. On our first date, John went with me to The American Ballet Theatre at the Metropolitan Opera House. I paid for the tickets; he bought me dinner at Victor's 76, a Cuban restaurant on Columbus Avenue. He fell asleep during the very long second act of *Sleeping Beauty*, but assured me he had a great time. I fell in love with him immediately.

John was honorable enough to worry that my divorce and annulment weren't finalized. He didn't give up, despite his concerns, and asked me to marry him as soon as the final decree was filed two years later.

John's family is Sicilian, the *real* Italians. We had a traditional church wedding, his first. I wore a white dress and no one said anything, at least that I heard. We had two sons, two years apart. My new in-laws were loving grandparents, but they just weren't Mike and Ellen. You can't replace your parents.

I thought the pain was behind me. I never minded getting stuck at the traffic light near the house, so I could stare into the yard and remember the happy times we spent out there on summer evenings. On a lucky day, I'd see Mike Sr. taking in the trash pails, kibitzing with the garbage men, still limping a bit. Little had changed, or so I imagined.

I was a busy working mom and hadn't heard from Michael since our dogs died over ten years earlier. The routine of one September day dissolved when I answered the phone in the middle of cooking dinner, expecting to give the telemarketer a not-so-polite brushoff.

"Carole Ann, it's Michael, your ex. I just wanted you to know my mom died today."

I felt like I had been knocked down—again. He just kept talking.

"She had lung cancer and died at home. We were all there. The wake is tomorrow, at McQuade's. We're going to bury her at Gate of Heaven; she'd like it there with all the trees and flowers."

"Can I come?" I managed to get the words out.

"Of course, that's why I'm calling you. She'd want you there. We all want you there." Michael spoke through his own tears.

I hung up, and my children crowded around me. "What's wrong, Mommy? Why are you crying?"

"Someone very special to me went to Heaven today." I wasn't sure how to explain the complexities of the relationship. They accepted it, not understanding the depth of my grief for all the deaths embodied in one woman's passing. I went to the florist and unloaded on the clerk.

"We're divorced, but Ellen was like a mother to me. I don't know what to do."

She just handed me a box of tissues. After I blew my nose and composed myself, she gave me a book to look at. "Pick flowers for the funeral home, and something personal for the family."

Those people must take counseling courses, too. I sent a fruit basket to the house, and wrote on the card that I'd never forget the years we had shared. Ellen loved red roses, so I sent her a dozen and scrawled the first words that burst out of my heart: "You were my second mother. I love you, Carole Ann."

When I walked in to the chapel, it felt like old times. All the neighbors and old friends were there. How could it be that they looked so much older, and I didn't?

"When we read your notes," Robin said, "there wasn't a dry eye in the house."

Mike Sr.'s eyes brightened when he saw me. He chattered on about how glad he was I had come, that Ellen loved me so much, and how he had just lost the love of his life.

"I gave her fifty red roses. One for each year we were married." He paused for a moment. "We should have made her quit. Why didn't we?" He looked so old, so sad. I promised to visit and take him to see my parents. I think we both knew that wasn't likely to happen.

Michael's hair and beard were still sandy brown, but he'd put on a lot of weight. His wife was kind enough to give us the space to hold each other, cry, and finally come to some closure for ourselves.

"You look fantastic," he said. "And you're the best nurse in the world, I know it. I hope you've forgiven me for what I put you through."

"I owe you a lot, Michael. I'm not sure I would have pursued everything without your encouragement and financial help."

We showed off pictures of our children, laughed, and reminisced about Ellen and the wonderful family life she had created. I had missed so much. Ellen became a senior citizen, had hip surgery, six grandchildren, and died of lung cancer. I regretted not calling out when I saw her, or having a chance to tell her how I felt before she died. I whispered my thoughts to the thin, peaceful lady in the coffin and hoped she'd heard me.

I drove home over the bridge from The Bronx to Queens as if I were crossing from one lifetime to another. I pulled into another driveway, in another neighborhood, walked through another garden and back to another family—my new one. The past had evaporated along with the young woman I once was.

"Should I go?" I asked my husband. "I want to find out what happened to Michael's dad. I'm afraid."

"Do whatever you think is best." John always tries to be supportive.

My resolve wavered, then I picked up the car keys. It was after two, and the sale was almost over. Best to get there when there wasn't a crowd. I drove the familiar Bronx streets, remembering the friends, the hangouts, the fun times. I parked my car, took a deep breath, and walked down the driveway and through the garden, unkempt and overgrown with weeds. Robin saw me first, then Tracy.

"Carole Ann! We can't believe you're here! How did you know about the sale? Come in, we just ordered pizza. Jimmy, Kevin, Daddy, look who's here!"

They hugged me like a celebrity. Tears flowed. Children I didn't recognize ran around, trying to figure out who the strange woman was.

Damn! Kevin and Jimmy had gray hair. Robin and Tracy looked like Ellen had the last time I saw her alive, minus the cigarette. Mike Sr., his shirt buttoned wrong, sat quietly watching strangers pick through his belongings, haggling to get the price down to fifty cents from a dollar.

His toothless smile brightened when he saw me. "Carole Ann, you take her yarn, all her sewing things, and her knitting books. Give them to your mother; she does all that craft stuff, too."

"You have to have pizza with us." Robin pushed me into a familiar kitchen chair. "For old times' sake."

The stove was covered in dust, no cast iron pot bubbling, no delectable smells. We ate off paper plates and drank soda from Styrofoam cups, surrounded by boxes and black garbage bags filled to bursting.

"Where's Michael?" I suddenly realized I had been there an hour and never missed him.

"He can't take this," Tracy said. "He can't face the truth or let go easily."

"Tell me about it," I said, and they all roared with laughter.

"Carole Ann," said Robin. "I never met anyone as tough as you. You haven't changed a bit."

Mike Sr. was silent, pizza grease dribbling down his chin onto his shirt. I gently dabbed it with a napkin. Robin and Tracy looked at me. We smiled, understanding, like the sisters we were, that taking care of sick and aging parents is the debt we owe them for the sacrifices they made for all of us.

"Can I walk through the house? I'd really like to see it again," I asked.

"Sure," said Robin. She and Tracy followed me into the dining room to explain the situation.

"My dad is okay, but he lives near me and goes to the senior center every day," said Tracy. "He never got over my mother's death."

"She's here, I swear," said Robin. "When we pick something up and try to decide what to do with it, she tells us. When my Dad was moving, we had this dilemma about the cat. Do you know that goddamn cat died? My mother had to have arranged that!"

I suddenly smelled Thanksgiving turkey, lasagna, and meatballs. I went into the living room, the furniture and rugs unchanged. Cigarette smoke curled upwards while Ellen sat in her chair watching television, her knitting needles clacking.

Robin and Tracy went off to do some business with customers. The tiny sewing room upstairs was empty. The master bedroom was full of boxes, the others dark and vacant.

Michael's old bedroom, where we used to sneak and make love when no one was home, still had the same shutters on the windows that we used to close out the world. I remembered two teenagers who thought they were going to be together forever, and heard Michael singing me the song, "My Brown Eyed Girl."

The new owners came to make measurements. I listened to them plan renovations. Standing in the stifling, bare attic, I recalled happier times when Michael and I stored all our wedding shower gifts up there. I felt Ellen's joy that the house was going to a family who appreciated it, to be filled with love and the sounds of children again.

Two books sat abandoned on the attic steps. One was *The Beautiful Bronx* by Lloyd Ultan. The other was an antique civil engineer's manual. I carried them downstairs and rejoined the group in the kitchen.

"Take those books," Mike Sr. said. "You gave me that Bronx book. I want you to have it. I found that antique manual years ago. Ellen said it was worth something."

And she saved them for me, I thought.

"Take whatever you want," said Tracy. "We'll pack up the yarn and sewing things. Can you come get them next week?"

"Sure." I can barely sew on a button, but Ellen trusted me to give her things to someone who'd appreciate them.

I looked at the treasures of Mike and Ellen's lives, strewn over dirty, dusty tables. I saw the photo caddy that had sat on their coffee table, filled with pictures of birthday parties, proms, graduations, showers, and my wedding. I wondered how many more pictures had rotated through that now empty item marked $1.

I took my books, kissed everyone and left quickly, not stopping to look at the other familiar things. Pieces of my life were attached to everything, being sold for pennies, as if they were worthless. I got in the car, nearly three hours after I arrived. The radio blared out "My Brown Eyed Girl." I cried all the way home.

John and I looked at the pictures of the old Bronx in the book, while I told him what happened. I opened the engineer's manual and caught my breath. The name scrawled on the inside cover was E. Weiland, the man who once owned the house in Queens where I now live. He was a retired civil engineer who threw his book in the trash before he moved out, only to be found by my former father-in-law, picking through the garbage heap.

Everything must go, Ellen. Yes, everything.

A few weeks later, Robin called to remind me to come back for the knitting books and yarn. The sign had a new date and, this time, Michael was there. I still knew him well enough to feel the pain of seeing his childhood home being torn apart.

"I know how hard this is for you," I said.

"Yeah." He averted his gaze, more distant and distraught than he had been at his mother's wake.

Michael helped me load boxes into my car. We made small talk about the ages of our kids and how things were going at work. He wanted me gone, quickly. There was nothing left between us; the separation was now complete. He was an acquaintance I hadn't seen for years, not the man I had been in love with between the ages of fourteen and thirty.

I declined the invitation to join them for their last round of hero sandwiches from our old haunt, Busco's. This time, Michael barely managed a weak pat on my back when I embraced him. Robin, Tracy, Kevin, Jimmy, and Mike Sr. hugged me tight.

"Goodbye," they called in unison.

Michael stood with his wife and kids in front of the sign to which they had added a line stating, "Everything free from 3-4 PM."

"*It's time to move on, Carole Ann. It's all gone,*" Ellen said.

I drove back over the bridge.

Autumn Meditations

James L. Foy

> *"There are things deep in us and you know what they are as well as I do."*
> —F. Scott Fitzgerald

I

In the copper-red and amber woods
Beneath the whisper of turning leaves
I rekindle my lost and found otherworld,
Rife with memories, dreams, desire.
Moonlight scatters on the ruffled lake,
Sunrise startles the birds from sleep,
Journeying geese honk in the quiet sky,
Salmon toil in whitewater on a frantic
Spawning run while a buck deer in rut
Crashes hell-bent through the meadow,
In late afternoon lengthening shadows.
This is the spirit path of transformation;
This is the only life, there is no other.

II

Four of us assemble at the trail head,
Young and old will hike to the waterfall.
The forest path draws us to the source,
Masts of western hemlock blaze the way.
The Sol Duc triple cascade is thrashing
And thundering both above and below.
We let the cool mist of it enter our lungs
And into our hair, faces, supplicant hands,
The wilderness bestows its own baptism.
Later at Lake Crescent we eat our meal
Facing the glacial blue water, the silent
Mountains surround us with their primeval
Promise of steadfast solace and consolation.
The only life is one we always remember.

III

November is for remembrance of saints,
A harvest feast when we count our blessings,
A time that strips down to bare essentials
With an overlay of early frost, light snow.
We retreat to the Blue Ridge and a cabin
Beside a pond that mirrors the shoreline,
The sky overhead, and dreams clouds by day
And stars by night. In a battered rowboat
We skim the surface stirring up sky colors,
And peer into the deep for the mythic fish
Who lives there in the wisdom of solitude,
While in the shallows the spindly blue heron
Stands still holding all her secrets forever.
The only life is the gift we already have.

IV

There is a recurrent element of autumnal
Sadness seeping along the edge of things,
A melancholy that safeguards inwardness.
Since a longing for life and the certitude
Of limits must be endured and affirmed,
I shall praise the transparency of winter
Trees and the dry husks of discarded days.
Lately falling asleep, I sometimes hear
My mother speak my name and dreams
Are peopled with my unforgotten dead.

Under the Full Moon

Mary R. Durfee

My niece always wanted to travel, to see the world. It was all she could do to get through college. Then came her chance. She became a Peace Corp volunteer and spent several years working in underdeveloped countries left ravaged by wars.

In the mid-1970's, while assigned to Nepal, a small, poor country wedged between India and Tibet in the Himalayan Mountains, she spent some time caring for orphaned children. One day, a tiny baby girl, whose mother had died in childbirth, was dropped off at the nearby hospital. There was no milk for the infant and no medicine. The baby lay on the dirt floor, very sick and in danger of dying.

Marge, my niece, cared for that baby, named Poonam, and as soon as she was well enough she brought her to the U.S. and adopted her. In no time at all, Poonam grew into a beautiful young lady and, upon graduating from college, her mom presented her with a gift: a trip to Nepal, the country of her birth. A desire to find her roots was always uppermost in her mind, even though expectations were quite slim.

And so it was that Poonam and her mom set off for Asia, their destination, Nepal, where their incredible journey had begun. They arrived in Kathmandu, the capital, and registered at a hotel. Marge was shocked at the changes that had taken place in the twenty-two years since she had left Nepal. There were so many more people and, though transportation had improved, apparent signs of poverty and pollution still existed. But the people were still wonderful and very friendly; signs in English were found everywhere.

Through a series of incredible and perhaps miraculous circumstances, they discovered Poonam's birthplace, a Tamang Village, just north of Kathmandu. But how to reach that village was another matter. The Tamang were an ethnic group from the hilly region of Nepal.

After many inquiries, they rented a van and a driver, who also served as their guide. First, they must go to a place called Gorkha, four hours northwest. Here, in this small country, trips are measured in hours, not miles. The first part of the trip was hard and bumpy. Some bridges were washed out or under repair, and huge rocks lay along the sides of the road. While on their hazardous journey, they saw beautiful hills and valleys, as well as the majestic Himalayan Mountains in the distance.

Upon reaching Gorkha, they came across a Catholic school that was operated by two Jesuit priests. Marge casually mentioned their mission to find Poonam's roots. About this time, a few families had gathered around at the sight of strangers and were listening in on the conversation. One of them came forward and said he was from Tamang, and he thought Poonam might have come from a village called Sahu Goan. "But where is that place?" they asked. He said he knew of a printer in Kathmandu who might be of help. So Marge and Poonam took the long trek all the way back to Kathmandu, where they found the print shop and its owner, who was a much older man. They told him about their quest to find Poonam's roots.

He seemed to be a very wise and learned man, and he remembered hearing of a child who had been adopted by an American woman, some twenty years ago. He suggested they go to a town called Trisuli and ask for a woman named Prim Kumari. She was well known in that town.

Marge and Poonam again rented a van and a guide to accompany them and to help interpret. They drove four hours around hills and curves. The ride was breathtaking. They caught glimpses of the snow-covered Himalayas, drove past huge mounds of radishes bound for market, and watched women carry baskets of forage supported by head straps on their foreheads.

They finally reached the town of Trisuli, a bustling area of business activity, and also the headquarters of the largest hydroelectric plant in Nepal. After asking several shop owners if they knew of a person named Prim Kumari, someone said, "Yes. She lives in Sahu Goan." Getting there meant several hours of hiking for Marge and Poonam, but they were determined. They packed their sleeping bags and started up the steep dirt path, not knowing what was ahead.

The path led almost straight up about 2,000 feet. Sahu Goan is the highest village above Trisuli. They met a young boy along the path, and he offered to take them to Prim Kumari's house. When they reached her house, the guide called for Prim to come out. She motioned for them to sit on what looked like a porch. Questions and questions followed, and answers unfolded as this little old lady mopped her brow and finally blurted out, "Yes, yes, I remember 'baba.' I take to hospital. Brother's wife, she die in labor, here on floor," stomping her foot.

"Lit'l baba gal. She sick, so sick. No milk, no med-cin. She die, stay here. Her name Poonam, meaning born under the full moon. I put baba on back. Carry down mountain. Take bus-car to Kathmandu, left lit'l baba Poonam with med-cin lady in hospital. She no sick no more? She go to America? No? Yes! Yes!"

Wringing her hands and adjusting her skirt, she slowly turned around on her seat and focused her eyes on Poonam. "You baba Poonam?" Then the tears streamed down her withered cheeks.

And as the story unfolded, so did the word spread. People appeared from everywhere. They were talking, laughing, and gazing in total wonderment. So she was that baby girl—all grown up. Her beauty shone through every movement she made and every word she spoke. But who were all these people?

An older man walked onto the porch and squatted down in front of Poonam. He was introduced. "This is your father, and he is seventy years old. And here is your oldest brother. He is forty-seven. And your sister, twenty-five." Soon, another brother arrived, followed by sisters-in-law, nieces and nephews, and too many others to list. It seemed Poonam was related in some way to the entire village.

In the midst of all the excitement, Poonam's father was watching her every move. A bit dubious, he began pointing to his hip. He described a birthmark he remembered on his child's hip. Poonam turned toward her father and said, "Yes, I have such a mark." How amazing that he should remember this! That was certainly proof positive.

Her father had remarried and was still living in the red clay house where Poonam was born. Conditions over the past twenty years had vastly improved, and there was water and electricity in the village. Everything in the house was neat and clean. Marge and Poonam spent the night in their sleeping bags, but Poonam was too excited to sleep. Everyone woke with the roosters, and a day of fun began.

Everyone put on their best clothes. Suit jackets for the men, and the women wore their wedding jewelry. Many pictures were taken. Each wanted a turn standing next to Poonam. A festive air prevailed, and all kinds of food were brought in. They ate fried eggs, rice and lentils, chicken curry, and drank buffalo milk. Yes, even popcorn and peanuts were available. Unfortunately, it was time to leave. All too soon, Marge and Poonam had to start the long trek downhill. Their mission accomplished. Roots found.

As they prepared to say their Namastes, Poonam looked around for her father. He was nowhere to be found. He just couldn't say goodbye a second time.

This was certainly a trip to remember. Tracking down and discovering one's natural parents is not unusual today for adopted children. But Poonam discovered more than she could imagine. She now knew who she was, where she came from, and how extremely fortunate she was to have found a loving family in Nepal. Best of all, Poonam knew how lucky she was to have her own loving family and friends in the United States.

Poonam is happily married, and lives in Baltimore, Maryland.

Uncle Charlie and Me

Ruth Weiss Hohberg

I'm a sickly, skinny, platinum-haired, blue-eyed five-year-old boy.

I have memories of sitting by the window of my parents' brownstone in Brooklyn, watching the kids play outside, too weak to join them, always tired. One day, my Uncle Charlie comes to visit. He invites me to come to spend the summer at his chicken farm in Toncanic, the little Pennsylvania town where he lives. Uncle Charlie changes my life.

As soon as I arrive, I just have a feeling that this summer will be lots of fun. My aunts, Gertrude and Martha, Uncle Charlie's sisters, welcome me warmly. I feel at home right away. In all that space under so much sky, I don't even feel homesick. There's lots to explore, chickens to chase, and an amazing sky filled with shiny stars to puzzle over at night.

For breakfast, there's always a glass of milk, fresh from the barn, at my place at the table, but the drink my uncle gives me at lunch and dinner is different; it's imported German beer. I've never seen or heard of it before, but like its strange new taste.

Aunt Martha is a hairdresser who owns a salon and likes to fuss with my long hair. Aunt Gertrude takes care of running the house and growing the vegetables in her garden. As soon as I know my way around, Aunt Gert assigns me chores.

She reaches for a beat-up aluminum dish. "The beans need picking. Here, I show you how. Go ahead, put them in this bowl." I'm happy to do her bidding and fit right into their childless, but loving family.

My Uncle Charlie is the best! He's tall and has big, strong muscles. He calls me Rohbert with the emphasis on the narrow "o" and a wide "ee" that sounds foreign. His heavy German accent and deep voice are commanding, but somehow funny. When I hear him say it that special way, I know he's inviting me to share in an adventure.

One day, Uncle Charlie calls in his special deep tone of voice, "Kom, vee go for a vok!" It's not really, not exactly a walk for a walk's sake. It's a purposeful march to the local barbershop. This is a trip with a special mission.

"Give my neview here a proper haircut," he orders the barber, an old crony of his. "He's five years old and still looks like a girl. It's stoopid!"

I have never had a haircut, and this is the moment to shed my Little Lord Fauntleroy curls. This is great! Aunt Martha won't ever be able to use a curling iron on me again! What joy! I almost jump into the barber's chair. When the job is done, I see the barber sweeping up blond locks scattered on the floor around the barber's chair. I look in the mirror ahead of me and gee whiz! I look like a real boy. I like it!

From today on, I won't stay with my aunts and their lady friends for Sunday afternoon teas anymore. I'll do boy things, like climbing up tree trunks and over fences, and go to Mr. Brundage's barn to see how he milks his cows. One of the cows, the one with big beautiful brown eyes, is my friend; we like each other.

Once, when I was milking, I got on the wrong side of her. She whacked me so hard with her tail that I flew to the other end of the barn. I never forgot. Now she stands quite still, swishing her tail back and forth, and I have a real good time talking to her while milking. I stay in the right place and don't get in the way of that strong, hairy tail-brush.

One sunny warm morning, Uncle Charlie calls, "Kom on, Rohbert, vee go take a ride in ze boat."

I'm ready. Barefoot, wearing only shorts and a blue-and-white-striped polo shirt, I follow as he leads the way down the muddy path to the river. His rowboat is resting upside down, halfway up on the riverbank to keep it from floating away. I help him turn it right side up. We push it to the water's edge, secure the oars, and climb in. I sit in the prow, watching the spot where the sharp triangular edge of the boat slices through the smooth, murky, brownish-green water, pushing it to both sides in a vee shape. Uncle Charlie rows away from the shore. The muscles in his strong arms make it look so easy. He can even make the boat glide smoothly against the current.

Suddenly, he reaches toward me very fast and gives me a shove that sends me toppling over the edge into the water. "*Shvim!*" he orders.

In my panic and terror I blow and spit water out of my nose and mouth. Terrified and inspired, I paddle for my life with hands and feet any which way I can. My uncle seems to be rowing away from me.

He keeps the boat just slightly out of my reach, watching my struggle.

"Verry goot, keep going." I dog paddle madly, trying not to swallow more of the muddy water than I already have. In a little while that seems very long to me, he stops rowing. I catch up, and he pulls me into the boat.

Triumph and pride light his smiling, sun-tanned face. "Verry goot! Now you know how to shvim. Let's go home and tell Auntie Gert and have lunch." He gives me a bear hug and a loving swat to my wet behind. I can't wait to go back in the water and try it again.

I return to the farm every summer. There's so much to learn; new adventures always await. By the summer I am ten, the farm is my second home. I know "the ropes" and am familiar with Uncle Charlie's and my aunts' habits.

On July 10, 1941, I hear my uncle call. "Kom here, Rohbert, here in the parlor!" It isn't usual for me to be invited to that special room, the one Aunt Gertrude keeps reserved for Sunday visitors, where every surface of the furniture is always spotlessly clean and not bearing a little boy's fingerprints, where every decorative knick-knack is in its carefully chosen place. Did I hear right? Am I really being invited into the parlor? I hesitate on the threshold. Aunt Gertrude is in the kitchen, and Aunt Martha is sitting on the loveseat, looking pleased and eager, encouragement sparkling in her eyes.

"Kom in, kom in. Gert, we are vaiting for you, mach schnell!" Uncle Charlie calls to his sister. Gert appears, wearing an apron to protect her dress, a dishtowel in her hands, as usual. Charlie is standing near the fireplace, holding a long, narrow cardboard box. He comes toward me and holds out his arms, offering it.

"Here, this is for you. Happy Birthday, Rohbert." The Aunts sing the birthday song, filling in "Happy *tenth* Birthday," and clap their hands as loudly as they can. I open the box in a hurry, tearing the cardboard in my impatience to find out what it is.

A .22 rifle for my 10th birthday! Wow! This is fantastic! I couldn't have wished for anything better. I'll be able to join the other boys in the neighborhood when they go "hunting in the woods." I feel so grown up!

Before I can run out to show the present to my friends on the farm next door, we lay the gun on the table, and Uncle Charlie begins to the take it apart. Slowly, carefully, one at a time, he hands me every piece to examine in detail and explains what it does. When they're all on the table, we put all the pieces together again. Now I see how they fit into each other. He makes me imitate his every move to show him I am learning how to handle it safely. Then he gives me a mandate: I am to keep the critter population—snakes, rabbits and other varmints that are destroying the vegetable garden—in check by shooting them before they trample, chew up, or pull out Auntie Gertrude's plantings.

And speaking of dear, good Auntie Gertrude! At breakfast in the morning, she is the only one who lets me have butter *and* jam on my bread, along with fresh milk from Mr. Brundage's farm next door. On the other hand, she assigns me the chore of pulling the strings from the green beans, something I really don't like to do. After such a good breakfast and being allowed to shoot varmints in the garden, how could I say no?

At the end of each enchanted summer, I go back to Brooklyn to start the next school year. I'm older now, still blond and blue-eyed, but no longer sickly and tired. I am tanned, have muscles, and am full of energy. In later years, it's revealed that, in addition to the loving, nurturing family and the open space and sunshine of the farm, the secret ingredient, the source of my strength, was vitamin B in the beer.

You Should Have

Kathleen A. O'Brien

You should have solace of stew this night,
    prescribed to put meat on your skinny bones,
selected to stick to your scarecrow ribs.
    A savory stew is as ancient as stones.

A trespassing cold front is pressing through
    with wind chill factored to 13 below.
Children muffled and mittened as mummies,
    grip parents' hands and trudge through the snow.

I'll heat the skillet so butter can skate
    across the black pan my grandmother used,
Next, I'll chop beef into 1-inch cubes
    and add the meat with white flour infused.

Carrots I'll free of filigreed leaves,
    and lop off like logs from a woodsman's ax;
then celery stalks I'll diagonally slice,
    and cleave onions, gleaming like globes of wax.

Tomatoes plump as Italian mamas
    with Sunday aprons cinched round their waists,
and potatoes peeled and quartered, I'll place
    in a crockpot; salt and pepper to taste.

You can stop by on your way home from work.
    All will be ready; you'll have nothing to do
(but maybe you'd like to sit down with me),
    for tonight's a night for simmering stew.

Untidy Cactus

Mardy Stotsky

Sprawling outside my
window, like
sun-hardened hoses
kinked and useless,
the Medusa of the cactus world:
staghorn cholla, twisted spiney
stalks bent into angles
stiff as steel
I look at this unwieldiness
and think oh, the stories
I haven't told

Harvesting the Cactus Apple

Zola Stoltz

The magenta fruit that crowns the prickly pear cactus is also called a cactus pear and, in season, those beautiful egg-shaped fruits beg to be plucked. The locals tell me they make an excellent jelly and syrup, as well. Discussions yielded quite a variety of uses, including adding to Jell-O, fruit mixtures, ice cream toppers, and meat marinades. If it involves food, I'd give it a try, as I'm most always up for a challenge. The thorns and spines on the plant and fruit make for a daunting experience.

As a new widow, I moved to the northernmost edge of the Chihuahuan Desert in 2003. A large variety of desert shrubs and cacti grows here, so most of my foraging was done near the tiny hamlet of Portal, Arizona in the Chiricahua Mountains. My home was at 5,200 feet elevation and four miles from the Portal store, which was roughly 4,700 feet elevation. I had a lot to learn about rural living, the wild life, unique plants, and their potential uses. Toward the end of summer, the prickly pear fruit started to fall, probably ripe, as evidenced by the number of wildlife feasting on them. Armed with heavy shoes on my feet, a long-sleeved shirt to protect against sun and stickers, a fistful of plastic bags, and some long-handled tongs, adventure beckoned. My truck bounced over dirt roads to a prime area I'd been told about near town. Some of the fruit was the size of lemons or extra-extra large eggs! The thorns of the cactus were not the only stickers. Mesquite and cat-claw acacia stuffed between some of the cacti made moving around a greater challenge than plucking fruit from the plant.

Both eyes and ears must be on alert every moment in the desert. Most rattlesnakes would warn, but once in a while, especially if the snake was caught napping, there would be no warning. No one would want to step on a less than friendly reptile. Keeping eyes to the ground had another plus—the sighting of bear and javelina scat. Talk about doing something stupid. I was about to raid a favorite snack area of the peccary and black bear. How intelligent was that? Well, it involved food, so I busily double-bagged plastic grocery bags; they have handles.

My scoop-shaped tongs seemed just right to cradle the 'apples', and the first few practically fell off. Most were a rhythm of grasp, twist, and pull, drop into the bag, and then repeat. The poor cactus plant, covered with blood-red smudges nearly everywhere I had removed the fruit, looked like I was killing it.

When the handle of the bag would begin to cut into my fingers, I knew it was sufficiently full, and I'd start loading another. After three such were loaded to my satisfaction, I drove home, while fretting about the next stage.

The fine spines on the fruit are difficult to remove and getting one or more on a hand or arm could be quite painful. I tried to hold one piece of fruit in the tongs and peel it. I'd be into the next summer doing it that way. Maybe they could be burned off. Waiting until the heat of the day lessened, so the sun would no longer be baking the patio where my barbeque was located, would make the chore easier.

At the cooler hour, I poured one bag of produce into a stockpot, half-filled a bucket with cold water, and proceeded to place the fruit in rows on the hot grill. Rubber gloves helped to keep unwanted stickers off my tender fingers. Each load was rolled around over the fire for three to six minutes, and then each dropped into the cold water. It's good I hadn't picked any more than I did. Once the pot was empty, it was rinsed and loaded with the drained fruit. That was sufficient for one day. I put the lidded pot in the kitchen and went about other pursuits.

Next morning, wearing rubber gloves and using tongs, I cut the blossom ends off and peeled the softened fruit as best I could. By the time I was at the bottom of the pot, I was squeezing the fruit out of the skins. At that moment I realized the kitchen looked like I had slaughtered someone or something. Had the sheriff shown up right then, he would have arrested me without question. The fuchsia color on those yellow gloves, along with bits of fruit and skin, looked just like pieces of bloody meat. Not only were my gloved hands a mess, but also the walls, floor, switch plates, stove, countertops, and the sink.

I found it interesting that nothing stained the vibrant color of the fruit, but those globes produce a waxy substance that leaves tannish-yellow stains on dish towels and the like. There was also a residue on the barbeque grill, which eventually burned off. I suppose a good cleaning agent would have removed it, but I was into cooking, not cleaning.

I rinsed the pot again, put the fruit back into it, and cooked the mix for a good hour—a nice round figure that sounded right. The next step was to put large spoonfuls of pulp into what I assumed was a berry press. It had belonged to my mother, but I never saw her use it. Like a broad funnel with the bottom half cut off and replaced with a heavy-duty strainer, it had a blade with a handle attached. I grasped the handle and turned. The blade was on an angle, so that one end scraped against the sieve while the raised end scooped the fruit under. Periodically reversing the clockwise motion, the blade would then scrape the leavings off the holes, and I'd dump the seeds and skins into a garbage bag. The prickly pear must be ninety percent rock-hard seeds, and those seeds kept popping out of the press and all over the kitchen.

I could have thrown out the seeds and skin for the critters, but had no desire to draw the bear to my property or wish a return of the peccary. Those voracious small barrels on stilts eat most everything in sight and left this property years ago for easier pickings, like in town, where thickets of the prickly pear grow in abundance.

So far, so good. The exquisitely colored juice was almost sufficient reward for all the work. It tasted sweet and more than acceptable, although it was obvious that it might, for many, be considered an acquired taste. Not yet done, I poured the juice through a very fine strainer, and then into a container for the freezer. Once the remaining bags were processed, the frozen juice would be thawed and strained through cheesecloth, probably two or three times. The cheesecloth was hiding—maybe in one of the cabinets in the garage. No stray stickers were wanted to mar my first efforts!

The second batch went a little easier. Perhaps eliminating the burn process and boiling instead might make the work with the press a little longer, but would eliminate a few steps, and overall might be quicker. Perhaps using the little propane torch would work, but I'd have to learn to use it first. Spread the fruit on the grill, burn over the lot, roll them a little and repeat until all were done. That way the fruit wouldn't be turned to mush inside the skin and might be more efficient to work with. It'd be a plan worth a try, perhaps some other time.

Friends say that there is such a thing as an extractor, where you put the entire fruit in, and it processes out all the seeds, thorns, and skins. I'd have to see it in action first before making a decision. In the meantime, I'd have to bite the bullet and finish what I started. I'd have all winter to decide how to properly process those magenta globes. Do you suppose folks on an Indian reservation would be willing to show me how it is really done?

Next year I should be prepared. A little over a quart was the sum of this year's adventure. Some mixed with sour cream and brown sugar turned into a deliciously brilliant shade of pink for a fruit topping. It was not bad used in a marinade for what I labeled scarlet chicken, with spices and a little chili oil. Selling it was not an option. In terms of time, who'd buy a questionable flavor at thirty dollars a half pint?

Posing this problem to some of my new friends, they all laughed. One said, "Hell, boil up what you harvest and strain it through a couple of clean old t-shirts and you're good to go." I should have asked first what to do with my harvest, not after the fact!

In Honor of my Mother

Gloria Salas-Jennings

In honor of my mother
    I pick through the freckled pinto beans,
        And spy that errant piece of gravel
            Hiding in the cellophane bag.

In honor of my mother
    I use the dark stone formed from an ancient volcano,
        firmly crush pungent garlic and cumino in her *molcajete*
            and I remember *fiestas* from long ago.

In honor of my mother
    I stir the simple grains of rice, turning them into a caramel brown,
        pour the golden broth slowly as she taught me,
            sprinkle in the spices, and taste memories of her.

In honor of my mother
    I pick yellow zinnias and white daisies
        from her garden, long untended,
            and pose them in the ancient blue porcelain vase.

In honor of my mother
    I liberate my black rosary from its red velvet pouch,
        go to her altar ablaze with candles
            and pray to *La Virgin de Guadalupe.*

In honor of my mother
        I kneel at the sacred place where she rests,

And in honor of my mother,

            I silently weep.

Market Prices

Helen Benson

"If I had a million dollars"
A game we used to play
When a Cadillac car,
A house at the beach
And three pairs of shoes
Seemed just about enough
To fill the pot
At the end of the rainbow.
We didn't know our bank account
Was already full
With legs than ran forever,
A mamma-filled kitchen
That smelled of bread just baked,
A couple of friends to share with.
Especially
We didn't know
There were no price tags
On moonbeams.

Grandmother in a Gray Flannel Suit

Joanna Wanderman

When I was very small, right after my mother was sent to a sanitarium and before I was sent to board at St. Cecelia's Convent School, I lived with Dama Schatzi, my seventy-eight-year-old Austrian-born grandmother.

Once a month on a Tuesday she took me to visit her youngest daughter, my Aunt Anne, who lived a few miles and many millions of dollars away. My grandmother made a special effort on those Tuesdays to look like she belonged in that affluent neighborhood. First, her teeth that had spent the night in a water glass on the dresser went into her mouth, followed by a generous gulp of Kimmel straight out of the bottle she kept on the closet floor. Then, properly dentured and well fortified, she took a set of clean underwear from the bureau drawer and began getting dressed.

My grandmother wore flannel underwear: gray wool flannel, the five-button trap door in the seat kind that made a kangaroo-mama pouch between her thighs. She waddled when she walked. Once she had the underwear in place, she slipped a lavender and pink paisley print dress over her head, sprayed homemade sugar water wave-set onto her hair, twisting the white strands into a bun, adjusted a tri-cornered, black Napoleon chapeau on her head, and together we went out on the front porch to wait.

Promptly at 10 AM, Aunt Anne's chauffeur picked us up and drove us to her home, a Tudor-style mansion on the golf course in Hancock Park with a porte-cochére that jutted out over the driveway. Aunt Anne was always in her bedroom when we arrived, recovering from the night before or revving up for the one to come. The large room took all of the upstairs floor space and was decorated in boudoir colors of aqua, silver, and duck-egg blue. Chiffon sheers hung over the vanity, swagged in place by satin cord tassels.

Aunt Anne greeted us with hugs and kisses, and we sat on plush velvet slipper chairs surrounding her platform bed. She told my grandmother about the recent appointment of her husband to Harbor Commissioner, the advantages of cigarettes over snuff (which Dama Schatzi used frequently) and, most important to me, my mother's progress in the sanitarium.

At lunchtime, finger sandwiches, hot tea, and Austrian crumb cake were brought up on a silver tray from the kitchen. We ate, sipped, and talked some more until she yawned and said it was time for her nap, leaving my grandmother and me free to roam around the house.

We stole everything in sight. Jewelry, a wristwatch, two cigarette lighters, a Fabergé egg, anything small enough to fit through the five-button trap door of my grandmother's underwear and slide down into the kangaroo pouch. "We're not stealing," she would whisper. "It's not a sin, it's for Boyliech (an endearing name for an Austrian male child), Bitsy, and Brother." Boyliech, Bitsy, and Brother, my grandmother's out-of-work youngest son and his two offspring. Boyliech, Bitsy, and Brother: their names sounded like a big rubber ball bouncing down the stairs.

Our most ambitious hoist proved to be our undoing: an old set of Rogers Sterling Silver found in the pantry, now nestled comfortably in my grandmother's underwear, ready to make the trip home. As she lifted up her arms to hug Aunt Anne good-bye, out of the pouch between her thighs, down through her pant legs and onto the floor landed a place setting for four.

Like my favorite movies of the day, this story has a Shirley Temple ending. Aunt Anne let us keep the silverware. She said it was the best laugh she'd had all morning. Soon after that, her husband rehired the two maids let go on suspicion of theft, but, best of all, my father took me back home to live with him until school started in the fall.

Back Porch Callers

Anna Mae Loebig

We children mostly used the back door for our comings and goings, especially in the winter. It was just easier to shed boots and book bags on the back porch and kitchen floor and, besides, the kitchen hot air register was only a few short steps from the back door, welcoming our cold or wet feet on a frigid winter day. As we grew older, the five of us graduated to the front door entrance, the same as our relatives, neighbors, and friends. We were then considered more grown-up, sort of.

Mum, though, had two gentleman callers who always used the back door when they visited, knowing each would receive a hot meal or sandwich, dining, of course, on the back porch. I'm certain she slipped them a few coins at times. In their shabby attire of dirty pants, old worn shirts and jackets, a few days' growth of beard on deep-lined faces, each appeared to be ancient to our young eyes. However, in hindsight, they were probably in their fifties or early sixties. The tallest of Mum's callers had long dangling arms extending from his five-foot, ten-inch frame. His thin face was lined with crevices across the forehead and alongside his nose and mouth, giving him the rugged appearance of an outdoorsman, especially if he had a beard.

The other back porch visitor was slightly built, weighing about 130 pounds, a little stooped over, with a soft, round face and soft eyes that reflected a gentle demeanor, in spite of his shabby appearance. This gentleman wasn't an ordinary beggar; he was an entrepreneur, his specialty being the sale of wooden matches used to light the kitchen stove and coal furnace. Mum was a softy to anyone in need, and she provided her callers with meals and some change before they left.

To my knowledge, our home and that of a neighbor, Mrs. Fields, were the only two houses on our block that greeted these men with some degree of hospitality. They always came separately and, we think, weren't always aware of each other. But, on the other hand, they may have been friends, passing along the word of a good place for a handout, which each received from Mum's generous heart.

Piles of Plenty, Stacks of Stuff

Celia Glasgow

I might use it someday,
but I probably won't.
I spent a lot of money on all this stuff,
but now it's merely clutter.
Someone in the family might want or need it,
but it's highly unlikely!

These recipes I clipped sound delicious,
but I'll never bake, fry, broil or sauté any of these dishes.

A friend gave this book to me, a friend long-dead,
but saving her gift won't bring her back to me.

Why is it so hard to let go?
Does a part of me go with my giveaways?
Most of my life may be over,
but there is still time to move on,
lightly.

Clutter: Too Many Good Things

Celia Glasgow

Yesterday, while standing in the checkout line with my milk and bananas, I noticed that several women's magazines featured articles on the subject of household clutter. My thesaurus gives "space" as the opposite of clutter. If we can unclutter, we can give ourselves breathing space to enjoy the rest of our lives.

Why do seniors, especially, have so much clutter? Americans have had more disposable income during the last few years, making it easy to acquire books, magazines, electronic gadgets, hobby equipment, and all the other items that overflow our homes. However, especially for people like me, born during the 1930s and '40s, it is much harder to get rid of these household objects. We were raised by parents whose mottos were: *Make do. Wear it out. Do without.*

Younger generations of Americans have grown up in a disposable society, where it is cheaper to throw away and replace equipment than to repair it. Modern computers, cameras, scanners, DVD players, cell phones, and other electronics become quickly outdated as newer technology emerges. Five years is considered the average life for a computer. When we were growing up, the idea of planned obsolescence was just emerging, with radical automobile redesigns every few years and electronics that wore out after limited use.

Over the years, most of us have inherited large pieces of furniture, albums of family pictures, extra sets of china, and other cherished possessions from family members who have passed on. Add to this all the gifts we've received over the years, all the latest household items we bought as soon as they hit the market, and all the individual and family keepsakes of a lifetime, and too often we end up with wall-to-wall furniture and closets crammed to the bursting point.

Eventually, we realize that household clutter is making us unhappy because we can't find what we need, we can't care for what we have, and we feel crowded and uncomfortable with so many objects around us. This is the time to start to unburden and clear out some of the flotsam of our lives.

We need to think about what our life is now. What are our interests? How do we spend our time? What do we think our lives will be like in the next few years? Then we need to start giving away, throwing away, or selling the objects we no longer need. We will then have the time and energy to clean, repair, organize, and use the things we decide to keep.

MAKE TIME FOR WHAT REALLY COUNTS!

It Rains

Irma Sheppard

It rains, and a fine-toothed wind,
bellwether of dark desires—obscure, forgotten—
combs the palo verde, the eucalyptus, the mesquite.

Fragments of all I ever wanted—the silence of canyons,
beaches and woods, blossoms in meadows,
home, buttered bread, tea—scatter.

Paired javelinas enter into the very center of the city.
Fearless, they root through burlap and birdseed, leaving them
as wounded works that linger in a museum storeroom.

Did I think I had never wanted a child?

The rain pauses, a scene unfinished.
Bark, leaves, seeds have already suffered
the attack of Tucson's August monsoon light.

I walk early in the slanted sun shafts,
the scent of creosote tight in each breath.
Old desires catch me unawares—

I am barefoot all over.

Exuberance

Nancy Sandweiss

Released from preschool
Noah rushes puppy-like
through the hall, flinging
his yellow windbreaker into the air,
tackling it with pintsize frame.
Again and again he tosses, dives
while older children form lines
to wait for busses.

I try to restrain him,
afraid that the gym teacher
with big biceps who patrols the hall
will spot his antics, bark
No running inside.

Noah flashes an impish smile,
wriggles from my grasp;
hurls the bright jacket, propels
himself to the floor.
Retrieving the yellow bundle,
I nudge him out the door,
watch him race to the car,
will his spirit to survive.

His Name Should Have Been Houdini

Henriette Goldsmith

"Are we *really* getting rid of him?" my son, Neal, gleefully asked. That's a very strange thing for an eleven-year old boy to say about his dog. I always thought boys were supposed to love their dogs. But Tevye wasn't exactly a dog…

It's been ten years since we said goodbye to him. My husband gathered up the dog's pedigree papers, and he and my son marched him off to the pound. It was a sad day—sad for everyone except the boy to whom he belonged. Neal could hardly conceal his delight.

I remember the day we decided to get a canine pet. It wasn't going to be just *any* kind. It would be a special one. He had to be very gentle, one our young son would love, and one who would be good to have around for our future grandchild, whose birth was imminent. I was hoping we would find an *unusual* dog. It didn't take long to discover just how unusual he was.

His name wasn't always Tevye. It used to be Charlie. But how could you call a beautiful St. Bernard "Charlie"? It was just too ordinary a name. His big, sad eyes reminded us of Tevye, the father in *Fiddler on the Roof*. So, after he came to live with us, Charlie had a new name—Tevye—and life was never the same.

We were so proud of him that we sent out birth announcements to all our friends to let them know of the new addition to our family. Because they were aware that we were expecting a new grandchild momentarily, you can imagine their astonishment when they read the news that a 110-pound baby had arrived.

Tevye liked company so much that he would do anything to be with us. The first night he lived with us, we decided that, since he was such a large dog, we would keep him in our yard. But he had other plans. He tore big holes in all the screen doors, and then managed to open the sliding door to come inside. No matter how I locked him out, he always managed to get inside. I don't know how he did it, and I began calling him "Houdini." I would lock him out, walk into the den a short time later, and there he would sit, waiting for someone to pet him. After several days and nights of these magical tricks on his part, we finally decided that he must be a house dog. So now he had a new place to stay—inside.

Having him in the house was like having a young horse walking around, although he was very careful and never disturbed my furniture or disrupted any of the bric-a-brac on the tables. He did, however, think he was a "lap dog," and several times tried to climb into my lap when I sat down on the sofa.

Taking Tevye for a walk in the neighborhood was quite an experience. You had to be prepared to be dragged down the street hanging on to the leash, while the dog galloped like a horse. When he stood quietly, he held the same attraction for passersby as a baby in a stroller or carriage. People stopped to ask questions about him, petted him, stroked him, pinched him, and smiled at him.

One day, Neal took him out for an afternoon stroll and, as usual, he encountered an admiring group of people. One man invited him to bring Tevye into his house, because he just *had* to show him to his wife. The boy sincerely tried to discourage this, but the man persisted. All went well until Tevye spotted a group of potted plants on the floor, walked over to them, lifted his hind leg, and sprayed a shower all over the plants and the lady's new powder blue crushed velvet sofa! With a mumbled, embarrassed apology, my son quickly left the house, dragging Tevye with him, who by now had decided he liked it there and didn't want to leave.

One of Tevye's favorite activities made him look like a child at play. He would come charging down our long carpeted hallway, working up such momentum that by the time he reached the entry hall, he would slide across the entire terrazzo floor (like a *Slip and Slide* game)—and then come to a screeching halt.

We began taking Tevye with us whenever we went out. He loved riding in the car. The fact that we had only a small coupe didn't bother him a bit. Heads would turn wherever we went. People would look with disbelief at the sight of this huge dog filling up the entire back seat of the car, his enormous head poked out the window.

One night, we went to a party and left Tevye locked safely in our yard behind the garden gate. Returning home at 2 AM, we found "Houdini"—he had done it again—sitting there in front of the gate, pleased as punch with himself, waiting for us to come home. As my husband opened the door of the car to get out, into the back seat vaulted Tevye. We coaxed him, pleaded with him, pulled at him, and pushed him to get him out of the car, but he wouldn't budge.

Suddenly, I had a brilliant idea and said to my husband, "Why don't you take him for a ride around the block? Then he'll be satisfied!" And that's exactly what happened. When they returned, Tevye was perfectly willing to get out of the car and call it a day (or night, whichever was the case).

Tevye soon found a favorite spot in the house to relax. He would plunk himself down in the hallway like a "troll" guarding a bridge and sleep there. Anyone wanting to walk to the other rooms would be forced to step over him. He was really quite harmless. He didn't care how many people stepped over him—that is, unless it was my son. For some unknown reason, he would become menacing whenever Neal attempted to walk down the hallway. He could be sound asleep, but when the boy started to walk past him, Tevye would open one eye, look up at him and growl. Needless to say, this was quite inconvenient—especially for Neal.

One summer, my husband's parents visited us from the midwest. I thought we might have problems with Tevye around, but was delighted to see my mother-in-law stop and pat him on the head every time she passed him in the hallway.

"Mom," I said, "I'm really glad and surprised to see how much you like Tevye."

"You think I like him?" she answered.

"Well, yes," I said. "I always see you petting him."

"Frankly," she said, "I can't stand him. I just want to keep on the good side of him."

I had a rather frightening (and, at the same time, amusing) experience one day when Tevye was in his dog run behind a tall chainlink fence in our back yard. He was barking rather urgently and looked as though he wanted to get out of the run. As I opened the gate to let him out, he lunged at me. Sidestepping him, I jumped into the dog run and quickly shut the gate behind me. Congratulating myself at being so clever and nimble, I started to leave the run—and then realized that Tevye had no intention of letting me get out. Every time I tried to open the gate, he began to growl at me.

Even from across the yard, he would race over to me and growl the minute I put my hand on the latch. I remained locked in my prison for the next two hours, until the gardener rescued me.

Neal's friends stopped coming over. One boy, who lived across the street, couldn't play in front of his own house when we had Tevye outside on a leash, because the dog would become ferocious whenever he saw the lad. We began to suspect a rather odd quirk in Tevye's behavior. *He didn't like little boys—especially dark-haired little boys!* Since Neal's hair was not quite dark or light, he was on the borderline of Tevye's ire.

One summer day, we had a large patio party with many friends and their children invited. I commented to my husband, "We had better watch Tevye carefully when the Gottliebs get here, because you know both of their boys have dark hair." With about twenty-five friends and their children already in our back yard and swimming pool, and no problems with Tevye, the Gottliebs arrived with their sons. The minute they set foot in the yard, Tevye started chasing the older one. We, of course, had to lock the dog in his run.

When Tevye came to live with us, we had a little kitten, named Goliath, who looked like a smokey ball of fur. One day, I rescued her just in time as Tevye was in the process of gulping her down. Goliath immediately found herself a new home down the street and never returned.

We were having so many problems with our pet that we decided he needed to be enrolled in a dog training school. He didn't last very long in the class because of the disruption he caused by galloping around, with the other dogs following suit and chasing alongside him. One dog in particular knocked down the lady who was training him. He dragged her by the leash for several yards. By the time he stopped, the poor woman had twisted her ankle, scuffed her knee, and broken her finger. The trainer asked us to leave.

Most of the time, our dog was fine in the house. He really didn't bother or upset anything. There was only one obstacle to keeping him inside. I was forced to keep most of the mirrors in our house covered because he would get absolutely fierce at the sight of his own reflection.

When we decided he needed a bath, I took him to a dog grooming establishment. The lady was all smiles when I dropped him off (reacting like most strangers did when they first saw him). She was talking baby-talk to him as I left. Upon returning, there was Tevye, looking amazingly like a fluffy, giant teddy bear with a bow on top of his head. But the lady looked a disheveled wreck. As I paid the bill, she said to me, "Next time, it will be ten dollars more!"

The most unforgettable of all the Tevye shenanigans was the dining room window incident. We had a circular bay window made of several panels of glass. When anyone knocked on the front door, Tevye would run to the window, jump up on his hind legs, and put his paws on the glass. After a number of times, the grouting between the panels cracked, and the glass became loose. I worried that, one day, someone would come onto the front porch, and Tevye would go right through the window. But window-repairing was a nuisance chore, so my husband wasn't in a hurry to get the job done.

The day wasn't long in coming. The doorbell rang and, as usual, Tevye went through his act at the window. Only, this time, he went crashing through! A typical response on my part would have been an emotional reaction to this scene. But, having expected it for so long, I calmly walked over to the shattered window, holding onto Tevye with one hand, and, with the other hand placed casually on my hip, said to the man at the door, "Yes, sir. What can I do for you?"

From my behavior, the unfortunate man probably thought this was an everyday occurrence with us. He stood there, petrified. I asked if he was hurt.

He said, "My leg is cut."

I could see it was only a minor laceration and offered him a Band Aid. He left rather hastily and didn't wait to discuss it with me. Besides, he was on the wrong street, looking for someone else.

Despite Tevye's clown antics, we realized that he was becoming a menace. His dislike of small boys was a potential danger that could surface at any time and lead to tragedy. Inevitably, the time came when we knew we could no longer keep our pet and would have to give him away. Due to his reputation, we didn't know anyone who would take him. My husband and son took him to the pound, knowing that he would find many people there interested in giving him a good home.

There were! They lined up five deep, all begging to take home this beautiful giant. The winner was a lady whose two little girls were tumbling all over Tevye. The dog looked as contented as a kitten at play. With a warning to her of Tevye's peculiar personality, my husband handed over the pedigree papers, and my son threw his arms around the dog for the last time and then walked away…never even once looking back.

Beach Treasure

Mardy Stotsky

I have borrowed my friend's dog for an early morning walk on the beach. The sun is just getting started, not high enough to bring warmth. My sweats feel cozy, but the damp will make them seem heavy soon. I try to stay out of the water, bare feet searching for hard-packed sand instead of sinking into ankle-deep mush at the edge of the surf.

The keen brown Doberman is far down the beach now, legs a blur, pounding his joy into the hard pack. His footprints remain a long time, they are so deep.

I search the coarse gray sand, hoping for moonstones I've found here before. In the shining water many small stones are tempting colors. My pockets are lumpy with them, and I rattle as I walk. The surf is gentle this morning as if tired after a night of crashing hard at the rocks that guard this small beach.

Now the dog runs back, passes me, circles, wants me to know his heart cannot contain the wonders of his running. Off again, he extends himself into his freedom—no limits, no purpose—just marvelous running, becoming one with all the world.

When it's time to go, I leave the beach—richer by far.

Juvenile Goshawk

Mimi Moriarty

I

Left alone to hunt, he keens into the quiet morning
he's hungry, adults no longer feed him.

This is how it is in avian tales, tantrums,
craving mice, sight and flight his talismans.

He will leave us soon. Every day he flies
farther afield, no longer from limb to limb

but corkscrewing over the earth, and like
my own children, he will leave not just a ripple

but waves.

II

We speak weekly, less in summer, the rubble
of their lives takes time to sort, I am at the bottom.

They purge by bonfire their past association,
or flush it, while I radiate anticipation

a call, a dropped note.

I am left to write straight lines in an empty pew
miniaturize their childhood into frames,

snap it shut, stand at the door,
watch the goshawk make his first kill.

First Runner-up: Best Fiction Contest

The Road Kill Chronicle

Marymarc Armstrong

"Mommy," Crystal sniffed in the back seat of the car, her face pressed against the window. "I don't see Puffy." She rubbed her snotty nose against the glass and whined. "Kelly let my puppy run away."

Kelly sat next to Jones, sulking as she had for the past month. They were looking for the puppy Crystal's father had given her. Kelly let the dog out of the apartment the night before, and he had not returned by the time Jones got home from work in the morning. The puppy showed up at the apartment the Sunday morning after Jones had moved herself and the girls out of her husband's house. It was in a crate on the porch, left there while they were at Wal-Mart stocking up groceries and household goods. Kelly loved the little white squirmy ball of fur until she saw Wayne's note. He had written: "To my Crystal, I miss you—Daddy." Wayne wasn't Kelly's biological father. It shouldn't have surprised Kelly—one of the reasons Jones left her husband was because of his lack of interest in her oldest daughter—but it did hurt, and Kelly had been angrier since. Jones guessed he was punishing them both.

Jones and the girls had moved into a small apartment above a garage owned by some Arabs who had a few motels down the road towards Interstate 10. It was the cheapest and quickest place Jones could find. There was only a miniscule bathroom, one bedroom with a closet so narrow it might hold a folded ironing board, and a slightly bigger room that was the kitchen-living room, which was perhaps twelve feet by fifteen feet and not large enough for a sulking teenager, a five-year-old going on four and a half, and a really pissed off, newly separated mom. Certainly no room for a dog.

As she had climbed up the apartment stairs, she heard what she thought was the television. Kelly slept with the TV blaring when she and Crystal were alone on the nights Jones had to work. The TV offered her a sense of security; she was only thirteen, too young to be babysitting her sister all night. But the clamor was Kelly trying to yell over Crystal's sobs.

Jones called Wayne as soon as she could get the girls to tone down and tell her what had happened. He laughed when she told him that Kelly had let the dog out.

"You're the one who gave Crystal the damn dog. You take the girls and go find it," she told him.

"I gotta work," Wayne answered.

"And I just got home from working ten hours in the pit. I have to go back for the four-thirty shift. I need to get some sleep. You never asked me if you could give Crystal the dog. By the way, you really hurt Kelly when you gave that puppy to just Crystal. It wouldn't have hurt you to put Kelly's name on that note. She trusted you. All she's ever wanted was a father."

"Hey, I have to go," he said. "The dog probably got run over on the highway. Dogs get killed there all the time. Just drive up and down the road a few times, then go home. That'll be good enough. It was just a mutt from the pound. I can get another."

"Oh, no," Jones said. She was in the bathroom where, she hoped, the girls couldn't hear her. They were having a hard enough time without listening to her screaming at Wayne. "Don't you dare get—" Jones started to say, but Crystal rattled the doorknob, then peeked in.

"Mommy. I want to talk to Daddy. I tell him to spank Kelly."

"No, Crystal." Jones tried to hide the anger in her voice. "We're talking. Okay? Go into the living room with Kelly." She pushed Crystal out of the room.

"Daddy's going to spank you," Crystal screamed.

Jones could hear Kelly kicking at one of the boxes piled next to the couch. They still had not unpacked, mostly because there was way too much stuff for such a small place. There was storage down in the garage, but none of them had a clue, yet, as to what they could live without. She watched herself in the mirror as she tried to talk Wayne into looking for the puppy. She longed to turn on the shower and let it steam up the room before she climbed into the scouring heat—she reeked of cigarette smoke and the alcohol that gambling drunks spilled on her.

Wayne refused to take any time off work to look for the puppy. He said he'd come over that evening and take the girls out to dinner to make up for it. Jones snapped the phone closed without saying goodbye. She turned on the faucet and splashed tepid water on her face. Her image shimmered in the mirror. It was raining hard outside and the lights flickered, slow to come back to full brightness. She inspected her face in the undulating light, put a finger under her chin to lift the slight sag she had just noticed, pulled the skin beside her eyes. She was decomposing, like those poor animals on the road, road kill, fading away. She imagined the puppy flattened like a figure painted on an Egyptian tomb wall.

Changing into jeans and a hoodie, she herded the two girls down the apartment stairs to the car.

"I'm hungry," Crystal whined.

"Yeah, Mom," Kelly said. "We haven't had breakfast." The girls usually ate breakfast at school, but it was Saturday.

"Well, neither have I. However, we're going to find that damn dog before it gets run over," Jones said. They sat in the car at the end of the drive. The morning traffic was heavy. Crystal's head swished back and forth as she watched the cars and trucks zoom by on their way to or from Interstate 10. Her whine went up a decibel.

"Run over?" She started sniffling again.

It seemed there was always fresh kill on the road every day that Jones drove the twenty-five miles to the casino where she had just begun working. Rice fields stretched in all directions and tenant trailers dotted the single lane blacktop, along with the bodies of the road kill. Mostly dogs, Jones realized after the first few weeks of driving to and from the casino. She'd watch the bodies in the process of decomposition, generally starting out as distorted but recognizable creatures. Sometimes, Jones couldn't recognize what was mashed on the road—a squirrel, a cat, a small rat terrier, red meat pureed next to the centerline or at the edge. Those kills disappeared quickly. But the ones that lay in the center of the road, or on the shoulder, they dissolved in layers to become shadows a little darker than the asphalt or grass, and then—gone forever.

Jones also noticed that the bodies tended to appear in groups, and she really hated that—seeing friends or family together in death was all too vivid in her mind. There had been two golden retrievers, three weeks ago. The parish crew had just cut down the weeds along the shoulders, which set the dogs out like a bronze bas-relief on a green carpet. After the initial rush of dismay, Jones took consolation in that they lay together, their noses touching. Jones imagined that, after they were so cruelty struck, one had crawled to the other so they touched in death, like the distraught hunchback crawling next to the beautiful, dying Esmeralda and pulling her into his arms.

She watched the two dogs blow up like balloons, then fur and skin sloughed off, and the bodies began to flatten, and little pieces began to disappear—a lower leg, part of the tail, ears shrunk, big holes gaped behind the rib cages. For days she watched the bodies fade into the ground, and the very last to go were their dark noses. Rose and Demetrius, as she had named them, remained faithful to the last molecule. She named them all; it was part of the job—a karma thing—someone had to notice that the animals' lives had been snuffed. Jones hated the thought of dying and no one knowing about it.

"Mommy, is Puffy run over?"

"Crystal, stop," Jones said. She prodded Kelly's arm. "Get in back and settle her."

"Hell, no," Kelly said. "She hates me."

"Well, you should have gone out with the puppy."

"I just put him out to pee."

"And fell asleep, I bet."

"I hate you. Bad, bad Kelly." Straining forward in the car seat, Crystal raised her fists.

Kelly crouched down and glowered out the window.

Jones knew it was just as much her fault as Kelly's. She could have taken a job as a clerk someplace, a nine to fiver, but she chose to work at the casino as a cocktail waitress in the pits because it paid well—she needed the money. And in order to get the good paying shifts, she had to work nights every third weekend. Wayne had given her some money, but he couldn't afford to support two households, and Kelly's father was dead. There was no other financial help.

Crystal continued to loudly grouse in the back seat and Jones ground her teeth as she turned north onto the road. It was within a quarter mile from their driveway that Crystal cried, "Puffy!"

Out of the side of her eye, Jones saw the white fluff of Eggy, a small white cat that had appeared at the roadside about six days ago. She didn't see cats too often, they being a shade smarter, or at least more cautious, than dogs.

"Puffy."

"No, baby. That was not your puppy."

"How do you that?" Kelly asked. "We're going sixty miles a hour."

"Because I know that cat."

"Whatta mean, you know the cat?"

"Eggy—she—it—got hit last week." Eggy had melted away with little resistance, leaving only a small rag of white fluff in the grass.

"Ya named it?"

"Well—" Jones grimaced. "Maybe it's a defense mechanism."

"Ahhh—" screamed Crystal. "Puffy."

A possum. Jones had to give it to her youngest, the rain was pouring down, and Jones guessed Crystal could mistake a brownish animal with a rat-like tail for her white Puffy. The possum, crushed a few days before on the roadway, was stretched out like a skin on a drying rack. Kelly craned her neck to watch it as long as she could.

"What's its name?"

"Milburn."

"Mommy, stop. I can't see," Crystal said. "The side goes by too fast."

Jones realized she was driving way over the speed limit. She tapped the brake gently. At fifty miles per hour, cars and trucks began to pass her when they had the opportunity. Jones took a deep breath and reached back between the seats to pat Crystal's knee. "Honey, we'll find Puffy."

Crystal toned down her sniffles and whines a degree. Jones swiveled her eyes side to side, watching the shoulders, trying not to drive too slowly or erratically. The traffic was fast and the rain heavy. "Look, guys." Jones pointed. "There's the fox that chased Eggy across the road." Beyond some weeds, down in the ditch, a long strip of red fur hung off a strand of barbed wire.

"How do you know that?" Kelly asked.

"Well, I figure that the fox—Edward, by the way—was chasing Eggy, and he caught her right in the middle of the road just when a Fed-X truck came and clipped them both. Eggy managed to crawl along for a few miles before she passed out and died from a loss of blood."

"You're nuts, Mom. You're inventing lives for—dead things." Kelly gestured with both hands towards the roadside.

"Yeah," Jones said. "It's like a daytime drama, I guess. But I think people who hit animals with their cars or trucks just think of them as—things in the road. No one stops. They ignore them like they didn't have a life. Animals should get the same dignity in death as humans. They say animals don't have souls, but I can't believe that. If there is choice, there is a soul, and animals have choice. Puffy had a choice. He probably barked at the door for a while and got really bored, then decided to go exploring."

"Yeah, bad Kelly," Crystal muttered.

"Shut up, stupid," Kelly answered hotly.

Jones looked sharply at her. With her brown eyes and blond hair, Kelly resembled her father, whom she barely remembered. He had died in a car crash, along with his brother, Emmett, and their mother when Kelly was three. It was raining and the curve was too slick, and they hit a tree going sixty miles per hour. They were coming home from Houston—12:30 in the morning. Jones hadn't received the call until noon. They lay in the crushed car, on a road like this road, in the rain, for hours before someone stopped. She overheard the coroner say it probably took several hours for Steven to bleed out. Jones could not think of them there, dying, for hours and no one knew. How horrifying to be so alone in death.

"We should bury them," Kelly said quietly.

Crystal stopped whining. "Yeah, Mommy. Let's bury them like Daddy buried my birdie. Ahh—there's one we can bury." The one Crystal pointed to was a large critter that had lasted a remarkably long time on the roadside. "What's its name, Mommy?"

Jones hesitated, then chuckled. "Cousin It," she said. "Because I don't know what it was. Either a big rat, or a nutria. Not sure. That one's pretty smelly, I bet. Besides, it's raining and—how are we going to dig a hole?"

"Actually, there's a shovel in the trunk," Kelly said. "It's one of those camp shovels. Wayne asked about it the last time we saw him."

Jones drove in silence for several minutes. It had never occurred to her to bury the carcasses, and somehow she did not find the idea preposterous. The kids didn't have to be anywhere, and she could maybe still get in a few hours of sleep before work.

"Look, Mom." Kelly pointed across the road to a large, crow-like bird, a small black dog, and a piece of rope.

"Stop, stop," Crystal cried. "I can't see. Did Kelly see Puffy?"

"No, Crystal. It's not Puffy."

"Yes, it is. I can't see."

Jones pulled the car over to the side of the road so fast the girls jerked sideways. She got over as far into the grassy shoulder as she could without getting stuck in the ditch. After Kelly got out, Jones handed her an umbrella and crawled out the passenger side door, too. Sure enough, there was a camp shovel in the trunk. She left Crystal in the back seat, over her loud objection, but Kelly insisted on going with her, so together they splashed across the road and walked back to the corpses. On closer inspection, the rope was a snake about two feet long with a tire-wide squashed spot in the middle of its body. The three odd friends were lying in a row at the edge of the shoulder, positioned like they were leisurely strolling. Jones had not noticed them when she had come home from work. This was stupid, Jones thought. It was a dangerous place for them to be standing and gawking at road kill. They stood getting soaked; the umbrella did little to protect them from the spray of the passing cars, and Jones could hear Crystal bawling from the back seat.

Jones scooped up the bird and the dog with the shovel. "Grab the snake," she told Kelly.

"Why? Yuck." Kelly pinched the snake's tail between her fingers.

"We'll bury them behind the car. It's too dangerous standing here. And Crystal can see then."

With the car between them and the road, Jones dropped the animals next to the ditch. She rolled down the window so Crystal could watch.

"What happened to them, Mom?" Crystal asked.

"I figure Ropedilly here," Jones gestured to the snake, "was hightailing it across a gravel road and was run over by a truck, and Wings picked him up and was flying home to feed her babies, but he slipped from her grasp over this road. Then Cat Biter, here, rushed out and jumped Wings just as she was pecking at Ropedilly and, you know, that same dang truck turned out onto the highway and got all three together."

"Jeeze, Mom," Kelly said.

"Look," Crystal cried, "their eyes are open. Can they see us?"

It was hard to tell if the snake's eyes were open, but the blackbird's eyes were deeply black, and the dog's eyes were a wide reddish brown, rimmed with white.

"Can we close their eyes?"

Kelly reached down, but Jones grabbed her hand. "Let me." Jones had to grit her teeth as she pushed one of the dog's eyelids down with her fingertip and held it for a second. But when she let go, the lid sprang up halfway. Cat Biter watched the road from under the car with one eye not quite opened, not quite closed.

"Was this like my dad and Uncle Emmett and Grammy?" Kelly asked, looking around at the wet, bedazzling rice fields as far as the eye could see.

"What's their names, Mommy?" Crystal reached out the window.

"I told you their names."

"Were their eyes open?" Kelly asked.

"Kinda." Despite the warm rain, Jones felt a chill. Kelly had never asked about particulars of the accident before. Jones identified the three bodies. She was their closest relative, other than Kelly. Lying on that flat, shiny table, Steven was an expression of cold, compressed death, and his eyes were wide open. She tried to pull the lids closed, but the skin wouldn't budge. He had been dead too long. She almost tore off his eyelids trying to close out what he could no longer see. Jones choked up. After a few deep breaths, she sent Kelly to get a handkerchief out of her bag. Then, certainly loosening some teeth, she tore it into thirds and tied a blindfold around each creature's eyes. The rain matted the material.

Kelly giggled. "They look kinda cute with their little bandanas."

Jones let Crystal get out of the car and stroke the dog on the back.

"I love her," Crystal crooned.

Jones dug a longish hole. Despite that it was soaked through, the tough, wild grass hung on to the dirt beneath with the tenacity of weeds. She had to stab through the grass, then peel it back, like pulling up sod instead of laying it down. Once she had the ground bared, however, it gave up its rich wet dirt. Jones didn't dig a very deep hole, and it kept filling up with water. She lifted the bodies of the three friends with the shovel and dropped them into their common grave, then pushed them close together before she scooped up the dirt and covered them. Lastly, she tossed the strip of grass on top of the wet mound.

"Thank God," Jones muttered to herself as she buckled Crystal back into the car seat. She tried to dry herself and the girls off with a towel she had brought in case they found Puffy. "Let's go to Waffle House for breakfast."

The restaurant was a short distance away from where they buried the three friends. As usual, Crystal insisted she have a plain hamburger for breakfast, heavy on the ketchup. When Kelly told her that the hamburger looked like one of those road kills, Crystal put her fingers in her ears and chanted, "I can't hear you."

Kelly and Jones shared a pancake special, mushy and syrupy, with crispy bacon and several cups of hot coffee. Over breakfast they agreed they would bury only the animals they could recognize, and they'd scrape nothing off the road—and nothing too smelly and only between Waffle House and ten miles past their apartment in the other direction, which was about twenty miles.

"And we'll bury them in a field instead of beside the road, where they can have a decent burial."

After carefully scooping them up and putting them in the trunk, Jones and the girls buried three dogs, Eggy's fluff, another cat, a small golden tail hawk, and three armadillos on the edge of a rice field. For each animal, they told a story. Jeb, Roy, and Dusty were buddies who lived on farms the next parish over. They had found a treasure map.

"No," Crystal cried. "They went looking for their princess brides—and—and on the way they ran into the dreaded pirate, Roberts."

Kelly and Jones smiled.

"She's probably right," Jones muttered to Kelly.

Ruth was a gray and black tabby. Her tail was missing. It was hard to tell if it was torn off when she was hit, or she didn't ever have one.

"She was a minx," Kelly said. "She was tired of being different, and she went in search of her tail."

"Kelly, you're wrong," Crystal said.

"Hey, this one is my story. She wanted a tail because her parents had tails, and she thought maybe on the other side of the world she would find her tail. But too bad, so sad. She learned that sometimes things lost can never be found, and she was going home when she got squashed."

Jones wanted to hug her daughter right then.

Shybird's story was a little more elusive. "I think she wanted me to have her feathers," Crystal said as she plucked several golden and brown striped feathers from the bird's tail. "They're magic." Jones tucked the feathers into Crystal's hair.

Finally, they dug a common grave for the armadillos, Armo, Armee, and Artree. "Ya notice how armadillos always die on their backs with their legs straight in the air? Funny, isn't that?" Kelly said. They stood solemnly over three armored backs planted solidly in the wet earth and twelve legs pointed towards the heavens.

"Yeah, quite the opposite of 'always landing on your feet', isn't it?"

"What's their story, Mommy?" Crystal asked.

Jones thought a moment. "Well, Artree was a daddy, and he and his brother and mom went to a wedding in Houston. But when they came back they got into a wreck. Artree was in a hurry to get back to his wife and daughter. He was so bummed he couldn't take them to his cousin's wedding that night. His mother's whole family was going to be there, and he was looking forward to showing his daughter off. He thought she was so perfect, beautiful, and smart. But she couldn't go because she had diarrhea."

It did not take but a minute for Kelly to figure out who Jones was talking about. She had never told Kelly that they might have been along that night with her father.

"We were supposed to be with them? They died and we didn't?" Kelly asked.

Jones thought of Demetrius and Rose. Their noses touching in death, an affirmation of their eternal devotion. "Don't go there, baby. I've been there, and it's an awful mystery." For the first time in months, Kelly let Jones hug her.

"Dear God," Crystal prayed. "Make Artree and Armo and, uh—Grammy land on their feet in heaven."

And the last they buried was Puffy. They found him about twenty yards before their apartment's driveway. It was Crystal who spotted him on the way home, lying in the weeds. Jones couldn't imagine how they managed to miss him. The rain had finally stopped and a hot, wet breeze blew on their faces as they looked down at the sopping, dead puppy. It looked like he got smacked alongside the head; his ear was partially torn off. But otherwise the poor dear looked peaceful, and his eyes were closed.

"I'm really sorry," Kelly told her sister.

Crystal's lips pulled down, she cried briefly, but accepted her dead puppy bravely. Kelly held her as Jones scooped Puffy up and put him in the trunk. They took him to the apartment and buried him under the porch, bundled up in one of Crystal's old baby blankets. They had to dig through several boxes in the living room to find the blanket. Jones found a picture of Crystal taken her first day of pre-K and gave it to her to wrap up in the blanket around Puffy, so that he wouldn't forget her.

"But what if I forget him?" she asked, as they carefully stamped the dirt down around the grave.

"You wouldn't. Trust me." Jones said.

"Did you bury a picture of me in my father's grave?" Kelly asked.

"No." Jones stamped on Puffy's grave a little harder than necessary. "Sorry, but I didn't think he'd ever forget you."

Jones doubted it would have been such a quiet, reverent burial if they had found the puppy just as they left the apartment to look for him. They had spent the morning—a wet, horns honking, harsh, smelly, and gross morning—saying goodbye to many lost souls, and somehow found some peace for themselves. Jones figured she had a few hours to get some sleep. But first she would shower. As they trudged up the apartment stairs, Kelly held Crystal's hand, and the golden feathers in Crystal's hair dripped down the back of her head, ready to fly away.

The Scarab Beetle's Persona

Ruth Moon Kempher

as a jade roach, he sits complacently to eat
his acid young; each increase in size is etched
like ribs around his carapace, or shell, but if
he sees his haggard wife, he turns his jaw to stone—
pretends he never ate his sons.

        Never noted for his grace, he's most
agreeable when left in peace. When menaced by
inquisitive cats or mice, he'll hide his vicious taste—
shouldering through the grass, seems all innocence
despite the weighty evidence of girth. If asked—
if he had speech—he'd mumble platitudes, how
dynasties survive, with growth at any price.

Lee Roy

Jan Rider Newman

"There's a baby squirrel on the ground." Sue, my son's girlfriend, rushed past me as I stood at the sink, running water for coffee. I followed her into the back yard. A grown squirrel chattered from the low branch of our hackberry tree, tail fluffed and twitching. Perched on the fence, a blue jay turned first one eye, then the other on whatever lay in the wet grass emitting scream after piercing scream. Sue stooped to pick something up. The screaming stopped. She stood and turned, hands cupped around a baby squirrel.

What if it has rabies? I thought.

"Poor baby," Sue said. "It fell out of its nest in last night's storm."

I had never thought of what happened to squirrels during high wind and rain. If I had, I might not have cared. A dozen of this baby's relatives claimed our back yard as home and felt free to dig up and eat our newly sown seeds and plants. We never got a single pecan from our tree—the squirrels ate them green. Squirrels were good-for-nothing rats with furry tails. Why had God bothered to create them?

As Sue carried the baby inside, the squirrel in the tree continued to fuss. *The mother*, I thought. *Will she miss her baby?* For the first time, I pitied a squirrel.

We gathered in the kitchen—my son, Paul, my husband, and me—as Sue wrapped the ball of fur in one of my hand towels. Its eyes were still seamed shut. The baby couldn't have weighed more than a few ounces.

I shook my head, still wondering about diseases. But we couldn't think of any way to get it back in its nest, and I remembered the blue jay watching from the fence. If we hadn't intervened, would the bird now be enjoying breakfast? Much as I disliked squirrels, I didn't hate them enough to abandon one to that fate, so I didn't object to having the baby in the house. It was cute and, after all, Sue and Paul were taking it back to Austin, Texas, the next day.

"We'll name it Lee Roy," I suggested, because Sue said it was a male. While they looked up the care and feeding of orphaned squirrels on the Internet, I went back to fixing breakfast.

The next day, Paul and Sue did return to Austin and their jobs and college studies. Before they left, though, Paul handed me instructions printed off the Internet, Sue handed me Lee Roy, and they waved goodbye.

What? I stood with the bundle in my hand, mouth agape. *They weren't taking it with them? What was I supposed to do with it?*

I had no room in my life for this silly thing. My father had recently died, and my sister was diagnosed with breast cancer two weeks after we buried him. Mom was a wreck, and we were all still grieving. I'd quit my job and was happy having flexible time to write, keep house, and go visit my mother and sister—in short, being mistress of my own time. The theory of keeping this animal alive was noble. Being in charge of the task myself? Forget it.

So, when the shock wore off, I called vet's offices to find out if they knew anyone who'd take the squirrel off my hands. A receptionist at one office promised to call a woman who might be interested. While praying for a return call, I read the literature Paul and Sue had printed.

"Squirrels are wild creatures and do not make good pets," one publication said.

Another cautioned: "Do not expect love from a squirrel."

I didn't need love from a squirrel. All I needed was someone to call and say, "I'll take that nuisance off your hands."

Until such time, I had to feed Lee Roy milk with a syringe, pressing out enough to satisfy, but not choke. I also had to make him void, which meant tickling his privates with a cotton ball till he emptied his bladder and bowels, because baby squirrels can't do that for themselves. I later learned newborn kittens can't, either. Their mothers have to lick them to get them to go.

"If that's what it takes," I muttered to Lee Roy, tickling away, "you're just going to have to explode."

During these intimate sessions, I concluded that Sue, the wildlife expert, had been wrong. This squirrel didn't have the right equipment to be a male. Lee Roy must be a girl.

Feedings frustrated both of us. I never knew exactly how much pressure to apply on the plunger or how much formula was enough, so I either choked or perturbed Lee Roy with too much or not enough milk flow. The milk itself was a problem, too, until we found out that formula designed for puppies didn't cause diarrhea.

And yet she got enough nourishment to thrive and developed a round, fat belly. While feeding, she flicked her fluffy tail and wrapped tiny front paws around the syringe like a human baby holding its bottle, except this baby had minute suction cups on the undersides of its paws and sharp, tiny claws. By the third day of caring for her, I realized something—I dreaded the phone call that offered Lee Roy any home but ours.

Whenever I heard her high-pitched cry, I dropped what I was doing and ran to her. Usually, she was hungry, or she had wandered away from the warm water bottle and was stumbling about in her box, a blind creature groping, crying out to be saved and fed and warmed, wanting its mother. I took to carrying her in my breast pocket, where she curled against my warmth and heartbeat with contented baby-squirrel grumbles.

Many nights, I woke in the dark hours, terrified I hadn't fed her enough or kept her warm. Suppose she died through some carelessness or ignorance of mine? In short, I agonized over her as if she were a human baby—my baby. The disdain I felt for her kind softened. I'll never like squirrels much as a species, and I never needed one to love me. But in the two weeks I cared for Lee Roy, she needed me to love her.

One night, I pushed out too much milk, and Lee Roy choked. Her sides heaved. Her mouth opened wide as she gasped for air. I rushed into the living room in hopes that my husband knew what to do. We rubbed her throat and held her upside down, but she kept gasping.

I killed her, I thought, and I wanted to give her my own breath.

Finally, I did the only thing I could think of. I grabbed the syringe, stuck it back in her mouth and, instead of pressing the plunger, pulled back on it.

That cleared the obstruction. Lee Roy breathed.

As our panic eased, Charles and I looked at each other. "I heard about a woman who runs a wildlife refuge," he said. "Maybe we should call her."

The next day we took Lee Roy to the refuge, where she would be nurtured until old enough to be released in an area where hunting was prohibited, an area better than our back yard in the city. The day we finally got rid of the nuisance, I cried. To this day, my pockets feel empty.

I still don't love squirrels in general, and I'm glad there are fewer now in our yard. But seeing them reminds me of the one who did steal my heart.

In the two weeks I had Lee Roy, she never opened her eyes. She opened mine. She reminded me how passionate and fierce and difficult love is. Lee Roy embodied for me the loss of my father and the desperate war my sister waged to stay alive. I focused on Lee Roy all my fear and compassion, my desire to heal and nurture those I loved. I couldn't save my father or sister, but I kept Lee Roy alive and learned that love, in any amount, for anyone or anything, is never misplaced. It sustains and guides us through this valley of tears.

Oh, the Longing

Annette Stovall

Oh, so you want a sister. I too longed for same,
I was your age. I had all the toys due
I could see handle. Several dolls were for me to
play with. Stuffed Raggedy Ann doll I loved so was
a lap face ragged as her name. Then was
before they made dolls walk and talk. I had
play china dishes, pots, pans, doll house where drab
the shifting furniture again. There was too
a wooden rocking horse, a rocking chair, and Oh,
the wood, round table with 2 chairs. Of else gifts,
no time for here mention. Did I accumulate
these all at once? Ha! laugh to that. At Christmas caste
for these imparted to me could stockpile the cache
tallied up in long years. My parents defy
this born all wrapped in satin sheets they tied
with threads in silk ribbon. You see that by where
we live. Our plain saffronly brown frame house resides
at rural rustic asphalt. So, toys and gifts then
could never equal sibling be it sister kin
or brother. It made no difference to me.
Oh God, was I lonely! It pained me to watch
other siblings! I even had my youthful
mother and uncle doing double duty.
You know, with playing the card games I reveled in,
and with giving this more attention I needed.
Oh, how my mother emphasized this I do have
half sister and a half brother. That placated
me some, though I was nowhere near them to play.
Daughter, child, look at it another on this wise.
You do have 3 brothers.

Letter to Rita

Kathryn Romey

Dear Rita,

Mary and Theresa have been giving me information on your welfare. I think of you hourly because of the many reminders of your celebration of life, everything from the garden work we both love to the races, Fox Chapel Boating Club, and just "bozoing" around.

When I put the newly-purchased African woman statue next to the one I already had, I smiled as this thought struck me: "These black women statues remind me of Rita and me! Maybe Rita and I are reincarnated African women."

Rita, remember when you took me from Shenandoah School to the hospital during one of my migraine headaches? I always wondered why I saw your name printed in my mind when I couldn't even spell, yet say, my own name. You must have heard my silent cry—mental telepathy. Even stranger, at the hospital I remembered the school's phone number. I really believe just your being near was the comfort that relieved the trauma and pain. So this soul sister from long ago would like to hug and squeeze your pain away today.

If you haven't guessed, I believe in reincarnation. I have been on this earth many times, probably because I am a slow learner and still haven't got it right. Being a good, but dumb soul, I'll be back for another try.

Rita, I don't think you got it right yet, also. So, spirit sister, we will meet again, even if we be black, yellow, or green with long fingers.

Please be comforted, Rita. Even though in body you may feel alone, know in spirit many souls are aching to comfort you.

In this life I am,

Kay Romey

P.S. — You will always know my spirit, as I will know yours, by any or many names. Looking forward to our continued friendship with much love.

Leaving

Margaret Susan McKerrow

I found her at home in her favourite chair
Her knitting at rest in her lap
Her gentle knarred hands firmly holding the yarn
The needles positioned with care

Her housework all done, pretty dress on the bed
The curlers were still in her hair
"Prepare for the party," she always said
"With plenty of time to spare"

Who called her to suddenly come from her nap
Her strong will responding at once?
It must have been someone she loved from the past,
No time for farewells to us

Friends said "what a nice way to go"—
Assuming that we were prepared—
But the children expected their Grandma for tea
Cream Puffs and Trifle to share!

No time for good-byes, so much left unsaid,
She shared her lessons so well
But the mystery of life, we're unable to solve,
And she is unable to tell.

Second Runner-up: Best Fiction Contest

All the Way to Heaven

Phylis Warady

Rosellen waited on the porch. Father came out wearing his best black suit. She handed him the Bible with the bumpy black cover before smoothing her dotted Swiss dress with her small fingers.

Hinging his crisp-cracker frame, her father pecked her fuzzy cheek. "Isn't that your best dress?"

She nodded. "Please, Father, take me with you. I so want to see Elizabeth go to Heaven."

"No, daughter."

With a meager shake of his head, he turned from her, the black of his jacket blotting out the morning sun as he descended the steps.

She watched him march briskly erect toward the horizon, a vanishing black pencil with a gray eraser top. At times she wanted to nag and whine and cry like her friends did, but Father would never cooperate.

Rosellen let out a defeated sigh, then went inside and up creaky stairs to her room. Father would expect her to take off her best dress, to put on clothes more everyday. Crooking both elbows, she fumbled for the top back button. Curds of mutiny clotted behind her eyes. She snatched up her favorite doll and ran downstairs and into the yard.

With a spoon borrowed from a kitchen drawer when Della's back was turned, she dug a shallow grave where the violets grew. She laid her doll in it and covered her with rich, moist dirt. Then, squeezing her eyes shut, she prayed like Father did from the pulpit on Sundays.

"Rosellen." The housekeeper's voice floated across the yard. "Come in, child, out of the heat and eat your lunch."

Inside the cool kitchen, Della scolded, "Is that your best dress? Land sakes, child, it's limp as a dish rag."

Rosellen squirmed in her chair. In her need to bury her doll, she'd forgotten about what she was wearing and had absently wiped her hands down its front. Would Della know about her friend, Elizabeth? Whether she was in the ground yet? Or how long it would be before God came and took her away to Heaven?

"What were you doing? Making mud pies?" Della asked. "Slip it off so I can put it to soak."

All afternoon, Rosellen waited. Father did not come. Maybe he was having trouble sending Elizabeth all the way to Heaven. The sun had shifted but she could still see waves of hot air zagging up from the sidewalk. She tried her hardest to wait an extra-long time. Worms of impatience crawled up her spine. If only she knew when.

A Model-T drew up and Father climbed out. As it moved on, he mounted the porch steps. Again, a dry kiss on her cheek.

"Has Elizabeth gone to Heaven yet, Father?"

"Yes, Daughter, she has," he said, going inside.

Rosellen huddled on the porch, scared, but not sure why. There wasn't much time. Soon Della would come to say supper was on the table. She crossed the yard to the violets. Kneeling, she began to dig, using her hands because she'd forgotten the spoon. Frantically, she scattered the loosened earth. Bits of the doll appeared like random pieces of a crazy quilt. A nose. A toe. A hand.

Her fingernails felt fat from embedded dirt. Where was Elizabeth, really? Sobbing, Rosellen clutched her doll and flung herself down upon the violets.

Just before the last ray of sun faded, Father came out and carried her inside.

One Night and a Quarter of Tomorrow

Susan Cummins Miller

Mother, the night you left us
the smoke trees wore a cloud
of tiny lavender blossoms
that looked gray and insubstantial
in the moonlight.

After the late-night news,
you and I sat on the porch, watching
the creamy saguaro buds unfold
as slowly as a solemn high Mass.
You told me how it pained you
that those flowers
had this one night
and a quarter of tomorrow
before they closed for good.
A microcosm
of a woman's life.

That's all I remember
except that it was Mother's Day
and I'd brought no gift—
just myself, sitting next to you
on the porch swing, listening
to the old stories one last time—
how you skinny-dipped
with your sisters in warm
Minnesota lakes, sang
with a big band at college, fished
for pike with Grandpa…

We rocked and laughed together
until, around midnight,
the bats fluttered in
to bury their wrinkled faces
in the soft saguaro blossoms
overflowing with pollen.

A Song for Bill

Joanne Ellis

Birdcalls echo, day slides into night.
Breasts of hills slip their outlines.
Small candles in camper's hands
light the rustic chapel
on the downside of the hill.

At the camp in the bend of the river
Sarah shepherds her flock of campers
to vesper service.

Hidden away in trees the campers sing
"Day is done, gone the sun…"
Sarah speaks, "Always have a magic hill,
learn of silence; learn of dance and song,
find a hill, a magic hill, a place of mystery,
soul and dreams."

I am young, on the edge of life,
her words seep into my bones.
I see again the flickering candles
like incandescent fireflies
circling back and forth down Magic Hill.

Your adobe home on Sweetwater Drive
grows into an oasis of Chilean mesquite,
desert willow, cholla and prickly pear.
Fountain sounds challenge the desert dove.
Home away from home for me
another Magic Hill.

Quail feed in the late December afternoon
as we sip our mulled wine.
Your little mother grows tired in her rocking chair
and sleeps next to the window.

Hopi pots, Navajo rugs, Papago baskets,
Kachina dolls
enclose me, bringing the warmth
of a log fire.

A cholla branch in the corner of the room,
pocked and dried,
stretches its snakelike arms
to lift small clay pots and scarlet berries
while Christmas poinsettias bow in at the window.

Nights around an open fire
you pluck the old guitar.
Your funny voice circles a Spanish love song,
you of the desert home whose laugh I love.

In June we eat gazpacho on the tile table
while summer rains gain on the arroyo.
You call and I come,
on the night a Mexican cereus blooms.

In the time of the fall planting,
the soil nourished now by your ashes,
when javelina gather
and the coyote calls,
we'll meet at the gate and dance
to the dirge of the wind
on another Magic Hill.

The Man Who Would Be Me

Tony Zurlo

watches from behind the face
that looks at me in the mirror.
The mirror face is mottled
and ragged like tree bark.

The man who would be me
has a face like a mountain lake,
each smile or frown from a pebble
tossed, but the ripples fade away.

The mirror face has too much space
on top, while gray shadows each side.
This face has road-map eyes with
detours that lead into the interior.

The man who would be me
has a plush forest of dark hair,
and sea-green eyes that suggest
endless vigorous adventures.

Through the night I lie wondering
if the man who would be me
will shatter the mirror face and
be there for me in the morning.

Getting Older

Kay Lesh

I had always planned to be a really cool old lady. You know the kind of woman I'm talking about. She is the feisty older woman who hikes the Grand Canyon to celebrate her 80th birthday, or the one who faces down the police while picketing the local recruiting office with the Raging Grannies. It seemed like a role I could slip into with little difficulty. Actually, I planned on it, as evidenced by an essay I found recently in a stack of papers I had saved from a creative writing class.

With the naivety I possessed in my mid-twenties, I had written about the possibilities I observed open to older women. It seemed to me that people cut you a lot of slack as you aged, and I thought I could make some choices. I could become the dynamic fashion plate older woman, the jock who keeps everyone surprised by her athletic accomplishments, the sweet, cookie-baking granny, or even the grumpy, crotchety old lady who chases the neighborhood kids out of her tomato patch. No one would care, one way or the other. They would just chalk it up to my advanced age and leave me alone. I was looking forward to experiencing what Margaret Meade termed "post-menopausal zest."

What I didn't plan on was the reality of getting older. In my fantasy, I expected to keep everything I had back then. It would all just be housed in an older version of me. Sure, there would be some wrinkles and lines, but, on the whole, I would be in control of how I aged. It turns out there were quite a few things I didn't plan on.

I didn't plan on the change in my appearance, and I never thought I would find myself avoiding mirrors the way I do now. Mysteriously, my body has reshaped itself. I have picked up about forty extra pounds from somewhere, and the weight doesn't want to come off in spite of daily walks, contracts with health clubs, stints with Weight Watchers, or flirtations with The South Beach Diet. The other miracles I see touted in the current women's magazines just don't work for me, either. Those pounds are simply here to stay. Here I am, wearing a size I never thought would he hanging in my closet, much less appearing on my body. And I have a belly. It doesn't matter how much I suck it in and hold my breath. It is just there. There is not a control panty in existence that can change that.

My hair seems to belong to someone else, as well. What happened to the shiny, thick mop I used to have? My hair is thinner, finer than before. I am graying in a strangely odd pattern. Grey around the temples is distinguished in a man, but on me it looks like my hair can't quite decide what it wants to do. And why do I find hair in places I didn't before, then find it missing in places where it used to be? This business with my hair unnerves and confuses me.

My energy level has changed in unplanned ways. I am no longer able to accomplish what I used to. Cooking has become a chore, not a pleasure. The dust bunnies are definitely winning the battle for control of my house. My reputation as a spotless housekeeper has faded to a dim memory. I pray that no friends drop in unannounced to see the mess my house has become. I don't feel good about it, but I lack the ability to do anything about it. The energy to cope with the cleaning and other chores necessary to maintain my life and still do my job is simply not there. My sleep patterns are different, too, and while I seem to need the same amount of sleep as ever, I am not able to get it. I wake several times during the night and have difficulty falling back to sleep in anything less than ninety minutes. So I have become dependent on fifteen-minute naps each afternoon, and am grateful when they revive me enough to keep going until my 9:30 bedtime.

I hadn't planned on the losses, either. In a cruel alteration of the natural order of things, I have outlived my son. I see my friends and co-workers dying and find myself surprised. We are far too young for that sort of thing, surely. Dying is for much older people. Yet, when I count up my losses, I begin to see that death is going to be a part of my life for years to come. My high school sweetheart died at age fifty. A dear friend of forty years was felled by cancer at age fifty-five. My office mate from my first counseling practice has been dead for four years now. Other loved friends are gone. I see the loss all around me and am aware of the fleeting nature of my own remaining years. Don't get me wrong. I plan to live to be at least ninety-two, the age my mother was when she died, but I am aware that this is another area in which I possess limited control.

So I find that this aging process is not quite the great adventure I thought it would be when I wrote about it in my twenties. It feels as if it is more about acceptance than about blazing trails. I am not the same me in a slightly older body. I am the product of all the experiences I have had along the way, the hurt and losses, and the joys as well. I am learning what I can control and what I can't. I am trying to keep a positive attitude, because the research seems to indicate that optimists live longer than pessimists. I eat healthy foods and exercise regularly. I do what I can. And I remind myself of the cliché about getting older being better than the alternative. So there are choices open to me. They just aren't the ones I planned on. That doesn't make them bad, just different.

I can live with that.

Midday's Sunset

Lena V. Roach

Behind me, the bus door wheezes shut,
And I hesitate on the sidewalk by her house,
Surprised to see her hatless in the yard
Daring the midday sun
Of a Louisiana August.

Tottering torso bent
In an inverted U
Hikes her red-flowered skirt,
Exposing ace-bandaged calves
As her naked hand plucks at brazen weeds
That embrace butter-lipped blooms of waffling daffodils.
She flings the grass aside and straightens,
But not past the hump of her shoulders;
A grimace, and she touches the back of her hand
To the cottony fluff of hair on her forehead.

Eyes focused on the ground,
She shuffles in calculated starts and stops
Toward a weathered plastic chair
Under the shady spread of a sycamore,
Corner of the yard.
There she sits,
Hands clasped on her lap,
Head swiveled in the direction
Of the lawn next door
Where the shirtless youth—
Long-legged, lean-hipped,
Muscles glistening golden sweat—
Races a thunderous mower
Past the edge of her lot,
Ribbons of dusty green arches
Staining the twelve o'clock air.

And still she sits and stares,
Relives? Regrets? Neither?

Not knowing,
Not wanting to know,
I give in to an urgency,
Round a corner and scurry home
To shake the shadowy glimpse
Of a midday's sunset
Slanting my way.

The Parting

Lolene McFall

Deep in your aging years, no longer spry,
I left you to fend for yourself,
Well-provisioned, but alone
While I jaunted to old haunts
Two days journey away.

As the miles between us sped on
Tears, unbidden, kept falling.
Could you make it safely to the store?
Had I forgotten something you'd need
Before my return two weeks hence?

One week quickly passed
With friends in favorite places
Yet all that had enticed grew stale.
I no longer belonged to the past;
Its charms had loosened their hold.

Agitation grew within. I drove
Two days in one to hasten back to you,
To see your pleased surprise.
Without words, I felt your relief;
Without words, you also felt mine.

I knew I would not leave again,
Yet one coming day I knew
You would be leaving me.

The Unguarded Truth

Tina Weaver

"Mrs. Wyman, here is your medication."

"Thank you, my dear. Do I know you?"

"Yes. I am Sarah, your caregiver. I know pills are hard to swallow, so I broke them smaller."

"Do I get to have tea?"

"I have it right here."

"He hated tea and would never have afternoon tea with me."

"Who was that?"

"Oh, he was quite the looker, that man was. I saw him before my sister did. He was dancing across the room with another girl. She was a loose one, that girl."

"Did you dance with him?"

"Of course! He danced with Anna, then stopped right in front of me and asked me to dance. We were meant for each other. I knew it the moment he took me in his arms."

"You married him?"

"Yes, eventually."

"So you had a long engagement?"

"No, it really was very quick. Father and his father came to an arrangement. He had no choice by then."

"You *had* to get married?"

"Oh, no, my dear. I saw them. They didn't know, but I saw them."

"Who?"

"They were crafty, but I was watching, and I saw Anna take him out the door and into the garden."

"You followed?"

"The garden was the most beautiful part of our house. Father brought plants from all over the world to grow in the garden. I studied books he wrote on each plant. He was a professor, did you know that?"

"I heard he worked for the University."

"He wrote what the plant looked like, what it smelled like, and if it were poison, sweet or bitter to eat. Some plants can heal if taken in small doses, but can kill if taken in large doses."

"You studied horticulture with your father?"

"He liked me to sit and listen while he talked about the plants. He smiled at me."

"Did Anna, your sister, study with you and your father?"

"We don't talk about her. She is gone to us."

"What happened?"

"I followed them into the garden, and they went right to the gazebo. He was kissing her, and then he was on top of her, and her ball gown was over her face. Her feet were kicking the cushions, and I knew there was mud on her shoes. Then he stood beside her and laughed, and when she sat up, he slapped her across the face and walked away. She was crying. I was glad."

"Why were you glad?"

"She seduced him away from me. She deserved to be slapped. What was she thinking, going into the gazebo with him?"

"Why didn't you tell anyone?"

"We were married right in the garden, in the gazebo, where she seduced him. I chose the spot. I wore a beautiful dress; it was white silk. And I had lovely roses in my bouquet."

"What happened to the girl in the gazebo?"

"I was so excited that night, but he never came to my bed. I thought he was being kind."

"He must have come to you. I have spoken to your granddaughter."

"I have a granddaughter? I don't think so."

"She comes to visit you every day."

"That is so nice of her. Who are you, my dear?"

"My name is Sarah. What happened to your sister?"

"She was never quite right. She was always thinking, and talking about what she thought. She read books she stole from Father's library. She put them back, but I saw the ones she took and told father. He put a lock on the door and said, 'Women should not read or write; it upsets the natural order of things.'"

"Anna just wanted to know more. What is wrong with that?"

"What for? Women don't need to know anything more than how to run a household, order food, sew, play an instrument, be a loving, dutiful wife."

"That is quite a list. Did you have to memorize it?"

"I have quite a memory. My father said so. I remember all the plants, and which ones are poisonous."

"How long had you been you married when you had your daughter?"

"She was such a beautiful little girl. We were so happy. I brought her home from my aunt's house."

"You stayed at your aunt's house until the baby was born?"

"That is where *she* was. Father sent her there after they found out that she was with child. He never looked at her again. I brought the baby home after she was born. No one thought she wasn't mine."

"Your sister Anna had the baby, and you took her and raised her as your own?"

"I bought the most beautiful clothes for her. She was the most beautiful baby."

"What happened to Anna?"

"Bella Donna."

"Is that what you named the baby?"

"You stupid girl, no, that is the name of a purple bell flower."

"What happened to Anna?"

"She loved tea. She drank it every afternoon."

"What kind of tea was it?"

"Bella Donna tea, flavored with rosehip."

"You poisoned your sister…?"

"Larkspur is another wonderful plant, along with Hemlock. Do you know someone famous was killed with Hemlock?"

"Yes, I know."

"May I have my tea now? Are there any scones?"

"Yes, but here we call them biscuits."

"You are so nice to talk to. You look like someone I know."

"Yes, I am your granddaughter and caregiver."

"That is nice, dear. Do I have a daughter?"

"Yes, she passed away last year."

"May I have more tea and scones? I do so love scones with my tea. My little girl loved to have tea with me every afternoon."

"Now I have tea with you."

"Do I know you? How nice you came to visit."

The Old Nuns

Anne Whitlock

> "O the mind, mind has mountains"
> —Gerard Manley Hopkins

The old nuns are dying
at the top of the mountain
where we planted geraniums on the hill.
Here in the halls
where we kept the great silence
the old nuns are keeping it still.

The old nuns are tended
like flowers in a garden
by young Filipino girls.
In the room where we studied Tanquerey
and Augustinian theology
the old nuns say their rosary.

The old nuns are upstairs
above the chapel
above the parlors
above the refectory.

What do I want from the old nuns?
I have left their community.
But I come up the mountain
through the rose garden
by St. Joseph's statue
where I had collation
and recreation,
past the chapel
of my reception
and profession,
past the parlor's parquet floors
polished on my knees,
past the refectory
where breakfast was accompanied

by the bloody deaths of the martyrs
up the stairs
to the rooms of the old nuns.

They are sleeping in my bed.
They are sitting in my chair.
They are eating porridge from my bowl.

What do I want from the old nuns?
One by one they are plucked
like flowers from a garden,
but when the dream comes
I go back to the hills
where we planted geraniums.

Old Brothers-In-Law Visit After Their Wives' Deaths

Seretta Martin

In his living-room, the younger, now ninety-one,
has demonstrated a half dozen transporting devices
and apparatus that pumps and undulates—"keeping him alive."

The older, ears bellowing below his crew-cut,
boasts a gold-plated belt buckle and bolo-tie
given to him by a new square-dance partner.

He asks where he can buy a darning egg to mend his socks.
The niece thinks it an odd request, though it may be
that he always has a hidden motive.

She searches in her mother's Victorian sewing stand,
finds a wooden darning egg, and tells him, "It's a gift."
He turns it in his knobbed fingers as if remembering.

After a lunch of tuna and grapes the men sigh
tilt back recliners, spread lap blankets
close watery eyes, weary with viewing photos.

On a flowered vinyl tablecloth the album yawns open
to the deck of their Alaskan cruise ship—glaciers ago
these brothers-in-law stood bundled together with their wives.
How juvenile the couples look strapped into orange life jackets.

When You Become a Widow

Anita L. Clay

When you become a widow, it feels like you are a sad rag doll someone has kicked most of the stuffing out of. Your body feels as limp as a new baby's, but at the same time you feel old, really old. Your eyes are sore from crying. If you close them, they burn. But if you open them, the tears come out in rivers. Your muscles have no strength. You want to do something, like get up or eat or use the phone, but you just can't. It's an effort to open your mouth. Your tongue feels like a piece of wood.

Focusing is impossible. Your brain seems split in two. One half is filled with a low wailing sound like a train whistle moaning, "Alone, alone, alone." The other half of your brain plays memories and words and regrets over and over, like a scratch on an old 78-rpm record. You wish you had been kinder, more patient, switched doctors, called 911 sooner, sat beside the bed longer, hadn't spoken so sharply—over and over again, you remember.

You are less sure of everything. Your feet don't seem to touch the floor. Your steps are tentative, as if you may stumble at any moment. Your driving is too careless and too cautious at the same time. You're way over or way under the speed limit, missing turns, changing lanes without looking, scaring yourself. You wake up at daybreak, and seemingly ten minutes later you look out of the window and it's dark. You've lost the day, but even if you hadn't, you wouldn't have known what to do with the time.

The time that's supposed to heal moves on, but doesn't help. You dump the last of the casseroles, uneaten. You don't remember when the people left. They come by and call less often now. Sympathy wanes, and people grow bored with your tears.

"You have to move on."
"It's your time."
"Now you can do all the things you've always wanted to do."
"Find yourself."

At sixty-seven years old, after forty years of marriage, time for what? I can't remember what it was that I always wanted to do. And where do you go to find yourself?

At first I went to Wal-Mart. I went every day when I couldn't stay in the house any longer, sometimes in the morning, sometimes late at night. Near me was a 24-hour Super Wal-Mart. It was a relief to roll the cart up and down those aisles. The anonymity was soothing. No one paid any attention to you. You could just roll that cart and let the tears roll down your face. The clatter of the cart covered up the sob you couldn't swallow. And, if it got too bad, you could sit in the bathroom nobody used in the back by layaway. In all those trips, I must have filled a hundred carts with stuff from every department, but I can't remember a single thing I put in those carts. I probably left carts filled with shoes, clothes, frozen foods, towels, and whatever else I passed by. I know I never checked out. I never bought a thing. I just walked out of the store. Wal-Mart may have everything, but I didn't find myself there.

Next I turned to church. I thought it might be comforting to attend the first church my husband and I had belonged to. I spent a long time deciding what to wear. I know church people. If a widow comes to church looking disheveled and sad, people say, "She's falling apart since he's been gone. It's such a shame. She'll never make it without him." But if the widow comes to church looking too good, eyebrows lift. "Looks like she's shopping around, and he's not even cold." I know. I used to do it myself.

I dressed with what I hoped was a suitable middle ground. I sat in the car for a long time, but I finally went in. I had anticipated the gossip, but unfortunately not the flood of memories. We had been young there. The future seemed limitless. All possibilities were within reach. How could I have forgotten that we used to be the "it" couple at church?

I was late enough that people couldn't rush up to me to hug and kiss me and say they were so sorry. I buried my head in my Bible to avoid the looks. I was determined to stick it out, but when the pastor announced a memorial service for the baby he and his wife had lost the week before, I flew out of my seat and ran to my car. I managed to get around the corner before I lost it. I may yet find myself in church but not that day, not that church.

I kept looking for myself. I went to my daughter's house, but found she had become *my* mother. I went to a therapist. I picked one at random, but found she was someone I knew slightly from work. It felt good to have a captive listener. I was trying to sort through some feelings of guilt, regret, anger, loneliness, and fear. She just listened. Maybe I was supposed to figure it out on my own, but wasn't that what a therapist did? It had seemed so simple on TV. I tried for a couple of sessions, but I didn't find myself there, either.

Perhaps, I thought, I should look back on my youth. There are a few precious years between the time you are someone's child and someone's wife. What had I wanted then? I remembered that I had always thought I would be a writer. So I wrote for my OASIS writing group, and people said nice things. Ah, that was a step. Then one day I laughed—laughed out loud, a belly laugh. The sound and the feeling startled me. I realized that that I hadn't laughed like that in the two years my husband was really sick. I remembered I used to be funny.

I was making my bed one morning, when I noticed how tired and washed out the comforter looked. I used to take pride in a beautiful bedroom. That same day I passed up the Wal-Mart store and bought a way too expensive bedspread, curtains, and sheets at a high-end linen store. I remembered how I used to love decorating.

I pulled a sweat suit out of the closet and realized everything in there was a couple of years old. You don't need much if you are a 24-hour caregiver. I bought something new and chic, a whole outfit, and I bought a stylish hat. The next Sabbath, I went to a different church, where hardly anyone knew me. I stayed awhile, but suddenly just got up and left. Not because I wasn't enjoying the service. I left because I could! I threw my suit jacket in the back seat of the car. The big fancy hat hit the back seat next. It landed on the floor about Shrewsbury Street. Down 1-44 at 75 mph, I managed to change my heels for some beat-up driving shoes. By the time I got to Lindberg, the wig I was wearing because my hair had fallen out was too hot. I pitched it next to the coat in the back seat. Past Eureka exit, I pulled out my partial dental plate—it had always irritated me—and tossed it into the ashtray. I rolled down all of the windows, even though it was cold, just to feel the air on my face. When I finally pulled into my driveway, I parked on purpose in my husband's favorite spot, instead of mine. When I unlocked my front door, the dog growled. He didn't recognize me.

The next morning I went out to find myself in the back seat, on the floor, in the ashtray. I picked up the pieces of myself—the teeth, the hair, the shoes, and the clothes—and I laughed for the second time. I'm still finding myself. I don't know where I'm going, or how I'm going to get there. I feel some stuffing coming back into that rag doll.

My husband's picture was still on my nightstand. At first, I couldn't look at it. I had turned it face down. After weeks, I sat it up, but I couldn't look at it without sobbing. This morning, I returned his smile and touched his face. I haven't found myself, yet but I'm looking.

He Died. Now What?
—*Operating Instructions for the Widow Business*

Vera Martignetti

When the memorial is over, when the casseroles have been eaten, when the kids have flown back to their out-of-state homes, I wake up one morning, stare at the ceiling, and realize there is stuff to do. There is the *business* of being a widow.

Unfortunately, losing your husband doesn't come with operating instructions. I am a member of the last generation of women who were raised to defer to men. Moving into a traditional Breadwinner/Homemaker life, we willingly allowed our husbands to "care" for us. In marriages that took place in the 1950's and early 1960's, there was a common division of responsibilities. Husbands earned, invested, made all the financial and many of the social decisions. Wives took care of the home, raised the children, cooked, cleaned house, and wore aprons and pearls. Pity the poor brides who, pre-Betty Friedan, married their sweethearts right out of high school before they even knew who they or their husbands really were. They moved directly from a household headed by their fathers to a household headed by their husbands—daughters became wives, mothers, empty-nesters, and then, finally, caregivers. The grim reality is that most of these women will outlive their husbands. And now, they're waiting to become widows, even though they don't acknowledge it to anyone, not even themselves.

We grew up in a world where the newspapers separated the want ads by gender, where banks denied women credit or loans, and where doctors talked to women as if they were children. Many of my contemporary friends have never had a checking account in their own name. A vast majority of these women have never paid household bills, let alone worked outside the home, have never dealt with a car salesman or mechanic, and have never had to get a quote on a large home maintenance job. In addition to the emotional impact, taking care of business after the death of a spouse will be overwhelming. For most, this means a barrage of contacts with banks, hospitals, insurance companies, government agencies and, worst of all (if they weren't prepared for it), the funeral home or mortuary. It will be difficult to stay sane during the whirlwind.

I found the multitudinous demands of the next several weeks daunting. There was no Plan A. Just when I was sleepless, had the least energy, and was having trouble concentrating, I had to take care of the practical necessities. All this activity, however, allowed me to put real mourning on hold. I've always been very good at compartmentalizing.

I accessed Phil's e-mail remotely, and there were twenty-five messages. Thankfully, I knew or could guess at the passwords to most of Phil's on-line accounts. They may be out there still: financial news, sports columns, political comments, and Comcast service announcements floating around in cyberspace. I scrolled down and hit *unsubscribe* to every newsgroup and journal.

Phil was a man of sharply expressed opinions. It's easy to see where he, a natural-born provocateur, got all those partisan columns to forward to friends and family with different political leanings. At least, there were no personal ones where I had to "break the news." As time went on, I realized that some of the Internet services were still automatically charging our joint checking account. The Dow Jones Financial Newsletter had to be contacted by phone to discontinue their services. On-line banking became my friend as I monitored our joint checking account for unexplained automatic withdrawals.

Luckily, Phil had already closed his on-line investment account. But there were still the bank accounts. In addition to our joint checking account, I've had an account in my own name for some time. I waited until there were no more outstanding checks before closing the joint account. My first call was to the Social Security offices to arrange to have my monthly benefit deposited into my personal account. Also, I asked that they start deducting my Medicare B and Medicare D drug coverage from that account. I spoke to a knowledgeable and sympathetic man based in their New Mexico call center. I had requested and paid for an arbitrary number of death certificates from the mortuary. What did I know? I thought six was a good number. Did he want me to send a copy of the death certificate to terminate Phil's Social Security payments? Not necessary, he assured me. The mortuary had notified them, but he did need my marriage certificate. A copy? A fax? No, the original. I hesitated to part with it. I said, "Believe me, we were so very married." "Sorry, Mrs. Martignetti, I can't issue you the death benefit and change your monthly payment to include your widow's benefits without the certificate. I'll send it back by return mail." And he did.

The hardly adequate Social Security one-time-only death benefit of $255 was deposited into my account. This figure has never been increased since its inception in 1950. In Jersey City, Phil's mother used to call this the burial money. "Rose won't be able to pay for Tony's funeral until she gets the burial money." "Holy Name Cemetery won't open a plot for Constantina until they get the government money." "We all chipped in to pay Quinn's. Grace'll pay us back when she gets the check." It must have been touch and go waiting for that survivor's payment.

The new monthly Social Security benefit for me, slightly larger than what I had been receiving, was deposited the following month. But, of course, Phil's payment had been discontinued. My new payment is nowhere near the total amount we both had been receiving, and my living costs (except for his vodka purchases and medical expenses) have pretty much stayed the same. There is no way around it. Unless you are the beneficiary of a large insurance policy, becoming a widow moves you into a lower income bracket.

"All our operators are currently assisting other customers. Your call is very important to us." Each morning, I sat at my desk in my tee shirt and underwear, made a list of which hostile customer service representative to call and listened to an eternity of Muzak. Although Phil was officially dead to the Social Security Administration, I still had to call AARP/Health Net and Humana to stop the automatic medical deductions in his name. They would have continued to make deductions from our joint checking account until they were notified. Kayla at AARP warned me that late submission of medical expenses might be denied, since I had cancelled his coverage. "Just submit the bills to our Atlanta office with an explanation, and we'll take care of it." Didn't happen. Those hospitals and pharmacies are quick.

I changed the utilities to my name as the bills came in to be paid. The Qwest man wanted to verify Phil's death by looking up the obituary on the Internet, which he did as we spoke, and I asked him did he see the irony in the fact that I (of the same last name and address) wished to assume the responsibility of paying the bill, and he was doubting me? "Well, harrumph, it's a government-regulated agency, and we need to verify." Because of the

Qwest customer service man, I was curious to see where obituaries are reprinted on the Internet, and I found www.legacy.com/Tucson/Obituaries.asp.

"Press one for English." I wish there were a number to press for a customer service representative who can really help me. What am I speaking—Russian? Is anyone even listening to me? Sprint apparently has no process in place for my phone call. I wanted to do what? "Put my account in my name only," I said. Well, she had to call a supervisor. The supervisor assured me that she understood. Five days later, I received a letter from Sprint to Philip (the dead one) thanking him for becoming a new customer. And the monthly Sprint bill came to Philip as usual. Two more phone calls finally got the name corrected, but they started charging me more per minute than my old plan. One more phone call finally got me back on the old plan and wishing I hadn't bothered in the first place. (Lesson learned.) Doggedly, I pushed on.

Automobile certificates of title should always be in both owners' names as *or*, not *and*. Vera Martignetti or Philip Martignetti enables either party to sell the car. Had the title been listed as Vera and Phil, I would have been obliged to prove Phil's death before I could sell his car. I sent a group e-mail to friends and acquaintances offering the car with a picture and list of the options, and it sold quickly to a friend. I cancelled the car insurance by phone, and the state registration on the Internet. The refund checks for the remaining months of coverage arrived the same week. Things were picking up.

With death certificate in hand, I visited the bank and spoke to our personal banker. He made a copy and gave me back the original. Phil had designated me the sole beneficiary, and it took just a few minutes for me to sign the paperwork to move his IRA into a retirement account in my name. I can withdraw any amount I want, but, of course, I'll have to pay taxes on it. Phil's IRA was not a Roth and, thus, was entirely pre-tax. Or I can leave the money in place, earning interest until I'm seventy and a half. At seventy and a half, the government mandates that a fixed amount of money be withdrawn each year. This is referred to in the land of the acronym as the RMD (Required Minimum Distribution). The RMD for my retirement account, I was informed, needs to be satisfied by December 31st of the year I became a widow—unless I turn seventy and a half during that year. Then I have until

April 1st of the following year to satisfy my first distribution. Huh? And then it gets more convoluted. I couldn't get a clear idea of exactly what formula is used to determine what I have to withdraw—more of a mystery than the Trinity. Hint: it has something to do with one's life expectancy. That makes me wonder if I can withdraw less each year if I prove I exercise, don't smoke, and eat blueberries every day. I'll know soon enough. I'll be seventy and a half in December.

Alaska Airlines has a bereavement policy that allowed me to move Phil's frequent flyer miles to my account at no cost. They just needed me to fax a copy of the death certificate. "We don't need an original," the customer service person assured me.

For forty-seven years, I called Phil when I had a car problem. Now I called my auto insurance carrier to ask about roadside assistance.

After his death, I contacted the three large credit information services—Equifax, Experian, and Transunion—to cancel Phil's account. Apparently, even the dead have their ID stolen. Police departments regularly receive reports of a deceased person becoming the victim of identity theft. The best way to prevent this kind of theft is to avoid including details, such as the day and month of your husband's birth, in published obituaries. Only the year should be listed. No details about a home address should be included to prevent a robbery during the services, when the house will be empty. Am I the only one appalled by this information?

An original death certificate is needed to submit to every insurance company. I would have needed one to collect life insurance, but Phil was not insured at his death. He had been insured through his employers and carried additional term insurance for most of our married life. "Annuities and universal life are for suckers," he'd say. But when he retired, he lost the company policy, and after the children graduated college and the term insurance premium increased exorbitantly at his sixtieth birthday, we dropped it. This is not unusual. Many people stop buying term life insurance after their children become adults or once a spouse dies. Their heirs will get nothing in the way of a payout. I was betting that Phil would live to be eighty, and we'd go broke paying the ever-increasing yearly premium. No regrets.

There has been no need to submit his will for probate. I have a will making me sole beneficiary, but there are no assets that will be contested. He and I met with our banker several times to confirm that Phil's IRA would pass to me as a retirement account upon his death. In any case, an IRA beneficiary designation, as a rule, supersedes a will. After his initial cancer diagnosis, Phil and I simplified everything. He had a will, a living will, and a medical and durable power of attorney made out to me. The only thing we should have had, but didn't, was an orange DNR (do not resuscitate) card. It hadn't occurred to us, but it is something that people with terminal illnesses are advised to consider.

I have a VISA and an American Express in my own name. Phil had thought to call and cancel all his credit cards except one, which we held jointly. It was important that he personally speak to the customer service operator in every case; only an account holder can make changes to the account over the phone. Had he not done that, I would have had to fax them a death certificate to close each individual account after his death. I wondered later why the operator took his word for it. Any male voice who knew his Social Security number could have closed those accounts. This is not to be used as a helpful hint.

At the Pima County Assessors Office, I was asked for a death certificate in order to transfer the house into my name only. Eureka!—a reason to have more than one certificate. But then a week later, I received verification that the house was in my name only, and they returned the certificate. So far, I still have every one of the six. I could make a collage.

We all know people who say that adversity was a gift—that their cancer, divorce, bankruptcy, or the death of a spouse made them better people, gave them a sense of purpose. Well, that isn't me. I don't feel like a better person. But as time moves on I feel less sad, less stunned, more in control, more able to speak up for myself. Maybe this is as good as it gets. For now.

A Bedtime Prayer

Ron L. Porter

Do you remember, Margie? "Sentimental Journey" started, I walked you to the dance floor, took your left hand in mine and pulled you close to me. Closer than you had ever been before. It must have been 10 o'clock. The fireworks were starting. Doris Day sang that line, "never thought my heart could be so yearny," and that's just how I felt. I moved my right hand higher on your back and bent over, putting my lips as lightly as possible on your neck, just above your shoulder. I waited three months for that night. "Moonlight Serenade" played next. It drifted into my mind the way your perfume had. Even the fireworks faded into the background. I knew there was no "I". There was us—only us. In every way possible in this world, you were everything. Your hand in mine, your scent, your hair against the side of my face, your dress. I felt it, I caressed it as we drifted right and swirled, and then I took you, and we shifted to the left and you followed. You moved as I did, knowing as I did where we were going, and you followed without hesitation, moved without doubt. You never knew I was struggling to keep a tear from escaping and betraying me; everything I was in that moment. I prayed, *this cannot be just another dance to her. Please*, I pleaded with God, *this cannot be just…another dance*. The fireworks grew louder; the intense colors from the sky were bleeding onto the dance floor. The sound split my attention from you, and I resented it for doing so. This was my time. All mine, I thought to myself—and hers. As unselfish as I believed myself to be, this moment I wanted never to end. "My God," I said, "I am so in love with you." It was the most honest moment of my life. Your perfume and your scent mixed with the gunpowder of rockets and sparklers, and I can still smell it today, White Shoulders. I still feel the material of your dress in my hand every time I pull the sheets back to get in bed. You looked so good in a dress. I sure miss slow dancing. Sixty-two years isn't really that long, when you think about it. It went by so fast. Too fast. I know we were just friends. Just supposed to be friends. You were dating someone else, that Major. I lied to you, Margie. I lied to you for six months. I told you for the first time at that dance. The truth is, I fell in love with you sometime between the first and second week of those classes we were taking. There was one moment when I actually heard it in my head: *she's the one*. I have thanked God for the G.I. Bill ever since. It was sixty-one years ago yesterday that we married, Margaret. I'll be eighty-four next week. That was my life. Back then. I never really left that dance floor. I never left Doris Day or Glen Miller or the Blue Danube behind. Life went on, that's not what I mean. You were my very own angel, and such a good mother. When your sister was sick, and you left to spend that week with her, I hardly slept a wink. I never told you that; I didn't want you to think I was silly. But I missed you so much. Not like I do now. Now is different. I needed you, Margie. I needed to come home to you every day. Your smile was my lifeline from the rest of the world. The world that didn't matter. The only world I have left now. Bills, appointments, television shows. The friends help. The kids still call once a week. Even our great-granddaughter called about a month ago. Can you believe it, a great-granddaughter? I go to Temple for you. But that and church is just a way to pass time. Sunday was always our day. I'm not unhappy, just alone. Like I was before that first class. Before that 4th of July dance. Before our wedding day. I miss you and I'm tired, Marge. I want to be with you again so bad, no matter what. Maybe tonight. Maybe tonight I'll go to sleep and dream of you. And be with you again. And we'll dance.

Second Runner-up: Best Poetry Contest

Before the Kiss

Steve Snyder

Massaging her back that summer's night:
the feel in her shoulders of that scapular unyielding,
below the doughy pliancy of muscle.
I suppose I could think it morbid, and yet
my thumbs along the bump-trail
of the spine are pleased to travel by touch,
blunt eyeless things that they are.
If sound waves have a consciousness,
then sonar might delight like this
when it strokes a ridge under the ocean.
A warm breeze played with her blonde hair
as I rounded her right shoulder,
her blue eyes wide with surprise.

Jane Pelczynski's Wedding Gift

Evelyn Buretta

In spring Don plowed the fields all day.
He hoped to give his sis a gift.
Jane's wedding day was set for May.

So young, so thin, he strove to lift
himself above the guys in town.
He didn't care if they'd be miffed.

He would not let his sister down.
He'd toil and sweat to earn some cash.
He'd beat them all. It's time: showdown!

The guys bragged 'bout the plates they'd smash
with bigger coins. It was the way
to show their skill and act so brash.

So Don worked hard without delay
for dimes, and nickels, pennies, too.
His love for sis he would convey.

Then came the day. Pa passed the brew.
Cigars were lit, the feast prepared.
The bridal dance would give the cue.

The polka music loudly blared.
The guys each hoped to break a plate.
Then with the bride each man was paired,

one dance, one chance, to show how great
he was to toss a coin and see
if he could make the plate a spate

of glassy chunks. No loud whoopee.
At last it was Don's turn to try.
He danced with sis. He thought, let me

show off my grit. His arm raised high,
he tossed with strength. His coin fell fast
and broke the plate. Don heaved a sigh.

The crowd cheered him; the fretting passed.
Sweet Jane hugged Don, his deed outclassed.

Trust in Magic

Lolene McFall

Love once seemed good and all went well.
We were oh, so young and trusting
When we envisioned a magic spell

To enclose our lives within a shell
Of wondrous powers. Love was singing;
Life seemed good and all went well

Until one day a warning bell
Clanged forth in tones that sent us reeling
So we envisioned a magic spell.

Yet no amount of faith could quell
The fear that held us in a sling.
Life once seemed good and all was well

But what transpired, what befell,
Shook us to our innermost being
'Til we envisioned a magic spell.

We placed our love in a wondrous shell
Which broke the grip of foreboding.
Life once seemed good and all was well
When we envisioned a magic spell.

Spring Break
—an excerpt from her forthcoming memoir, Swimming Upstream

Constance Richardson

The all-night train to Barcelona leaves from Paris' Austerlitz station on the *Quai Austerlitz* and *Boulevard de L'Hôpital*. Frances and I have third class tickets, but instead of trying to find the appropriate car, we throw our luggage on the first car we come to, climb on board, and collapse on top of our bags at the end of the corridor. The train starts to move, gradually picking up speed. Passengers with luggage begin to pass through interconnecting coaches. Each time the door opens, a cold blast of air jolts us. When the conductor arrives, asks for our tickets, and motions us towards the back of the train, we get up. Seven cars later, we take our seats, stowing luggage underneath and overhead. Exhausted from the exertion, I immediately fall asleep, my head rolling against the cold window.

Twelve hours later, on a very bright Barcelona morning, we catch a boat for the Balearic Islands. From the deck we watch Palma, the capital city, appear. In Palma, we take the electric train that rattles over the mountains before making its descent into Soller's station and on to Port de Soller, our final destination. At the small family hotel right on the bay, we meet some of the German exchange students who selected this vacation spot. Willie Paulsen, short and athletic, knows Frances from New Jersey. They hug, and Willie introduces us to the others as they straggle in.

The Hotel Miramar faces a sandy beach on a horseshoe-shaped cove dotted with palms. Adjacent to and left of the lobby is an outdoor terrace and restaurant/bar shaded by hibiscus-covered trellises. Tables and chairs covered in soft pastels welcome patrons. A young mother and her child sit at one of the tables; the child, in a highchair, is busy drawing with crayons on her tray, while her mother sips a colorful drink.

I cross the lobby and step outside. On the beach, gentle waves roll in and out, and small boats bob up and down offshore. The combined sounds of gentle surf, sea gulls, outboard motors, and laughter form a "relaxation symphony."

At dinner in the hotel's dining room, I meet everyone again. They know one another as students in Munich, except for Willie and Frances, who know each other from their hometown, Short Hills, New Jersey. Diminutive Willie is the loudest and most aggressive of the four.

Talk shifts to boats and water skiing. I excuse myself and go to my room to unpack and settle in.

The next day I am up early to find Frances already having breakfast in a sunny corner of the dining room.

"They're planning a hike after breakfast," she says. "Want to come?"

"Thanks, but I'd rather paint," I reply.

By midmorning I have set up my easel, a folding chair, and tubes of paint under a palm tree facing the bay. I place a small canvas on the easel, take a charcoal stick, and roughly sketch out the curve of the bay with the horizon above and a tree trunk in the foreground. Next, I gather the colors I see: Cerulean Blue, Naples Yellow, ochre, Mediterranean Blue. I pour a little turpentine into a small cup and oil medium in the other. Starting with a large brush, I paint the canvas with a wash of diluted color.

"Constance!"

Seeing no one, I step back from the easel a few feet. Then I see a figure mostly hidden behind the palm tree. He turns to show his face—Stani's. As I am about to yell, he puts a finger to his lips, indicating that I should keep quiet.

"Stani, what are you doing here?" I ask. "Why the secrecy?"

Shaking his head, he answers, "It makes no sense. I'm not sure. I had to come, to meet Frances' friends."

"Why hide, then?"

He shrugs his shoulders. "Would you please explain I'm here? If she is angry, I will find another hotel."

"Of course, Stani. She went on a hike. I'll tell her when she comes back."

We hug. He looks somewhat relieved as he walks towards the parking lot. I resume work on my painting and reflect on why Stani has suddenly arrived. I introduced them three months ago, and they've been almost inseparable since. Stani is my second cousin. My guess is that Stani wants to know Frances' world, and that sounds serious. He looks so French with his long hair, horizontally striped French polo, loose pants, leather sandals, and small rucksack.

Around noon, I schlep my equipment and chair to the hotel and wander into the restaurant, where the menu offers a vast array of choices. After explaining to the waiter that I want something small, he suggests *tapas,* an assortment of hors d'oeuvres that includes olives, prosciutto, and calamari, all of which I enjoy.

In the afternoon, I put on a swimsuit, get a beach towel and some magazines, and plunk myself down on the sandy beach, where I doze. When I open my eyes, the sun is no longer overhead, but sliding down in the western sky.

I knock on Frances' bedroom door. When I tell her about Stani, she is shocked, but not displeased.

"Where is he?" she asks.

I shrug, turning empty palms. She hurries from the room.

I descend to the lobby. In the restaurant, the others have gathered at our table. Presiding over the table is Willie, who announces he has rented a large Citroën and plans to drive around the island tomorrow morning. Noticing Frances' absence, Willie asks where she is.

"She'll be back," I mumble.

"From where?" Willie asks.

Just then, Frances and Stani appear. Frances introduces Stani to Willie and the others, and an extra chair is pulled up. Gradually, the animated conversation resumes. Frances and Stani decide not to go on the drive around the island, while the rest of us agree to meet the following morning at nine.

The next day, five of us pile into the Citroën sedan. Willie is driving. Bob McDaniel, with his long legs, sits in the passenger seat. At over six feet three, Bob deserves his nickname, "Stretch." I sit between John and Fritz in the back. The circuitous route north to Port de Pollenca winds along rugged headlands that drop straight down into the sea. From the port we head east to Arta, Mallorca's most historic hilltop fortress. We park on the main square and, after a ten-minute climb, reach the fortress-church built on the site of an Arab castle. The views over the rooftops are spectacular. Seven kilometers southeast of Arta are the Coves d'Arta, thought to have inspired Jules Verne's 1864 novel, *Journey to the Centre of the Earth.* Being claustrophobic, I decline the tour, but am happy to loll about in the sun. I buy snacks at the small concession stand and eat them at a picnic table decorated with pots of flowers.

From Cove d'Arta we proceed south over the winding, narrow road that hugs the coastline. We fall behind a slow-moving vehicle. The longer we are stuck behind it, the more agitated Willie becomes, shouting insults in German. Suddenly, Willie pulls into the oncoming lane to pass. A blind dip in the road ahead obscures the view. Terrified, I press my face into John's neck, shutting both eyes. I hear the car accelerate as we pass and feel it swerve back into the right lane. I open my eyes. We are still alive.

"Wilhelm, cool down," says Stretch. "We're in no rush. Want me to drive?"

"No! I can manage. The guy's a jerk. I can't stand jerks!" shouts Willie.

I wish Stretch *would* take over. What is the matter with Willie? Does he have a Napoleon complex? I wonder.

We follow the interior through almond groves, apricot orchards, and small farms to bustling and crowded Palma. As the city recedes in our rear-view mirror, the traffic and humanity thins.

Later, when I spot John alone, I ask, "Why is Willie like that? I was really scared. He could have gotten us all killed."

John nods his head as if to say, "What's new?"

When I try to talk to Frances about Willie's aggressive driving, she changes the subject.

"I'm glad Stani came," she says. "He doesn't much like the others, though."

"He's so French," I exclaim. "You only realize it when you see him next to a bunch of Americans."

The next two days are lazy ones for me. The guys have found a place to rent motorboats and gear for water-skiing. I pursue my oil painting at the same spot on the beach and watch dot-sized humans flail about on water-skis a long way off. Frances and Stani hang out together.

One afternoon, John invites me to join him for a walk. The trail follows coastal hills as it gradually climbs to overlook the horseshoe bay. We chat about his family, my family, our siblings. I learn that he's a junior at Wesleyan University in Connecticut. When he asks about my plans once we're back in the states, I confess to feeling confused and overwhelmed about what to do.

"I was so naïve before coming to Europe," I tell him. "Life seemed so simple. Now, I know how much I don't know, but I have no idea what to do—or even if I *should* apply to college."

"I think you should," John says.

"Why?"

"I think you are perceptive, smart—cute, too."

I check his expression as he watches me. Then he bends down and plants a soft kiss on my lips. No one has kissed me for a long time. I touch the place where he kissed me. John tilts my chin up until our eyes meet.

"If you go to college in the east, we can see each other next year," he says. His smile is so welcoming and inviting that I think about possibilities all the way back and for the rest of the afternoon.

John and I, Frances and Stani decide to sightsee in Palma our last day in Mallorca. As we ride the electric tram over the hill, Palma seems dwarfed by its Gothic cathedral, La Seu. Walking its myriad streets, the city takes on a different dimension. It feels like a big city, with its chic restaurants and cafes, modern art, and shops selling local arts and crafts. Along the waterfront, palm trees line a promenade that winds past a fishing port and a yacht club. After lunch, we buy souvenirs at several gift shops.

For our last evening I dress with a decided effort to look soigné. In my limited wardrobe I find white pants and pair them with a beloved Guatemalan striped shirt, dangling earrings, and thong sandals. Downstairs, John escorts me to a chair and sits next to me, placing his left hand over my right While he holds the menu for us both to read, we make our choices, which he relays to the waiter. He orders a bottle of white wine.

Willie is holding court at his end of the table with loud remarks about their water-skiing adventures. Stretch makes an attempt to include us by asking how we liked Palma, but Willie lobs the conversation back to his court.

Looking at Stani, Willie says, "I guess the French are more interested in food than sports, right?"

Stani shoots back, "I was a contender for the Junior French Olympic Ski Team in 1950."

"What happened?" taunts Willie in a sing-song voice.

Stani pauses a moment, then says, "My mother got sick. She died. So I didn't go to the finals."

It is suddenly deadly quiet around our table, except for the waiter, who happily explains the dessert selections. Conversation finally resumes at a more moderate level.

After dinner, John and I wander outside to the shoreline. The stars overhead and scattered lights from boats in the harbor and surrounding villas create a luminous backdrop.

"I'll miss you," he says.

"I'd like to know you better," I say.

Abruptly, he kisses me as if he were dying of thirst and I am water. The urgency of our embrace makes me wonder if I am still standing. We cling to each other, swaying in the sand. Hearing approaching voices, we pull apart. Willie and Fritz are laughing. John takes my hand and leads me towards the hotel. As we cross paths, Willie says something to John in German. Suddenly, John drops my hand, swings around and grabs Willie's shirt from the back, turning him so they are facing. John swings with his right fist and hits Willie in the face. Fritz just stares, his mouth open. Willie raises his arms to shield his face, so John punches him in the stomach. When Willie drops his arms protectively to his gut, John hits him again in the face. Willie drops to the sand, hands covering his face.

"Maniac," screams Willie.

"Shut up, you cretin!" John yells. "One more rotten word, and I'll kill you!"

Fritz bends down to assist Willie.

"*Komm, Willie, lass uns gehen.*" They stand, and Willie hobbles with Fritz towards the hotel lobby. I step close to John, still not understanding what prompted the sudden violence. John is breathing fast and massaging his right hand with his left. I take his right hand in both of mine and gently press it to my lips.

"You shouldn't have heard that," John says, shaking his head.

"I don't speak German."

"Good."

"What did he say?"

"Never mind."

"Because we were kissing?"

"Implying more, in dirty German slang." John puts his arm around my shoulders as we go inside the lobby. He looks distracted as we say goodnight.

In the morning, Fritz and Willie appear in the dining room. Willie's black eye is swollen shut. They sit on the other side of the room from where John and I are sitting with Frances and Stani.

"My God," remarks Frances. "What happened to Willie?"

"There was a fight last night," I tell her.

"Who? Why?" she asks.

"It was me," interjects John. "Willie was out of line. Way out."

Standing up, John announces he doesn't want to travel back to Munich with the others; he needs to work the telephones. Stretch comes over to say goodbye. We agree to meet in the lobby in an hour with our bags.

While I'm packing, I wonder if I will ever see John again.

Sexed on a Kona Balcony

Ellaraine Lockie

All his lovers have fed the birds he says
This is after I've sprinkled the balcony
with pieces of pancake

Well, we can't help it
Our wombs command the role
as surely as the moon dictates the slap
of waves against lava rock below the hotel

We are hardwired to feed hunger, if not in children
then in pets, plants and wild things
I especially like the wild ones
The touch between feral and female
A scrap becoming energy that burns in both directions

The myna who is empowered to squawk and walk
the perimeter as if giving orders
Zebra doves too dumb or smart to pay attention
House sparrows hopping like wind-up toys
as they pick up pieces for babies in a nearby palm

All of them fueling to follow their own destinies
And me with the same small flame that must have
kindled Annapurna when she filled Shiva's begging bowl
It burns through my morning bath

When I come out wrapped in a towel
to find more food for the birds
A saffron finch with fluorescent head
is eating macadamia nuts

that my man chopped with his pocket knife
He calls it male bonding
The nuts are coffee-coated, sugared and salted

Affair

Betty Birkemark

I looked in your eyes and what did I see?
Some new kind of heaven waiting for me.
We gently touched hands, and what did I know?
Wherever you went, there I must go.
And locked in your arms, what did I feel?
Unbearable joy, too sweet to be real.
One last, parting kiss, and how did it seem?
Was it reality? Was it a dream?
I watched you depart, and then my world fell.
We did love unwisely—but always so well!

The Party

Jan Rider Newman

You sat apart
but focused west
toward me.
The hair on my skin
pinged to your scan.
I knew you'd approach.

I could have kissed you.
Your blue eyes young
but not innocent.
I took off my sunglasses
to let you see mine.
A lean over, and your mouth.

But no dissection could adjust
The circle of my life
Into an angle where you fit.

Ships That Pass...

Frank Frost

In the fall of 1945, Oregon State College (now Oregon State University) was about as close to heaven as any nineteen-year-old, freshly in from nine months of sea duty, could expect to find on this earth. There were 180 of us in our V-12 (officer training) Unit, about half of us in from the fleet and half right out of high school. It seems all rather silly now, realizing that just one year earlier I would have been one of those greenhorn schoolboys, but at the time it seemed to make a world of difference. Half of us thought of ourselves as sailors, and the others—well, they were really still kids. Despite that minor, internal distinction, we quickly became a close-knit group. We were still on active duty, and our "undress blue" uniforms were our daily campus attire. Away from campus, or for more formal occasions, we had uniforms identical to those of a Naval officer, but without the gold braid. We thought we looked pretty spiffy.

The Navy had taken over a dorm where we were housed as the only residents. We were still subject to the familiar Naval discipline, including weekly inspections and all that rigmarole. We also had fairly strict hours during the week. Other than those minor annoyances, we were simply students, like everyone else, and all of the social and extracurricular activities available to any student were equally available to us.

In the fall of 1945, the colleges and universities had not yet felt the influx of returning veterans. The ratio of girls to boys must have been around four or five to one. Bright, young, wholesome, attractive, and friendly girls were everywhere. One all but tripped over them. To a young man who had just spent months—in some cases, years—scarcely being able to so much as speak to a girl, this was heady stuff. There was no such thing as a dateless weekend, and the availability of social events seemed endless. Every few weeks, some organization, dorm, or sorority arranged to host a formal dance. At least once a week, a "sock hop" dance was open to all, without invitation. There were football games and pre-game rallies. Short "coffee dates" could be set up anytime, and even library study times could easily be turned into minor trysts. As I said, this was as close to heaven as it got.

Despite the attractions offered by a sometimes frenetic social life, we were students and, by and large, serious students. As an entering freshman, I was required (by the college, not the Navy) to take a battery of placement tests. I did quite well in them—too well, I realized later. I had long ago decided I wanted to study engineering. My reasons were somewhat vague, founded on nothing better than a fascination with how things went together, and an understanding that the designing of how things went together was what an engineer did. My problem was that the poverty-stricken country high school I attended had provided me with no foundation in either math or the sciences, even though I had taken every math class offered. They consisted of one term of high school algebra and a couple terms of general math.

Somehow, I managed to score high enough in my math placement tests that I skipped college algebra entirely! It was an impossible situation, and I was naïve enough that I didn't even recognize the warning signals until it was too late.

I was a reasonably decent student, and managed to escape flunking my math and physics classes, but just barely. I had no trouble with the rest of my courses and, for the most part, I thoroughly enjoyed being a student. I carried a heavy class load and worked hard. Still, I didn't let classes interfere with the pure joy of being there.

I was back in the Northwest and in a climate I knew and loved. The late summer sun that warmed the campus and my heart when I first arrived gradually lost its dominance. Soon, autumn leaves began to form a joyful red and yellow carpet to be sent swirling and rustling with every step. Then the inevitable fall rains turned the colorful mass into a slippery mush, and the campus was transformed into a bleaker, but no less vibrant place.

We sloshed around, hunched in pea coats. More importantly, the girls all disappeared, cocooned within winter coats and headscarves. And wooden shoes—schizophrenic things sporting a thick wooden sole that elevated the wearer above the puddles, but which were held in place by a leather upper that left half her foot bare. They did make a delightful "clippety clop" rhythm that echoed all over campus.

With the coming of the fall and winter rains, basketball replaced football. The number of formal dances multiplied. We started taking our dates to the movies instead of on bike rides or canoeing. Social life didn't diminish; it just tended to move indoors.

I seem to have strongly weather-related memories of that year. I suppose it is partly due to my classes being strung out all over the campus, so that each class change meant a walk to some other, usually far distant, building. Whether fall, winter, or spring, I was exposed to the weather for a significant part of each day.

During finals week, at the end of fall term, the Willamette Valley was in the grip of a cold snap. I had just come out of back-to-back physics and math finals and, in a state of near mental collapse, I wandered down into Lower Campus to regroup my senses. There was not a breath of wind, and a dense, freezing fog blanketed everything, turning the trees into ghostly, rime-cloaked silhouettes against a backdrop of gray nothingness. A girl materialized out of this eerie beauty. We greeted each other impersonally, the way strangers do, and exchanged a few banalities. She, too, had just survived back-to-back finals. We commiserated with each other and began walking together and talking. Eventually, we sat on a bench in the frigid afternoon fog, sharing a sort of final exam communion. I remember that she was pretty, and she had red hair. The cold soon forced us to retreat to our separate havens of warmth. We kissed, and she disappeared again into the fog. I never saw her again—and I think I'm glad. To be sure, the memory of that magical half hour has been romanticized over the past sixty and more years, but somewhere there is a lovely, redheaded girl who will forever remain young and pretty and just a little mysterious, and who, even in my dotage, has the power to invade my mind at unexpected moments.

Twenty Nine Times

Janet Kreitz

Bill Maddox
small town youth
volunteered 1942
to defend America
saw Texas, California, Florida
courtesy of the Air Force
stationed in England
drank warm ale
caroused at Piccadilly
saw Glenn Miller
ached for home
enemy target
high in the sky
twenty nine times
witnessed friends lost
in spiraling planes
tension iced missions
smoking engines
flak ruptured wings
treetop landings
came home
raw nerved
hollow eyed
worked
raised a family
loved America

The Box in the Attic

Jack Campbell

I was feeling rather pleased with myself after finishing a memoir that dealt with a boyhood friend who had died in the skies over Europe during WWII. The piece was based on the air log left behind by this young airman, and my direct association with him as a friend of the family. The dog-eared air log gathered dust in my closet for quite a few years after acquiring it from his brother. I had accepted it with a promise to write his story for surviving relatives and friends. Somehow, the years sped by, propelled by a fast-moving career and a growing family of my own. I had flirted with writing through the years, but it wasn't until I retired that I could really concentrate not only on my memoirs, but also my short stories.

I took the finished memoir with me to my local VFW post, where I not only enjoy the bull sessions with my fellow veterans, but also the cold beer and a hot game of pool that will generally fill a pleasant afternoon. One of my buddies, a Navy vet from the Vietnam War—let's call him Dick—read my piece. He thought the idea of resurrecting a lost diary after all these years was cool and asked if I would be interested in doing it again. After assuring him I was always interested in fuel for a new story, he went on to tell me about his mother's brother, who had been killed in Europe during WWII. Apparently, Dick's mother came into custody of her brother's records after her folks passed away. She eventually sent them to Dick, knowing he would be happy to know more about the uncle he had never met. After a lengthy inventory, Dick had stored the items in his attic and got on with his life.

"Do you think there might be a story in that box?" I asked

"Well, let me think…as I remember, there were some war medals and service-connected papers in it. Might make a good story for you."

Well, it took a week or so, but Dick finally remembered to bring me the now famous "box in the attic." I immediately asked for temporary custody until I could make copies and return the items.

"Hell, yes, take your time. It's been sitting in my attic for years…no hurry!"

My pool game suffered for the rest of the afternoon, as my gaze went intermittently to that box now resting on the end of the bar. I kept thinking of lame excuses to end our pool game, so I could get that box home. My imagination had been running wild with the thought of resurrecting another hero from the past. "He won medals," Dick had said. The young man in that box gave his life for his country so, yes, there's a story there.

"Dick, it's late, I gotta go," I finally blurted out.

"Hey, man, I hear ya." Dick gave me a sly grin and hung up his cue. "See ya next week, guy. No hurry with that box, okay?"

Driving home, I labored to maintain my lane on the road, the box beside me a magnet for eyes and fingers. Alone in my computer room, I set the box down on my desktop and prepared to resurrect a forgotten life, a hero, no less, to his country so many years ago. I sat down in my chair and leaned back to contemplate the moment. "There were medals and testimonies in the box," that's what Dick had said. Well, it's time to say hello to this long-forgotten soldier, I thought. Let's resurrect his deeds and display his awards. Let's go back almost seventy years when the whole damn world was at war, and see what this good man did to help bring that war to a successful conclusion.

I carefully removed the tattered lid from the cardboard container, which was about the size of a large shoebox. Lined up neatly, consuming the entire length of the box, were three flat leather cases. They undoubtedly contained the medals Dick had mentioned. I retrieved the first of the three, noting a thin coating of dust. I reached for the cloth I kept handy for cleaning my monitor and rubbed sheen back to the tan leather case. I did the same for the other two cases and lined them up, side by side, before me. With no outward indication as to what each box contained, I took one in hand and, with breathless trepidation, eased back the lid and peered down at what I immediately recognized as the Distinguished Service Cross. I think I stopped breathing for at least half a minute. I was in awe.

This medal is just one step below the Medal of Honor, and is awarded for Extraordinary Heroism in action. I placed the open case on my desktop, my lamplight accentuating its slightly tarnished splendor. This was one hell of an introduction to my mystery soldier. I was pumped, nervous anticipation doing a job on me as I opened the lid on another case. My God, the Silver Star! What had this young man done to rate two such prestigious

THE BOX IN THE ATTIC 187

awards? This medal was awarded for "Gallantry in Action." Adding that to the previous one for "Extraordinary Heroism," I had to ask myself, who was this man? Hopefully, the remaining paperwork left in the box would tell me. I placed the Silver Star next to the Distinguished Service Cross, a slight tarnish on both clouding their full glitter potential.

I now found myself in a stunning ambiance as I looked to open the last leather case. I fingered it in a restrained fashion, running a guessing game with myself, not sure what I might find inside. The "Purple Heart," of course. This young man had two of the highest decorations a soldier can earn, and the natural assumption would be that he was wounded in the process. I leaned back in my chair, trying to get a handle on this man before examining the paperwork left in the box.

Technical Sergeant William B. Hawk Jr. from Radcliff, Ohio had already shown me the depth of his valor. Now I wanted to know the path he had taken to garner this much respect from his peers. For the next two hours, I scanned the remaining documents—"pages of history," if you will. They painted a distinct picture in my mind of a man who came to the aid of his country when asked and subsequently gave his last full measure of devotion to that country—his life.

The writer in me said, "Let's get to work," but the patriot in me said, "No. Sit here in the company of this fine soldier. His credentials are set before you. Absorb them and garner the words you will need to praise him to the world. Do not go in haste."

Sergeant Hawk won the Silver Star before his death, but never saw or envisioned the awards lined up here on my desk. They were all awarded after his death in Germany and presented to his grieving parents months later. This scenario was played out in every corner of America over the four years of WWII. It would appear that Sergeant Hawk not only used the skills taught him for war, but implemented them with a high degree of courage and on a regular basis until his death in action.

The following are some of the details from the short life of Technical Sergeant William B. Hawk Jr., serial no. 35867136. No records as to his pre-war life were available, only highlights from his time served in the Army.

William B. Hawk lived in Radcliff, Ohio. There were no records in the box to indicate when he entered the Army or where he trained. The records I have before me tell me he joined Company G, 334th infantry, 84th division, known as "The Railsplitters," in April of 1944. In November of 1944, he earned his Combat Infantry Badge and was promoted to the rank of Technical Sergeant. He was leader of the 3rd platoon by February 1945.

His division was part of the 9th Army, which, during the Battle of the Bulge, was moved into Belgium to stop the German advance. After pushing the Germans back into Germany, they went back to spearheading the 9th Army's push across the Roer River and towards the Rhine.

On January 9, 1945, Sergeant Hawk won The Silver Star in the following action: leading his men across an open road, fire from a German tank kept them pinned down. He gave suppressing fire, while constantly exposing himself to the enemy in the process, until all of his men were out of harm's way. He then volunteered to lead a patrol that ultimately forced a German unit, trying to flank his position, to withdraw.

His citation ended with, "The cool courage, disdain for danger, and commendable conduct displayed by Technical Sergeant William B. Hawk are worthy of high praise, and are in accordance with the finest traditions of the Military service of the United States of America."

From all accounts, Sgt. Hawk was not a glory hound. It would appear the man had a real affinity for keeping his men safe in moments of compromise, often exposing himself to deadly fire to that end.

I leaned back momentarily to recall the intense combat that was the name of the game as the Third Reich crumbled in the spring of 1945. This young man had spent almost a year with his unit, always out on the point of 9th Army's offensives.

The final definition of Sergeant Hawk's courage came on March 1, 1945 in the vicinity of Eiglen, Germany. He and his men were pinned down by a deadly machine gun crossfire. With the usual disregard for his own safety, Sergeant Hawk crawled forward almost fifty yards, often exposing himself to that same fire. He got close enough to toss a grenade into the position of the first machine gun nest, wiping it out. He was wounded during that action, but proceeded to crawl close enough to the second gun emplacement to throw another grenade and silence their fire. He was mortally wounded in that effort.

His actions allowed his Company to move forward, and prevented the many casualties that surely would have befallen his men without his daring sacrifice. For his actions that day, Sergeant Hawk was awarded the

Distinguished Service Cross. The next highest award would have been the Medal of Honor.

Ten days later, on the 11th of March, General A. R. Bolling, the commanding general of Sergeant Hawk's unit, sent the following letter to Mrs. Clemmie S. Hawk, his mother. In part it reads:

> It is with the deepest condolence that I inform you of the death of your son, Technical Sergeant William B. Hawk Jr. ASN: 35867136, of Company G 334th Infantry, who was killed in action on March 1st, 1945, in Germany.
>
> Your son, who was 3rd platoon Sergeant, was leading his unit in an attack in the vicinity of Eiglen, Germany the afternoon of his death. His advance was slowed by enemy machine gun and rifle fire. Despite this, however, he continued to lead his men forward until he was struck by fire from an enemy sniper. His body was recovered immediately and was prepared for burial in an American cemetery in Holland.

The letter continued to relate some of Sergeant Hawk's exploits during his service under General Bolling, and assured Mrs. Hawk that her son's personal belongings would arrive in the following weeks.

In August of 1945, Mrs. Hawk received the following letter from her son's Company Commander, Captain Charles Hiatt.

> Dear Mrs. Hawk:
>
> Perhaps my name is familiar to you, since I commanded G Company of this regiment as a Captain while Bill was in it. I have wanted to write you, to tell you something about Bill as a soldier, but have delayed doing it for some months because I have a very great affection for him, which makes writing about him somewhat difficult.
>
> As Bill may have told you, he was one of my bodyguards for several weeks after we went into action. Being together in danger so often established a bond between us, which is no salvation, I know, for the loss of your son, however, I thought you would like to know.
>
> Believing that you would like to know more about the engagements in which Bill took part, I have arranged to have a copy of the Division history sent to you when it is published.

I realize fully that nothing I can say can compensate you for the loss of your son, however, in tribute to Bill, I would like to say that he was one of the finest soldiers I have ever known, and with him, I lost a valued friend. He was the kind of young man who should have lived to help make this a better world.

Please feel free to write me if you desire to.

Sincerely yours,
Charles Hiatt

Postscript: Technical Sergeant William B. Hawk Jr. was buried in a United States Military cemetery in Margraten, Holland, the final resting place for almost eighteen thousand American soldiers in WWII. I chose to write about this great patriot not only because of his glowing credentials, but because he was just one of the many brave servicemen it took to once more assure succeeding generations that there will be freedom! And, as in any war, though the means will always be cost effective, human life, I'm afraid, will not.

From the D-day invasion on June the 6th, 1944, it took eleven months to push the Germans back inside the walls of Berlin, resulting in their unconditional surrender. Of the over 16,000,000 U.S. men and women called to duty in WWII, 291,000 died for that cause, almost 672,000 were wounded and lived. As of this writing, there are 4,700,000 surviving veterans. I am proud to be one of them.

Nomen Dubium

Andrew J. Hogan

I'd almost finished reading the final papers my students had submitted for the Advanced Paleontology Workshop on the Rio Limay excavation when I got a telephone call from my brother, Felipe.

"You've got to come out to the ranch right now. There's an investigator here from America. He says he's got information about what Dad did in Germany during the War. Dad's locked himself in his study."

I rushed to the ranch outside Senillosa, where I found Felipe sitting at the dining room table with a man in a yarmulke who introduced himself as Daniel Aarons of the Simon Wiesenthal Center in Los Angeles. I saw a recent photo of my father with his arm stretched out in front of him; it was one of the photos taken at the press conference I'd organized at the beginning of the semester to announce the discovery of the Antreisraptor. There were also several old black and white photos on the table, mostly group shots of men in uniform.

Felipe was studying one of the black and white photos with a magnifying glass. He handed it to me; his eyes were red, on the verge of tears. In the photo were fifteen men assembled under the main gate of Der Zoologische Garten. In the center was Adolf Hitler. On the right side were half a dozen men in black or brown uniforms with swastika armbands. On the left side were men in business suits, all with swastika armbands. I took the magnifying glass and looked at the faces of the soldiers; my father wasn't there. But then I found him, the fourth business suit on the left. "Berlin, Mai 1941" was written in white letters on the bottom left-hand corner of the photo.

"Dad was a Nazi," Felipe said. "He ran the Berlin Zoo for Hitler during the War."

"Actually, he was the curator for animal welfare from 1939 until he abandoned his post in April 1945, just before the Allies entered Berlin," Daniel Aarons said. "The Zoo used political prisoners and Jews as forced labor during the War, and there were some serious allegations against your father."

"What kind of allegations?" I said.

"Mostly the usual—harsh treatment, starvation, inadequate housing. These were very common at the end of the war," Aarons said. "Food and clothing were scarce for everyone; prisoners were the lowest priority. The only reason the Center became involved was the reasonably credible allegation by two Jewish prisoners that your father fed sick and dying prisoners to the Zoo animals."

"I don't believe it," I said.

"We've seen many war criminals become model citizens in the communities to which they escaped after the war," Aarons said. "In your father's case, we didn't find enough convincing evidence to recommend any kind of prosecution. During the bombing of Berlin, before the Allies entered the city, several of the prisoners working at the Zoo were seriously injured. When the Allies entered the city, they found many unburied corpses. Your father may have fed the dead bodies of injured prisoners to starving Zoo animals."

"So what are you going to do now?" I said.

"The documents we've assembled will be released to the public. Before doing this, the respondent of an allegation is always afforded the opportunity to review our documentation and make any corrections that can be verified. Your father has refused to answer any of our correspondence. I was in Buenos Aires to meet with Uki Goñi about the Argentine angle on Operation Last Chance, so I came here personally to offer your father a final chance to set the record straight."

I went to the door of my father's study. "Dad, open the door." No response. "If you don't open the door, I'll break it down." I waited. He was moving around on the other side. When it didn't sound like he was coming to the door, I pounded on it again. There was a click, then an explosion. Felipe and I broke down the door. My father was lying with his head on his desk, a pistol in his hand.

It all began with the press conference in January. My father had always been terribly shy in public, in spite of being an excellent speaker at family gatherings and private business meetings. I knew he would never agree to stand up in public, to call attention to himself, so I hid the details of the press conference from him. I managed to get him up on the stage with me, but he was very nervous. I thought he would loosen up once we got started. I went up to the podium.

"Honorable Mayor of Neuquen, esteemed trustees of the Ernesto Bachmann Paleontological Museum, Mr. Marco Sentini, Neuquen's representative on the Argentine National Soccer Team that will win the Gold Medal at the Atlanta Summer Olympics—" Cheers interrupted me; many in the crowd stood up and turned toward Sentini, clapping. I continued, "—members of the press, ladies and gentlemen. Thank you for coming here today for the announcement of the discovery of a new species of dinosaur, Antreisraptor Bayeri, a bird-like dinosaur closely related to the Neuquenraptor and Buitreraptor, both of which were discovered in this region by my fellow paleontologists from the Neuquen University Institute of Paleontological Research. The Antreisraptor was a carnivore who appears to have hunted surreptitiously, lying in wait for its prey to pass by the entrance of the caves in which it dwelled along the banks of the prehistoric Rio Limay, pouncing on its victims and dragging them back into the cave to eat. Unlike the Neuquenraptor and the Buitreraptor, the Antreisraptor did not hunt in groups. This cave-dwelling raptor wasn't above eating carrion and may have specialized in preying on the sick and wounded to feed itself and its young."

Out of the corner of my eye, I could see my father fidgeting in his chair. I'd placed him at the end of the first row, a place of honor, right next to Sentini, who was attracting a lot of press photos. My father had gradually moved his chair back into the second row, next to a large university assistant vice president, shielding himself from public view of the right half of the auditorium.

"We at the Neuquen University Institute of Paleontological Research think the Antreisraptor Bayeri represents a turning point in the debate about the independent evolution of dromaeosaurs in Gondwana. The Antreisraptor is clearly the descendant of the Utahraptor of Laurasia and the missing link between the Utahraptor and the Neuquenraptor and the Buitreraptor. The evidence suggests that the Antreisraptor evolved from the Utahraptor in Laurasia, probably somewhere in what is now Europe, and as the result of some climatic or astronomical disaster moved south across the Caribbean land bridge that formed 120 million years ago as Pangaea broke apart into Laurasia and Gondwana.

"To the species name, Antreisraptor, the cave-dwelling raptor, I have added the specific epithet, Bayeri, in honor of my father, Frederico Bayer, who, like the Antreisraptor, migrated here from Germany after the cataclysm of the Second World War to evolve a new life in Argentina. To those of you who know him, my father may appear a simple rancher, but it was his incredible knowledge and love of animals, which he passed on to me, that led me to become a paleontologist and to make the discovery we are announcing today. Dad, please come up and say a few words."

The color drained from my father's face; the skin around his skull seemed to contract. Standing beside me on the podium, facing the audience, the photographers and cameramen taking pictures of him, he seemed a bleached-out fossil himself.

"I...I don't know what to say." My father froze up. "Thank you, my son, for this honor." Everyone clapped. He wasn't smiling when he sat down. I had expected him to say more; I didn't think he would be so camera shy.

Once the press conference had ended, reporters and photographers came up to the podium. My father retreated toward the exit behind the stage. A photographer rushed over and snapped a photo. My father held up his hand. The photographer kept shooting; my father reached for the camera. Afraid there might be a scene, I rushed over to calm the situation. The photographer took a couple of shots of me on the way over, and my father slipped out the rear exit.

"What's going on?" I said.

"I don't know," the photographer said. "I just wanted to get a good shot of your father. He crouched down behind the podium, and the microphone was partially covering his face. I didn't mean to upset him. This is a press conference."

"He's always been camera shy," I said. "Even at home he avoids being photographed. I don't have a picture of him myself. Let me see if I can get him to come back."

I found my father in the restroom. I tried to convince him to come back to the conference room.

"I'm leaving. I don't feel well," he said.

As soon as he came out of the restroom, he went to his pickup and drove away. Later, when I used the restroom myself, it smelled of vomit.

I apologized to the reporter for my father's behavior and asked if I could possibly reschedule an interview.

∼

When I was growing up, my father had insisted that everyone speak Spanish at home all the time, although my brother and I did learn to read German well. My father had acquired a large collection of books on general biology and animal behavior in German from his Aunt Helma, who had taught biology before the Nazis forced most women out of the workplace and back into the home. Although many of Aunt Helma's books were outdated even when I read them as a child, they sparked my interest in animal biology, which eventually led to my career in paleontology. Reading those biology books under my father's guidance was the only time I spent speaking to him in German.

My father told Felipe and me that he was born in Bavaria just before the First World War; he studied animal husbandry at the University of Ingolstadt, where my Aunt Helma had been a professor of biology. He returned to the family dairy and hog farm after graduation. My father was found to have a heart murmur and was exempted from military service. The family farm was in ruins at the end of the War, when all the animals were confiscated by American troops; they said the animals were needed to feed the local population, but hunger was still widespread among the surviving Germans months later. His patrimony destroyed, my father decided to start over as a cattle rancher. It wasn't easy for Germans to travel after the War, but a German bishop at the Vatican, Alois Hudal, helped my father find a new home in Argentina. His heart condition improved, the cattle ranch was a success, and my father was still going strong at eighty-seven years old.

I'd always assumed my father just translated his original name from Friedrich to Frederico. He never kept in contact with any relatives or friends from the Fatherland. He said his whole family had been wiped out during the War. I suppose there must have been some friends or distant relatives who survived, but he never mentioned them. He was a bit of a loner. There are others of German descent living in and around Neuquen, but my father was never really close to any of them.

The evening after the press conference, I drove to my father's ranch. That time of day, he's usually in his office, doing some administrative work or reading. When I arrived, the housekeeper said supper was almost ready; she set a place for me at the table. A few minutes later, Felipe showed up for dinner with his wife.

"What did you do to Dad at the press conference?" Felipe said. "I've never seen him so upset."

"What do you mean?" I said. "I asked him to come to the podium and say a few words."

"You named a carrion-eating lizard after him," Felipe said. "Dad said he's never been so embarrassed."

"You don't understand. That carrion-eating lizard, as you call it, is a major link in the debate about the evolution of dinosaurs. Dad has always been fascinated by this kind of research. It's a major honor to have your name attached to a new species. Nobody cares how the animal made a living."

"Well, maybe you should have consulted Dad first before you embarrassed him in front of the whole world. What are his relatives back in Germany going to think?" Felipe said.

"What relatives? He's never mentioned anyone by name back in the old country to me. Did he mention anyone to you?"

"No, not specifically. He just said something about what would they do back in Altoetting if they saw this," Felipe said.

"That's where he grew up in Bavaria?" I said.

"I think so."

My father came out of his office. "What are you doing here?" he said to me.

"I came to see if you would be willing to talk with the reporter from the press conference. She's doing a story for *Der Stern* on the German connection to the Antreisraptor discovery," I said.

"No."

"It'll be just the three of us. We can do it at La Parrilla restaurant," I said.

"I don't want to be interviewed. Why is where I came from important to the discovery of your new lizard? I wish you hadn't named it after me."

"I thought you would be proud. Your name will be associated with a major discovery in the history of paleontology," I said.

"What? Being named after a lizard that eats dead animals is an honor?"

"In all the years you taught Felipe and me about animal biology from Aunt Helma's books, you never once judged an animal by its behavior. Every animal has his place, you told us," I said.

"Let's talk about this after dinner, okay?" Felipe said. He touched my elbow and led me to the table. My father stood there, seemingly paralyzed. His face was red; his eyes bulged. I couldn't tell if he was angry or afraid.

"I'm not hungry," my father said. It sounded like an afterthought. He grabbed his hat and left through the back door, heading toward the barn.

I rose to follow him, but Felipe grabbed my arm. "Let him go; give him time to cool off."

"I've never seen him act like this," I said.

"I think maybe he's getting senile," Felipe said. "He's almost ninety."

"Have you noticed him forgetting things or getting confused? Has he stopped doing his regular activities, keeping the accounts, stuff like that?"

"No, not really," Felipe said. "But this could be something sudden—like a mini-stroke?"

"Maybe we should get him checked out at the clinic?"

"Good luck with that," Felipe said.

We ate dinner without my father. I was afraid he might be riding around in the dark just to stay away from me, so right after we finished dessert I went out to the barn. I found my father in a stall, brushing down his horse, Relampago, after their ride.

"It was too late to go riding," I said.

"I'll ride whenever I please," he said. "This is still my ranch."

He swung Relampago's saddle off the railing of the stall and onto its saddle stand several feet away, more like a fifty-seven-year-old than an eighty-seven-year-old.

"Dad, are you all right?" I said. "I really thought you would consider the press conference today an honor. I wanted to show you how much I respect you."

Tears ran down my father's cheeks. I thought he was going to say something, but then, as though he were trying to lift a massive weight, his face hardened and turned red. "I accept your apology," he said, almost in a whisper. "Now don't ever mention it to me again."

He turned his back on me and finished brushing down Relampago. As I left the barn, he said to the horse, "Lebe wohl, mein langjaehriger freund." I went back home to Neuquen.

Later that evening, I called the *Der Stern* reporter to say my father had the stomach flu and wouldn't be available for an interview.

For the next several months, I checked the *Der Stern* website for the human-interest article on the cave-dwelling raptor. Finally, I gave up. My relationship with my father gradually thawed, and we avoided any discussion of the news conference or the Antreisraptor Bayeri. I tried a few times to get him to talk about his youth in Germany.

"Something to tell the grandchildren," I said.

"Maybe you should get married first, before you worry about what to tell your children about me," he said. "I'd rather the bastards you've fathered know as little as possible."

I shrugged off the insult. "What about the children Felipe and Rosa are planning to have?"

"When Felipe fathers a child, he can ask me himself." Then he left the room.

At the same time, my father's health visibly declined. The night he rode in the dark rather than have dinner with me was the last time he mounted Relampago. Felipe took over complete management of the ranch, and my father mostly stayed in his study, looking at the old books he'd brought with him from Germany. Both Felipe and I tried to get him to go to the clinic for a checkup, but he refused. We all knew something was wrong. My doubts simmered, but like any paleontologist, I let time and nature do most of the work unearthing old skeletons. Then Daniel Aarons arrived from Los Angeles.

Aarons left shortly after being interviewed by the police. He told Felipe and me that he would wait a couple of months before releasing the documentation on our father's case, to give us the chance to go over his papers and contact anyone back in Germany to verify our father's past.

In my father's desk, we'd found the letters his Aunt Helma Schuetzer had sent her nephew, Dr. Errando Ablehnung, Direktor von TierBetreuung at the Zoologische Garten on Hardenbergplatz 8 in Berlin. The last of Aunt Helma's letters had been sent to my grandmother, Marlisa. Aunt Helma had, by this time, moved from Altoetting to Berlin to care for the few remaining animals in the Berlin Zoo, abandoned when my father deserted his post just before the British occupation. Aunt Helma said she was still too angry to write to my father directly, but she was glad to hear he had safely escaped to the Oberer-Weilhart Forest in Austria. She prayed my father had done nothing that would cause him to be brought before the War Crimes Tribunal in Nuremberg.

In the month following my father's suicide, Felipe was preoccupied with the day-to-day management of the ranch, so I found a regional paleontology research symposium for early January in Amsterdam that would pay for my travel to Europe. Even though the submission deadline had long since passed, the North Sea Paleontology Society was more than happy to squeeze a presentation by the discoverer of the Antreisraptor Bayeri into its session on the Laurasian-Gondwana land bridge.

After the symposium, I made my way to my father's hometown of Altoetting, Bavaria. I brought my parents' one wedding picture with me to help me verify that my family name really was Ablehnung.

I wasn't prepared for the snow and cold in Altoetting. Standing in front of the Hotel Koenig Ludwig, the snow-covered Alps formed a backdrop for the town, just like our snow-covered Andes back home. I knew now why my father stopped running after he reached Neuquen.

A second-hand clothing store on Neue Gasse catering to visiting pilgrims unprepared for the weather provided me with a coat, hat, and gloves. The manager of the store suggested I begin my search at the Stiftskirche, where parish records dating back to the early Middle Ages were kept.

I knew my father's birth date, but I didn't know if he'd borrowed it from a deceased prisoner or associate at the Berlin Zoo to disguise his identity and make his escape from Germany. The sacristan of the Stiftskirche led me to the library, where I found the early twentieth-century birth records and an entry on my father's birthday: Errando Friedrich Ablehnung, born to Marlisa and Otto Ablehnung in Altoetting, Bavaria on August 6, 1909. Further searches through the parish records showed that both my father and grandfather were only children; my father had told the truth; there were no more Ablehnungs in Altoetting. On my grandmother's side, the Schuetzers, there had been three sisters: the middle sister, my grandmother, Marlisa; the oldest, my great Aunt Helma, the university professor whose letters I had found in my father's desk and who died while working at the Berlin zoo in late 1946; the youngest, Petra, who married Albrecht Meier and had a son, Theodor, who I learned from the sacristan was an usher at the Gnadenkapelle, the Chapel of the Miraculous Image, the most visited pilgrimage shrine in Germany.

"Herr Meier would be just a little younger than your father," the sacristan told me. "They probably attended some of the same schools. He ushers for the late morning mass; it's the least demanding this time of year. His mind is still sharp as a tack. He can tell you the stories behind hundreds of the votive drawings on the Chapel walls."

At the Chapel next morning at 9 AM, I found every inch of the exterior walls and ceilings covered with pictures drawn or painted by pilgrims seeking a glimpse of the Miraculous Image of the Black Madonna.

"This one is from the 1940s," an elderly gentleman said in a strong voice. "See here, a young girl stumbles on an unexploded bomb. Her mother runs directly to the Gnadenkapelle to pray to the Black Madonna for her daughter's life, while the older brother rescues the girl, after which the bomb explodes, killing only a lonely dove, which represents the mercy of Jesus."

"How many of these votive drawings are there?" I said.

"Too many to count," the man said. "In better weather, we display the new ones on easels. A committee replaces the old ones that have deteriorated with the newer. Between what's on the wall and in storage or discarded due to age, there have been more than five thousand over four hundred years."

"I came here to meet Theodor Meier. That wouldn't be you, by any chance?"

"Yes, it is." He handed me a slip of printed verse with a drawing of the Gnadenkapelle at the top and a cross on the bottom. "Did you come here on a pilgrimage long ago? Did I give you one of my poems?"

"No," I said. "I think I am your second cousin."

"I didn't know I had a second cousin," Theodor said.

"I am the son of Frederico Bayer, who was called Errando Ablehnung before he left Germany for Argentina."

The poems in Theodor's hand fell to the ground; he leaned against a drawing on the wall next to a sign: *Please, Do Not Touch.*

"Are you all right?" I said.

"I'm sorry. It's been such a long time since I've heard that name," Theodor said. "Not since 1946, when the British Military Police came looking for him. The Zoo where Errando worked was in the British sector of occupied Berlin. Errando fled across the border. We sent him word about the military police. Both of his parents passed away shortly after the War. None of the Schuetzers ever heard from him again."

"He died two months ago."

"I'm sorry," Theodor said. "I imagine he was successful in his second life. He was very ambitious as a young man. Do you know he was only thirty years old when he became the chief veterinarian for the Berlin Zoo? He was always in the papers, mostly because of the auroch back-breeding project."

"Auroch?" I said.

"It was a prehistoric ox, now extinct," he said. "Hitler saw it as a symbol of Aryan strength. Restoring it was part of the mythology of the Third Reich, the resurgence of the Aryan race. Of course, by the end of the war, the entire Zoo was in ruins. Errando was afraid his prominence would make him a target for revenge by the Allies or the Jews who'd escaped the concentration camps. My Aunt Helma, who'd always championed Errando before the War, came to despise him. She wouldn't even speak his name. She went to Berlin to save what was left of the zoo animals after Errando fled. Your father came here first, but he feared Aunt Helma might turn him in, so he escaped into the forest across the border in Austria. We never heard from him after that. Was he successful in Argentina?"

"Yes, but it was a very private life. My father eventually came to own a large estancia, a cattle ranch, outside of Neuquen. It's a farming and cattle region not far from the Andes. You can see them off in the distance, just as you can see the Alps from here."

"I'm surprised you've come in person to visit after all this time, and this isn't the best time of year. It's cold here now for pilgrims who live in the tropics."

"My father was accused of war crimes by the Simon Wiesenthal Center. He killed himself before he could answer the charges," I said.

"Oh, no," Theodor said. "Suicide is a terrible crime against faith. We must have a mass said to beg for his forgiveness."

"The Simon Wiesenthal Center is going to make public the allegations against my father unless I can uncover information that might exonerate him."

"I hope you won't involve the Schuetzer or Meier names in the matter." Theodor was moving away from me. "We don't have any records that might help you. Please don't mention us."

"What did the British Military Police accuse him of?" I said.

"It was some kind of mistreatment of forced labor, but we never saw any documents. We told the Military Police we were only distant relatives. I know they talked to Aunt Helma about Errando; it was shortly after she died that they came here looking for him." Theodor looked at his watch. "I have to get inside; mass is going to start soon. I'm sorry you came so far for nothing."

"Perhaps we could get together tomorrow? You might remember something," I said.

"I'm sorry. I have an appointment all day tomorrow at the clinic. Prostate problem, you know." He rushed off.

I caught a flight out of Berlin back to Argentina. Before leaving, I stopped at the Deutsches Historisches Museum to donate my Aunt Helma Schuetzer's letters; they've been stored in Folio 4198, along with thousands of other personal accounts of the experiences of ordinary Germans under Nazi rule during World War II.

Back in Neuquen, the University was just getting ready for the new semester after the Christmas break. The Advanced Paleontology Workshop was full, with a waiting list long enough to fill the class twice over. Students were lured by the possibility of having their names associated with the next fossil discovery. Only a year ago, I'd put my father on the podium at the news conference on the cave-dwelling raptor. My desire to give him fame had instead unearthed his prior disgrace. But I learned there was someone else in my family who deserved the honor of having her name remembered.

In the Department office, still nearly empty of students and faculty, I stood in front of the fax machine. My department chair would send me a nasty note about the expense of faxing a letter from Argentina to London; administrative funds were always scarce. I put in the letter in the slot, pressed send, and saw the address vanish into the machine:

Ronald Taylor, Ph.D.
International Commission on Zoological Nomenclature
Natural History Museum
Cromwell Road, London SW7 5BD UK

Dear Dr. Taylor:

> There was a clerical error in my recent submission, Case #2468, submitted on March 18, 1996. The specific epithet for the Antreisraptor in the submission was listed as 'Bayeri'. The specific epithet should have been 'Schuetzeri'. Would you please make the change to our application? We apologize for any inconvenience this error may have caused the ICZW.
>
> Thank you for your assistance.
>
> Sincerely,
> Pablo Bayer Mueller, Ph.D.
> Neuquen University Institute of Paleontological Research

During the War:
Memories of Lives through Food

Kathy Hayduke

Starvation is a horrible curse no matter where it happens.

During WWII, living in Detroit, I remember rationing of flour, sugar, butter/oleo, coffee, and gas. We always ate well and never went hungry. There was always plenty on the table and meat four or five times a week, with chicken on Sundays. Anywhere we wanted to go, we walked or went by bus.

My husband, living in a remote village in Ukraine, remembers none of his family meals because it was always the same: potatoes, kapusta (sauerkraut), black bread, borscht and other soups. Meat was saved for extremely special occasions and often still not available.

I remember going to the Detroit Farmer's Market, and my dad carrying a bushel of corn on one shoulder, onions on the other. My mother carried a bushel of green peppers, and my brother and I each helped carry red peppers. When we got home, Mom spent the day peeling, cooking, and canning homemade corn relish. When she was done, she took the jars down to the cellar and placed each one on the shelf with loving care, knowing this and all the other jars of canned meats, vegetables, and fruits would see us through the winter.

My husband remembers looking at the sky and seeing the Russian and German planes fighting overhead. He remembers the Germans crossing the village bridge in the middle of the night in September 1943, telling everyone to get out of the village because they were burning it down. He remembers father leading the cow, mother gathering the bread that she had and whatever else would fit into her apron, carrying baby Bernie. Walter, the oldest at twelve, held three-year-old Mary's hand. Jerry, ten, and Harry, seven, carried what they could. And so their march began. Through the night, Walter often carried Mary because she was crying so much. When dawn came, they realized Mary had been crying all night long because her shoes were on the wrong feet.

My husband remembers that, when they stopped to rest, people rushed to drink water, and mother rationed out the bread she had to her family. Father milked the cow, giving his family something nourishing to drink. Father never could figure out how the cow continued to give milk without having time to stop and graze. Mother always believed it was because the eyes of God were watching over them. The villagers marched for three days, and then were put on the trains to Dachau.

I remember coming home from school, the smell of warm, fresh-baked cookies filling my nostrils with love, and the aroma of furniture oil each fall and spring, when Mom did her cleaning.

My husband remembers being stripped of all clothing, everyone being shaved of all hair, going into the showers to be de-loused, and then given prison clothes. He remembers eating a little piece of dark bread and broth—you couldn't really call it soup; there was nothing much in it. He remembers one of his brothers refusing to eat. Mother, fearing he might starve, hid his piece of bread in his little cap to eat later.

I remember going fishing with Mom and Dad and my brother, cooking the fish over an open fire right outdoors, how happy and content we were.

My husband remembers his family being transferred to a work farm, and mother pleading with the soldier to let her family sleep in one room in the barn, so they would not be separated. My husband remembers walking the road along the farm with Walter and Mary, going up to each house along the road and begging for something to eat, women slamming the door in their faces. He remembers one woman coming back to the door with a hard piece of old stale bread covered in mold. He and Walter looked at it, neither one of them able to stomach the thought of eating it. He remembers Mary grabbing that piece and devouring it.

I remember picnics at Grandma's house. All of us kids would be playing baseball with our uncles. Food was everywhere. We had as much as we wanted. Aunt Thelma always arrived with her kids late, and so it was determined that she could bring the dessert. She was the richest of the family, and so we knew we would get Sander's ice cream in wonderful creamy flavors that melted in your mouth.

My husband remembers mother being called first thing in the morning: "Auchsten"…get up. She would nurse baby Bernie quickly or get beaten, and then go milk the cows and work all day. One of the women took her little girl into the barn one day. The child cried because she was hungry. The mother squirted some milk from the cow's tit into her hand and gave her little girl a drink. With that, the soldier shot the mother and the little girl.

I remember going out in the fall and picking fruit that Mom would can. We picked pears, peaches (my favorite, peach pie), cherries—wonderful tasting fruits.

My husband remembers coming to the United States in 1949 on a ship with other immigrants. He remembers a sailor giving him an orange. He started devouring it, and the sailor laughed at him and showed him how to peel it. When he bit into the flesh of the orange, it was love, love, love. The same thing happened with a banana. My husband thought any country that had such delicious foods must surely be the best in the world.

When we met and started dating, my husband told me he would never want a lot of worldly goods, and if I were that type of person, it was best to get out then. He knows that no matter what you think you have, you can lose it all in just a minute. To him, food has always meant security, love, comfort, and good times. We have had many wonderful dinners with friends, families, and strangers. We operated a motel for quite a few years, and we often invited people staying with us to have dinner at our table, enjoying their company and the wonderful feeling we felt, offering people food, the ultimate sign of security.

The motto in our house has always been:

"Everyone is welcomed here. We may not have much, but we have good food."

My Favorite Game

Jane Boruszewski (1926 – 2009)

"Hey, Marek, why do you always have to be the first guard of Dwa Ognie (Two Fires)," I shouted at a sturdy boy holding a ball in the crook of his arm. He stood at one end of a grassy field that was marked off with sticks and stones.

"…ooo…nie nie nie," the edge of the nearby East African jungle echoed my Polish words.

"Ya, tell us why?" someone else wanted to know.

About a dozen youngsters, milling within the boundaries, waited anxiously for Marek to begin the first round of the game this morning.

His dark eyes went to Bolek at the opposite end of the field. Bolek was the other guard, who, with Marek, was supposed to keep the ball flying from one end to the other, either above our heads or between our bodies. Their aim was to hit a contestant. Even the slightest graze was enough to send us out of the game.

Marek laughed. He dropped the ball to the ground and dribbled it awhile. Then he caught and raised it slowly over his bushy head and held it high for everyone to drool over. Making big circles with it, he yelled, "It's because I have the only ball in this camp, in Tengeru."

"Bastard!" called out Stasia, the biggest girl in the group.

Marek pretended to ignore her, but he lowered the ball to his side and, staring into a space to her left, sent it spinning straight at her. With the speed of a cannonball, the ball hit Stasia's chest, and she fell to her knees.

"You are already out," he hissed.

"Yes, you are out!" cried the others in the field.

"That's not fair," she said, getting to her feet. "Marek, you didn't say that Dwa Ognie had started."

"Out! Out! Out!" the others shouted, amid much laughter.

"Get out before I hurt you again," Marek warned.

"I'm going…going," she mumbled. On her way out, she smacked small Edzio across his back.

"Fatso!" he called out after Stasia, sticking his tongue out at her as she staggered off the field. Edzio was the best player among us. He had developed the art of ducking the flying ball and using others as a shield at just the right moment. Most of time, he was the last one left in the game. As winner, he was handed the ball to start the next game with a partner of his choice.

I hated the little squirt.

And now, as soon as the ball went into action, we players turned into wild creatures. Running backward so we were always facing whichever guard had the ball in his hands, we swore and screamed. "Come on, Bolek, get me if you can…Marek, you think that you are tough, eh? You are nothing but a bully…" We called the boys names I can't put on paper.

Caught up in a fearful excitement, I ran about as if seized by madness. I avoided the flying object by jumping up, ducking, or leaping backward. We kicked and elbowed one another, but felt no pain, only a fury of anger. Right now, in the midst of this madness, I was not a child who lived in Africa, but a nine-year-old grownup, ducking bullets with our Polish soldiers, fighting off the Nazis in 1939. In the distance, Jaroslaw was bombed every day while I watched it burn and smoke, flames shooting up to the sky. I had cried to see our captured countrymen being kicked and whipped by Germans. In the beginning of the war, Nazis rode in tanks across our village or rode on horses, but when they left, the Russians came to stay for good. Both invaders robbed me and my friends of our childhood.

And who was robbing us now? Marek? But he had been robbed, too. He had lost both of his parents to typhus in Uzbekistan and crossed the border with a group of Polish orphans, strangers to him.

Suddenly, I saw the ball coming straight at me. I spread my arms and caught it. Bolek had thrown it at me, hoping to get me out of the game, but he failed. I couldn't believe my luck. As I hugged the ball, I felt sweet success filling up my heart to the brim. I grinned, knowing I was temporarily saved from having to leave the field. I savored my precious moment. I had conquered the ball the way I had beaten the typhus that tried to claim my life in Russia.

"Don't just stand there gaping, you stupid goose," I heard Marek's voice behind me. "Let me have the ball!"

Slowly, I turned around and stared at the ruffian, grinding my teeth. With his arms folded across his chest and his legs wide apart, he looked like a short Lensky assembling our grownups for all-day labor in the Siberian forest. Lensky and his helpers kept the Poles confined to a place of imprisonment in the district of Omsk on the shores of the Irtish River. For two years, my parents worked for meager food alone. For two years, we children were too hungry, too cold or hot, and always humiliated by Lensky. And here in Tengeru, biting my lips hard, I was about to throw the ball, not to Marek, but at him, wanting to hit his nose, wanting to see it bleed. But he caught the ball with ease and laughed his awful laugh.

"Communist!" I called him the one name we Tengerians hated and despised.

Marek seemed to ignore my insult, but I knew he was up to no good. As I thought, he sent the ball whizzing at me again. Today, his and Bolek's shots were harder and more twisted than ever before. The two bullies kept aiming at our heads or chests. At this moment, I was one of four contestants left in the game, and I wanted to win this turn, even if it killed me. My fingers itching and palms sweating, I braced myself. "Ready for another catch," I muttered to myself. "Be careful," a small voice inside of me warned. But I did not listen to its advice. I spread my arms, but forgot to jump up a bit.

Woops! I felt a hard blow on the left side of my face. A million stars exploded before me, and then faded away. I went down to the ground, and the ball rolled away from me, laughter floating about me.

"Another loser," someone sneered. "Got what you deserve."

I got up with effort and staggered off the field to join the players grouped outside the boundaries. With my cheek numb from the blow, I sat down on the ground next to Wanda, the shortest girl of us all, who was sniffling, as always. Her hands embraced her knees, and she looked like a fetus curled up in its mother's womb. From the time I met her in Pahlevii, our first friendly camp on the other side of the Caspian Sea, I had felt compassion for this playmate. She told me then that her papa was shot in Warsaw by the Nazis for hiding a Jewish family in his cellar. After his death, Wanda's mama went to live with her cousin in Eastern Poland, which was occupied by the Russians, and they had deported the woman with her daughter to Kazakhstan. Two years later, they both found themselves in Iran, where her mama died of dysentery.

I had lost my little brother in Siberia, a month after our arrival at Bialy Jar, the Russian settlement. Extremes of climate and lack of proper nourishment killed the poor baby at nine months of age. We buried him in a hole we dug in the woods. A month later, my aging aunt died, for what reason, I never knew.

"Janka, you got a whopper there on your cheek." Wanda's voice brought me back to Africa and my gang. There were still two players left in the field, and I wished I were one of them. But now my head was getting hot, and I felt dizzy.

"Have to go home," I whispered, glancing at Wanda's sweet profile, outlining itself against Mount Meru on the western horizon. I smiled sadly. The mountain was always there, like a loyal friend, for everyone who wanted to look at it and be consoled.

"Don't you want to stay for the next turn?" asked Wanda. "You usually wait to the end of our games."

"I...I don't feel well," I moaned, touching my face. It felt hot and lumpy. I tried to stand up, but sat right back down in order not to fall on my back.

"I'll walk you home," said Wanda.

Before I could say no, she helped me up and put her arm about my waist. I leaned on her thin shoulder. Listening to our playmates hollering, we plodded toward my hut, where I lived with my big sister, Marysia, Mrs. Nadzieja, and her daughter, Irena, who was my age. Wanda helped me to get into my bed. It was one of four leaning against the round, white-washed walls and shielded carefully with a snowy white mosquito net. We were all told that mosquitoes here carried malaria and were advised to keep the nets down at night.

No one was home, and I was glad. "Sit down, Wanda," I said, pointing to one of the wooden stools that embraced the round table in the middle of the hut. Everything here was round to match the walls of the round hut. The pointed roof was covered with palm leaves, and the earthen floor was smooth and hard.

Wanda looked around. "Where is your washbowl?"

"What do you want it for?"

"To bring water from the faucet." Tengeru had no water inside our shelters. Each group of huts had stoves, laundering tubs, and water pipes installed outside.

"I'm not thirsty."

"A cool compress on your face will stop some of the swelling."

MY FAVORITE GAME

After Wanda left me with a wet rag on my face, I fell asleep. Right away I plunged into a nightmare from my past:

I am lying in the hospital bed next to Marysia's. We are both ill and hurting all over. Marysia tells me I have a very high fever, and she begs the nurses to give me some medicine, but in vain.

"Where is Mama?" *I keep asking.* "I want my mama."

"Janka, don't you remember? She and the rest of our family are on the train that is supposed let them off in Bukhara."

I nod. Tears fill my eyes, and I'm blinded by the naked light bulb above my head. I keep asking the nurses to shut it off...

Someone shook me by the shoulder, and I woke up in the round hut.

"What's the matter with you, Janka?" Marysia said, leaning over me.

"It hurts," I said, touching my swollen and throbbing cheek.

"They hit you with the ball. Have I not asked you to stay away from those bullies? But you don't listen."

"I wish Mama was here," I moaned.

"Ya, if she were here, she would know how to deal with you."

I turned away to face the wall, and she walked away.

Mrs. Nadzieja made delicious potato and beef soup that late afternoon. The good woman checked my face over very carefully and told me I was fortunate not to have lost my eye. I waited for her to scold me the way Marysia had, but she did not. For the last several weeks, she had advised me to stay away from Dwa Ognie. Ever since we moved in with her, she had been pestering me to hang around with her precious Irena. Irena herself wanted to be my friend, but I thought she was too boring and not very popular. Today, everyone left me alone after supper, so I could recover from being hit.

Next morning, my eye had closed from the swelling. Irena told me that the lump on my cheek had turned black and blue and was as big as a hill. I had a slice of buttered bread for breakfast, and a cup of coffee sweetened with sugar and whitened with powdered milk. The powder made grease dots on the surface of the coffee; one had to get used to such a drink. Today, I was excused from washing the dishes, and I stayed in bed.

"Would you like to play a guessing word game?" Irena asked, after she had done her share of housework. I liked to hear her speak because she never hurried or skipped any syllables, and she rounded her mouth for perfect O's. But I shook my head.

An hour later, I saw her drawing something on a piece of brown paper on the table. All she ever did in her free time was draw or scribble. From my bed, I watched her pencil getting shorter and shorter from being sharpened so many times, and I could hardly wait for it to get too little for her to use. Then I got bored and was about to nap, when she noticed that my eyes were open. She returned to my bed and offered to stay with me in the hut. Her dark, expressive eyes seemed to search my soul, and I resented the look.

"Leave me alone," I hissed. Hurt or not, I was not going to be stuck with her company.

Without a word, she left. Where did she go? She was always so polite, and that also irritated me.

Now I was alone again. Marysia had gone gallivanting with her friends, as usual. She told me they were going to Duluti Lake with someone who was supposed to take pictures. Irena's mother was doing laundry at the outdoor sinks, which had built-in washboards and running water. With no one to disturb me, I could think clearly about things and people I did not think about often. Maybe I should quit Dwa Ognie. I was getting hurt, and I hurt others by kicking, shoving, and hitting. Down deep in my heart, I didn't like what I was becoming. Yet what would I do without my gang and the ball? I would have nobody to hang around with except Irena. Maybe she could be a good friend, after all? Eck. No. Even that leafy young tree in our back yard would be more fun than she, if one wanted to climb to its top. Irena did not fit with my crowd because she was neither brave nor active enough, and she was such a good daughter and perfect child that it made me sick to my stomach. But what about the gang itself? How many of my so-called playmates had bothered to visit me in the hut? None, so far. And who would be next to get hurt by the ball?

On the third morning after I was hurt, I got out of bed and moved about the hut. I gladly helped Irena with washing the dishes and making up beds. I also swept the floor, simply out of boredom.

"Since you are up, Janka, what are you going to do today?"

I shrugged. "I want to go back to play Dwa Ognie, but I don't want my friends to see me looking so bad."

"Come outside with me?"

"No way. I'm not showing my bruised face to anyone."

"Let's climb up my tree."

"What can we do up there?"

"You will see," she said, grinning.

Twenty minutes later, she and I had settled down in the tree house she had made up there. "So this is your secret hideout, Irena." A spark of interest stirred in me for this skinny, long-legged girl with straight, brown hair.

She nodded and smiled. Right now, her round face not only looked interesting, but almost beautiful. I asked how she had made this cozy room in the elbow of the branches. And she said that she found pieces of cut boards behind the outhouse and nailed them to the tree. She made three walls and a floor, which she lined with grasses and leaves.

"You are clever, Irena," I said sincerely. "But what do you do up here all by yourself?"

"Daydream," she whispered, staring into a hole in the foliage toward Kilimanjaro, which sprawled like a giant haystack to the north of Tengeru, about fifty miles away. The mountaintop was covered with snow even though it smoked or shot flames upward sometimes. It was volcanic, we were told, but not expected to erupt for hundreds of years to come.

"What do you dream about?"

She paused for a long time before answering. "I try to imagine how it would be to go back to Poland after the war ends."

"It would be wonderful to see my farm," I said. "Our house was big and had smiling windows. The barn and fowl shelters and the silo were surrounded by a white wooden fence, and so were the flower gardens—"

"But I also think of something else." Irena interrupted the thread of my thoughts. "And I dream of..."

"Of what?"

"I wish...to have...a boyfriend." She giggled into her fist.

"You do?" I looked sideways at her.

"Yes, I do. But most of all, I would love to have a best friend."

"I see," I said, adding to myself, *Don't look at me, kiddo.*

"And I do something up here."

"Huh? If it's something weird, don't tell me."

"I draw pictures, silly, and write poems."

Thinking that I would be bored looking at her things, I was about to suggest we descend the tree and go back into the hut. But when I opened my mouth, I said words that surprised me. "Can I see your pictures?"

From under planks used as a table, Irena pulled out her sketches of Meru and Kilimanjaro, with huts in the foreground and trees umbrelling them. Her drawings were simple, but full of details. She had captured the image of the rocky top of Meru, which was pointed and constantly hugged by fluffy clouds. Even Kilimanjaro smoked its pipe, like it always did. She even drew monkeys swinging from tree to tree.

"You're an artist," I said, envy kicking at my guts. How I wished at that moment that I could create something constructive, too. Maybe, just maybe, I could start a diary. If I only had a tablet and a pen. These things were hard to find in Tengeru until after our people began to organize schools. "Yes, you are good at drawing," I repeated, picking up the image of a monkey sitting on the roof of a hut. "This one is my favorite."

Irena stood up and, bending over like a monkey, sang out, "Eech, eech, eech." She scratched her underarms, and I imitated her. Soon we both were laughing, making monkeys sounds and giggling until noontime. While I was with her, I forgot about the bruises on my face and about my gang. Then Irena showed me the poem she had written. In it she described how she missed her birthplace and her father, who signed up with the Polish Army while still in Russia. I thought the poem was beautiful, but didn't tell her so, because I was now jealous of her talents, of which I had none. Maybe because of that feeling or because of sitting up in the tree so long, I suddenly turned off Irena's voice. Now I was listening to the screaming of my gang, playing Dwa Ognie in the distance. Suddenly, I wanted to be with them. But I said nothing about it to Irena.

Early next morning, Marek showed up on my doorstep before the game started. I came out of the hut and, standing before him, I asked, "What do you want?" I had pulled my light brown hair over my ugly bump. With one eye, I stared at him, an old hatred stirring in me. He doesn't look so big or mean now, I thought.

"Came to see if you were all right," he said.

"I'm still living, no thanks to you." Now I brushed the hair from my face. "See what you did?"

"Wow!" His mouth opened wide. "I'm sorry," he whispered, blinking and stepping back a bit. Yet, after a short pause, he said, "Coming back to play with us?"

I ached to say yes, yes, yes. But instead I blurted out, "And who else did you hurt lately, Marek?"

"No one, and I'm sorry, again, for hitting you."

"That's all right," I heard myself say. "What's going on with everyone?"

He scratched his head. "We're still playing, but now we don't have enough people in the field."

"Huh?"

"You see, some kids stopped coming."

"Why?"

He shrugged.

"Is Wanda…?"

"She quit the day Stasia elbowed her in the stomach and made her throw up right in front of everybody."

"Dear Heavens!"

"The twin sisters attacked Edzio and broke his arm…"

"My God! Marek, you, I, and the whole gang are bad, very bad."

He stood in silence, looking down at the ground.

"You know, I don't think I'm going back to play with any of you anymore."

"I…I don't blame you for feeling this way." With his head still down, Marek, the bully, shuffled away. He looked like a confused boy of thirteen now, which is what he really was.

That he was changing for the better, I knew then. And that I was changing, too.

The Final Flourish

Deni Compere

The year was 1945. Another generation's war was winding down, troops were returning home, and the nation's relief now erupted into a euphoria of socializing and entertainment. As a result, the formal dining room of the Book Cadillac Hotel, replete with orchestra, was well occupied when we arrived. Thankfully, our reserved table for ten was ready.

American Airlines had long planned and recently implemented their system-wide Air Cargo Division. All systems were 'go' regarding operations at Willow Run Airport, as was the organization of sales and engineering in the downtown offices. I had been the last to be hired.

This particular evening was to celebrate the inaugural flight to Detroit of a planeload of shoes from Sandlers in Boston. It had arrived following a full day of coordination meetings between our management/sales staffs and three complementary executives from Chicago.

As the newest member of the Detroit office, and with the lowly position of secretary, I was astonished to be included in such august company. Parental admonitions, hopefully absorbed long ago, circled my brain: "Mind your manners; don't talk too much; remember names and use them; stand up straight; have a firm handshake." And "You'll be fine, dear."

During dinner and the ensuing conviviality, I enjoyed and participated in the animated bits of conversation, hoping that I was at least making a favorable impression.

The orchestra had played medleys of quiet background music throughout the dinner hour but, after their break, the tempo and variety perked up, and I was asked to dance by my seating partner, one of the Chicago executives.

All went well as he three-stepped me in a test run around the floor, and then began to experiment with a variety of hesitation moves. He was an excellent dancer and a strong leader, and I was having a marvelous time.

He had just released my hand and stepped back a pace, as had I, and was guiding me back toward him again when the orchestra leader let out a whoop. Some musicians missed a beat; others hit sour notes before dissolving into snickers. The entire room suddenly quieted, until the comments began.

"What happened?"

"Why did they stop playing?"

"Did someone yell?"

Hesitant titters soon exploded into hilarious, continuing, and ego-shattering laughter as the leader, on the slightly elevated stage and in full view of all, put his hands on his hips, stifled a snort, and glared down at me.

It seems that, as I was returning to my partner, my right hand, wafting gracefully to the rhythm of the music, had slid under his coattail, and I had goosed the orchestra leader.

Oh Joy!

Esther Brudo

practicing the newest steps
the latest moves
in the back room
of the little grocery store

thelma shows the twirls
and double steps
to the boogie woogie beat
the needle on the phonograph
bounces
ceiling light sways

getting ready for the party
check for new pimples
pull on the pleated skirt
stockings and garter belt
black patent leather high heels

on the streetcar
cinderella me
dream of dancing all night
will he be there
will he ask me
will there be someone else wonderful

down the stairs to the recreation room
dah dah dah de dah
dah dah dah de dah
smooth pulsating rhythm
we're dancing low to the floor

all night the skirt slaps around
nylon thighs
flying
the body knows the beat

finally the last record
a slow piece
body heat and arousal
then heading outside to the street

home later
washing my nylons in the bathroom sink
balls of my feet burning
imagining next saturday night

Song and Dance

Neal Wilgus

Wife and mother-in-law gone to Mexico
so father-in-law Alfred and me,
we're off to Kykotsmovi to see the dances.
Alfred is a member of the Hopi tribe
so he knows better than anyone
that you can't take pictures,
can't tape-record the songs.
Nevertheless, he takes along a recorder
the size of a house
and asks me to carry the damn thing.

A long drive to K-Town as some now call it
and then we make our way to the plaza,
Alfred shaking hand
with old friends and family,
me tagging along with that damn recorder
in tow, sweat rolling down my face.
A long wait in the hot sun,
a gritty wind sandpapers us
as we sit on folding chairs
in the brown adobe pueblo,
the recorder on the ground between us.
More waiting as the clowns come out
to pick on the people in the crowd—
I always worry I'll be the target
but they usually leave me alone.

Finally the dancers begin to come out
and the singers bring the drum
and the clowns ease off
and help organize the lines of dancers.
That's when Alfred begins to fiddle with
the recorder, testing to see if it works,
getting ready to record the songs.
I'm nervous but at first no one seems
to notice what he's doing, or they
ignore it, knowing him.

But when the drums begin
two or three of the older men come over
to speak to Alfred in Hopi
and he answers but of course I can't
understand, but fear the worst.
Then a spokesman says in English:

"You know you can't record the songs.
You must put the recorder away
or we'll have to confiscate it."
A silence, then I notice Alfred
is looking expectantly at me,
as are the others—I'm on the spot.
I don't even know how to run
the damn thing and I fiddle with it
in vain until Alfred cuts it off
and tells me to take it to the car.

All eyes are on me as I lug it away
from the plaza and return it to the trunk.
The sandpaper wind is still blowing
as I hurry back
but wouldn't you know it—
they started without me!

Deleted Scenes

David Ray

About to send the Netflix back
we discuss whether we shouldn't keep it
longer and watch the *Deleted Scenes*,

and I wonder if the movies of our lives
would also have quite a number we must
have deleted, and perhaps that's the reason

we decide not to look at what's left out of
the film where more than enough nudity
of body and mind were already shown,

and if what we never got around to telling priest
or doctor or lovers or even ourselves in dreams
might overwhelm the veneer of a film,

fling our lives back into chaos, deprived
of a plot, believable characters, spectacle
enough to please viewers and reviewers,

and maybe win an academy award or two.
But a movie having no chance at all unless
we restore enough deleted evil to be believable.

Attitude Adjustment

Sherrie Valitus

Bill is a typical macho male. He has to decide where, when, and how everything will be done. He does not want a woman to initiate or suggest. He wants to be completely in control. Nevertheless, I did surprise him once, and with him, that's not easy. First, I had to get around that bullheaded, stubborn streak.

We were on vacation in the Arkansas Ozarks. We have friends in Fayetteville, and I have an aunt and cousins in Mountain Home. Bill decided to take me there on vacation. Not for any of the above-mentioned reasons, these reasons were just the bait to reel me in—his real motive was the fishing. Arkansas has fantastic pristine lakes and, consequently, the fishing is marvelous. It was a perfect plan. We were enjoying our friends, and the relatives in Mountain Home are ones we both like. All of the men fish back there, so he had plenty of fishing buddies. While the men are fishing, the women go to the craft fairs, and they're a lot of fun. Sometimes, the craft shows are held on historic Civil War sites, where famous battles were fought. Now, they are tourist sites, with handcrafted items to sell. People in Arkansas do a lot of whittling, crocheting, embroidering, woodworking, and making hooked rugs—all of the old-fashioned things people used to do in the good old days. There were many items to choose from, and I had to stop myself from buying too much because we had to go home on the plane. We had flown into Fayetteville and, after we finished visiting our friends there, we rented a car to go to Mountain Home, where we had a nice visit with our relatives. Bill was happy; he caught lots of fish in his favorite lake, Bull Shoals.

Now that it's time to travel back to Fayetteville to catch the plane home, Bill decides it would be nice to spend the weekend in Eureka Springs, where the Rockefellers used to vacation. We had been there before, and it is a beautiful, quaint little town nestled in the trees in the Ozarks.

"Bill, it's Friday night, it's June—the height of the tourist season—we don't have a reservation, and I don't think we'll be able to get a room."

"Oh yeah," he says, "it's a short drive. We'll get there early, and they'll have some rooms left."

Bill always hates my practical approach; why use any logic? He wants to do whatever he decides without any preparation. I enjoyed Eureka Springs so much when we were there before, so I just let that slide.

The roads in Arkansas leave much to be desired. They wind and twist like a snake, are very narrow, single lane, and generally not in good condition. Because Bill did not allow for all of this, we were still on our way to Eureka Springs after dark.

We are up in what they call the mountains. Compared to Colorado or California mountains, they aren't mountains at all; they're more like foothills. But because of the winding, twisting roads, it seems like quite a ride. It's like the road to Hana in Maui, Hawaii. Bill's getting tired now, but we're almost there. We start coming to motels along the way.

"Bill, why don't we start trying to get a room for the night?"

"No," he answers, "I want to get all the way up the mountain. That way, we don't have to get up and start driving in the morning. We'll already be there, and we'll be ready to have fun."

We continue up the road, and I repeat, "Honey, please, let's try to get a room now, before they're all gone."

He is so tired, he finally agrees, but every place we stop is full, and many places we just have to pass by because the 'No Vacancy' sign is already up. By the time we make it to the town of Eureka Springs, I am really getting worried that we aren't going to find a room.

"Sherrie, I'm starving. We haven't had any dinner yet. I want to find a restaurant first."

I'm thinking, *oh, no, we won't have a chance of finding a room if we do that,* but I don't want to say anything, because he's so tired and hungry. I know it will just start an argument. I see a motel with a vacancy sign. I'm delighted. "Look, Bill, a 'Vacancy'—stop here."

"Okay, Sherrie, you go in and get the room, and I'll gas up at the gas pumps out front. Then we'll be all set for tomorrow. I'm so tired, I just want to get something to eat and crash."

I go into the motel and ask for a room. The clerk tells me, "I'm sorry, all of our regular rooms for $89.95 are taken. All we have left is our specialty rooms at $169.00."

"What is a specialty room?" I ask. "And why do they cost so much more money?"

"We have pictures of them in this album, if you'd like to take a look."

He hands me a picture album and goes to wait on other customers. I open it, and Oh My Gosh, now I see why it costs so much! It's a huge room with a Jacuzzi big enough for four people covering one wall. *Bill will throw a fit if I get this expensive room. He's dead tired, and he's not going to want to get in a Jacuzzi, but I have never stayed in a room like this. It looks exciting. And, besides, where are we going to get another room tonight?*

When the clerk comes back, I tell him, "I'll take it," thinking, *I'll just put it on the credit card, and then I won't have to hear the ranting and raving tonight over how much it costs. I can tell him that later.*

Just as I am signing the credit card slip, Bill walks in the door. "What's taking so long?" he asks. When the clerk hands back the credit slip, Bill reaches out his hand and takes it.

Oh darn, I think, *now I have to go through all this!*

"What? $169.00! Why didn't you get the one for $89.95? What was wrong with that room?"

"They didn't have any left, Bill. They only have their specialty rooms left."

"For $169.00, it sure as hell better be pretty special! What could be so special it would cost that much money?"

We get our luggage from the car. All the while, he is throwing a fit. We are outside, walking to our room. People are walking along the sidewalk on their way to the restaurant, or coming from their rooms to go out for the evening. Everyone is staring at us. "Honey, I think you'll be happy when you see the room," I say, trying to appease him.

Bill is still mumbling and grumbling as he's turning the key in the lock. He throws the door open and steps inside. He is completely speechless.

The first thing we see upon entering the room is the Jacuzzi. It's huge! There are candles on the ledge, bordering the mirrored wall behind the Jacuzzi. There's a bottle of champagne sitting in a bucket of ice, with a silver drawstring pouch sitting next to it. The bed is covered with a black satin comforter, along with black satin sheets and pillowcases. The headboard is tufted black velvet. The wall behind it is silver paisley. The ceiling over the bed is done in mirrors and the white carpet is deep, like fur.

Bill goes immediately to the silver goody bag to see what's in it, while I head for the bathroom to check it out. The commode and sink are done in a blue gray. The toilet seat is black, and the towels are fluffy black ones, as big as beach towels. There are two plush terry cloth robes hanging on the wall. I go back into the bedroom. I'm anxious to see what Bill thinks of the room. He's sitting on the side of the Jacuzzi filling it with water.

"What are you doing?"

"I'm filling the Jacuzzi."

"You can't do that now. We're going out to eat. I thought you were starving."

"Oh, I forgot," he remarks.

"What did we get in our goody bag?"

He hands it to me and I look inside. It's neat; it has matches to light the candles, soap, bubble bath, oil, and body lotion. It also has a big natural sponge. "Whoa, I like this!" I exclaim.

Bill's attitude has completely changed. I don't think he would complain now if the room cost $300.00. He drives me to the nearest restaurant he can find. I'm sure he doesn't even care if he eats, this man who was starving two hours ago. Now, I'm sure all he can think about is getting into that Jacuzzi.

The restaurant is nice, white tablecloths and candlelight.

"What do you want to eat?" I ask, when we're seated.

"Oh, I don't care," he says.

"You're just so tired, you want to hurry up and eat, so you can get some sleep?"

"Oh, I'm not tired," he says with a smile.

You can't believe how peppy he has become, now that he's seen that room. It's a crack-up. I've never seen such a change in a man. He's all animated now, with a twinkle in his eye. His voice is satin smooth. All the anger's gone. I'm getting a big kick out of this transformation in him from a moth to a butterfly.

When we get back to the room, he dashes straight for the Jacuzzi. He turns the faucets on full blast and begins taking off his clothes.

"Wait, Bill, don't get in yet."

"Why not?"

"This is a Kodak moment!" I tell him. "This is a once in a lifetime experience! I want to take pictures."

"Pictures of what?"

"Of the room. I want to show my cousin, Jody, and tell her to come here with Troy for their vacation. Get the movie camera while the tub is filling. I'll go into the bathroom and get undressed. I'll come out with a towel wrapped around me and step into the Jacuzzi. I'll lower myself into the bubble bath, toss away the towel, pick up my champagne glass, and tell Jody and Troy to spend their vacation here. Now don't forget to put the bubble bath in the water."

I go into the bathroom, come out, and go through the whole scenario just as I have mapped it out. When I finish telling the relatives to spend their vacation in Eureka Springs, Bill throws the camera on the chaise lounge and jumps into the Jacuzzi.

"Wait a minute. Don't you want some champagne?" I ask.

"Forget the champagne," Bill murmurs, as he pulls me into his arms.

This Jacuzzi in the room bit was so romantic it would turn anyone on. I had heard about rooms like this and seen them advertised in magazines. You know the ad, "Spend your honeymoon in the Poconos and have a heart-shaped Jacuzzi right in your room."

Every time I saw an ad like that, I thought about how nice it would be, but you really have to experience it to appreciate it. It's better than you can imagine! Heaven only knows what time we finally went to sleep, because when we came out of the Jacuzzi we found ourselves in a bed with mirrors on the ceiling, and Bill was ready to start all over again. We sure got our money's worth out of that room!

The only fly in the ointment was when we got home and ran the movie. It turns out I had forgotten about the mirror on the wall behind the Jacuzzi, and, while I'm holding the towel in front of me, my bare hind end is reflected in the mirror. Needless to say, we couldn't send the movie to Jody and Troy.

Toilet Talk

Nancy Sandweiss

"Do not stand on the toilet" reads the sign, a sort of Bathroom Lesson #1 for ESL students learning First World ways. I wonder if broken seats, shattered limbs, had prompted the warning with its diagram and admonitions to flush, never throw toilet paper in the trash.

In India I once squatted over an open hole, struggling to keep my clothes dry. There the folks would feel similar unease on a hard raised seat; would shrink from wasting soft white paper, look for water pail or spigot to splash themselves clean.

The high-tech Japanese know a thing or two about hygiene: their heated commodes provide dual-area sprays and a drying draft of air. You'll never find them standing on the seat.

King of the Roost

Mel McLain

For a few years following World War II, we spent our winters in Eloy, Arizona, helping with the cotton harvest. With irrigation, what once was desert bloomed like a garden and began to produce some of the best cotton in the whole country.

One fall, we parked our trailer house and temporarily homesteaded the lot behind Mayhew's place. As we were getting settled, to our surprise we found that our neighbor had a big Rhode Island Red rooster that patrolled the path to the outhouse. That rooster took his job seriously and would attack anyone who ventured toward the outhouse during daylight hours.

As a scrawny eight-year-old, I was in trouble. I was afraid of the rooster and afraid of the dark.

One day, as I was making a mad dash for the outhouse, the rooster caught me. I started kicking, first with one foot, then the other. With each kick it was like kicking a Weed Eater. I turned and ran for the trailer house as the rooster got the backs of my legs.

In the excitement of the attack, I forgot where I was going and what I was going to do when I got there. And I didn't need to go anymore, because I already went.

When I got back to the trailer house, Mama saw my wet pants and asked, "What happened to you?"

Through tears, I answered, "The rooster got me!"

Mama got mad, and then she got a little crazy. For a moment or two, I thought I might get a whipping for wetting my pants. But Mama turned, grabbed her broom, and headed for the outhouse, saying, "I'll bet I can teach that rooster a thing or two!"

Mama was a short, rather plump lady. But for the next few seconds it looked like she was training with the major league. When Mama got near the outhouse, the rooster was waiting. With his wings held out and slightly downward, he was strutting like he was king of the roost. It was obvious he didn't know who he was dealing with.

He lowered his head to attack, then threw his head back and his feet forward to nail Mama in the leg with his spurs. That's when he should have ducked, because Mama swung her broom, catching him solid on the side of the head and sending him on a double flip flop. He got up, staggering like a drunk, leaning mostly to the left.

But Mama wasn't through. She swung again and again. By this time, the rooster had a few broom straws sticking out of his feathers. He finally got his senses working well enough to make a run for the hen house. He stayed there a few days.

As the rooster's courage began to grow, he would come out near the path to the outhouse. But all of us kids had learned from this experience, too. When we went to the outhouse, we would take the broom with us. Once in a while, I would chase that rooster with Mama's broom, just to see how fast he could run.

Rafting on the Good Ship Muckaway

Eleanor Whitney Nelson

When I mention the subject of rafting, most people smile as pleasant images fill their heads. They remember the adrenalin rush as, once again, they feel their rubber raft leap through the rapids coursing down the Grand Canyon, and the surge of relief when smooth-flowing water embraces them on the downstream side of the frothing cataract. Others may remember the icy blue water of an Alaskan stream colored with rock flour from the glacier grinding downward through the valley above them. And some may picture themselves floating across a lagoon in the South Pacific, lazily trailing a finger in the clear aquamarine sea above schools of fish, rainbows of color darting in unison in an erratic dance. Reams of purple prose pass through their minds while they daydream of adventures yet to come.

When I think of rafting, I think of sewers.

Our house on Bell Haven Road was a pretty, white frame structure capped with a sloping wood shake roof. Located on the outskirts of Reno in a residential section known as Southwest Suburban, it looked out across a pastoral setting to Washoe Valley and the city below. All around, custom homes of every size and representing an eclectic collection of architectural designs dotted the hillside. Neat pastures separated by split rail or white board fences, some by fieldstone walls, surrounded most of these homes. All were filled with pampered horses and cattle. It was an idyllic setting routinely traversed by sightseeing buses making a scenic detour as they transported tourists to other destinations.

Our 2,500-square-foot house, while far from the newest or fanciest home in the neighborhood, was tightly constructed and had been well maintained when we bought it in 1986. It kept us cool in summer, snugly warm on frigid nights, and secure from gale-force winds that swooped down the eastern slope of the Sierra Nevada, shaking the structure to its core. Because of the semi-rural nature of the area, the house had its own well, and often friends from town came to fill their jugs with our delicious water. It had a sensible floor plan and, overall, we found it remarkably trouble free.

A one-story home, it sat over a crawlspace that had been dug three feet into the ground. This space, which provided access to wiring, water and drainpipes, heating and cooling ductwork, and other essentials, was entered through a small, brick-lined notch located outside the north face of the house. Inside this notch was a removable panel, just big enough to accommodate an average-sized man. Fortunately, we rarely needed to explore this nether region.

One day, after we had lived in the house for about a year, I remember hearing a faint trickling sound in the hallway as I approached the front door. Because the entryway was situated between the guest powder room and the kitchen and was close to the laundry room, the sound of running water might not have seemed unusual, except that I could not remember hearing water flowing in that area before. Now that I was aware of it, I wasn't sure. I checked the powder room to see if the toilet handle was stuck and needed a jiggle—it didn't—and everything in the kitchen and laundry seemed to be functioning normally.

Over the course of the next few weeks, the faint gurgling was sporadically audible. Although I tried to convince myself that it was nothing more than water draining normally through the pipes below the floor, something about the sound bothered me, but not enough to mention it to my husband, Frank.

One day, as we were leaving the house for brunch at a nearby restaurant to celebrate the first day of Frank's annual vacation, he paused by the front door and said, "I'll be right with you. I just want to pop in here a minute." He pulled open the door to the powder room, a room he rarely used. A moment later he called out, "Do you hear that?"

"What?" I asked.

"Running water in the little bathroom. It seems to be coming from the air vent in the floor."

"I've heard that, but I thought it was just water in the pipes."

"No, it sounds peculiar. I'd better check it out."

"How?"

"I'll have a look in the crawlspace and see if I can spot anything."

RAFTING ON THE GOOD SHIP MUCKAWAY

After changing his clothes, Frank squeezed into the access notch, pulled aside the panel and stuck his head into the opening. The side of the house was in shadow, and it was even darker inside the crawlspace. "Hand me the flashlight."

I wrinkled my nose. "What's that...?"

"Holy—"

I will not repeat the words that flew from his mouth, but under the circumstances they were entirely understandable—there was a lake under our house. Off this lake wafted a smell that churned my empty stomach. In fact, the longer the panel remained open, the ranker the odor became. Oddly, until the panel was removed, not the slightest hint of what lay below had reached our olfactory senses. A sewage lake, I thought. The house was, indeed, well constructed.

When Frank stepped out of the access hole, I knew it was one of those times to keep my mouth shut. Suggestions—at least at that juncture—would not be welcome. Today, twenty years later, he would calmly ask me to get on the phone to a plumber, but at that time he performed most home repairs himself.

"We must have a broken pipe, but I can't see where the noise is coming from," he said. "I'll have to go look. Find me the oldest, rattiest clothes I have, while I dig up some plywood."

There is always a positive side to every catastrophe. Here was the perfect opportunity to rid his closet of at least one set of clothes, old favorites that long since should have been donated to charity or relegated to the ragbag. Knowing there was no way to distance myself from this project, no matter what I had planned for the day, I also scrounged up some threadbare jeans and a frayed tee shirt for myself.

Luckily, we had an ample supply of scrap lumber left over from construction of our horse barn, and together Frank and I managed to wrestle a hodgepodge of plywood sections through the small opening into the crawlspace. Overlapping them one on top of another, Frank fashioned a loosely connected raft that would be sufficiently buoyant to support him.

"Well, here goes nothing," he said, easing his feet into the cold water. It was about a foot deep, leaving another two feet between the surface and the floorboards. He wriggled his belly onto the raft, but when he tried to raise his head to see where he was going, his skull cracked against one of the joists, the two-by-six planks that supported the floorboards at five-foot intervals across the entire underside of the house. Traveling at right angles to the joists, Frank had only eighteen inches of clearance. With much effort, he turned himself over and lay on his back. Because the bulk of his weight was toward the stern, the bow of the makeshift craft rose above the surface, allowing his scalp to remain dry.

Frank paused to catch his breath. "I don't hear anything. Turn on the water in the bathroom just a little and leave it running."

When I returned, the steady splash of trickling water was audible. It was faint, but distinct, a tiny beacon of sound emerging from the inky gloom.

"Here we go again." Frank took a deep breath and shoved off from the wall with his legs. The raft lurched forward. "The Good Ship Muckaway to the rescue! Admiral Nelson at the helm." Frank's words boomed across the murky water. With his lamp beside him pointing upward, he reached back over his head, feeling for the two-by-six joists. Gripping these between his fingers, he drew himself forward.

"Cripes! It's loaded with spiders…black widows and brown recluse. Jeez, they're right in my face. At least, I haven't grabbed one yet." The progress of the Good Ship sloshed to a halt. "Get me a pair of hay hooks. I can pull myself along with them."

Before dashing to the barn for the hooks, I could see him slowly returning to home port, pushing against the joists with the lamp, his fingers well away from the mandibles of those tiny, eight-legged creatures.

The second launch was more successful. With leather work gloves covering his hands, he grasped the hay hooks and drew the valiant craft along. Soon, all but the spot of lamplight had vanished into the darkness.

Minutes passed and I waited. I ducked my head inside the opening, but the lamp was no longer visible, its pinpoint light blocked out by a forest of upright floor pillars. Finally, I heard a muffled, "I found it. You can turn off the water now."

"What's the problem?" I shouted.

"A section of PVC pipe has separated from the main cast-iron sewer line. It looks like all the water in the house has been draining out here."

For weeks, I thought, a surge of guilt flushing my cheeks. "Can you fix it?"

"Piece o' cake."

Right, I thought. Where had I heard those words before? I am a follower of the glass-half-empty school, because it saves me from unrealistic expectations that lead to inevitable disappointment. Frank, on the other hand, is the eternal optimist.

"It looks like a support that held up the PVC came loose from the ceiling…the floor…you know, overhead…and the ring clamp holding the two pieces of pipe together pulled apart. I think I can fix it without getting anything from the hardware store."

Sure, I thought. When had we gotten away without going to the hardware store—at least once—for any project?

Ten minutes later, the Good Ship appeared on the horizon, having traversed almost the entire width of the sewer sea. The problem would, of course, have to be located on the opposite side of the house. It had something to do with someone named Murphy.

As Frank hauled himself into the entryway, I handed him a glass of cold water from a jug I had filled while waiting for him to return from uncharted regions. He leaned back and stretched his arms and shoulders. "I'm going to need some tools," he said, reciting a list of supplies for me to collect from his shop: wrenches, hammers, pliers, screws.

Twenty minutes later, he was off again. While I hovered on the brink awaiting further instructions from the skipper, I could hear the occasional grunt or expletive. Then came the depressing but not unexpected news that he needed more tools.

While once again he crossed the ocean, I procured the requested implements and was waiting with another glass of water when the gallant ship pulled in. This time, Frank did not disembark, but set sail immediately, reinforced with heavier ammunition.

Another thirty minutes later, an explosion billowed across the water. "You're going to have to go to the store for me."

I changed in the barn, where I had set up my command center, now stocked with fresh, dry clothes, towels, sodas, and snacks. Armed with a fistful of cash, I left for the hardware store.

Forty minutes later, the rested but muscle-sore Captain Nelson sallied forth on a new expedition, but once again the outcome was dismal. "The ring clamp won't tighten up. I'm going to need some more plumber's putty and a new clamp."

I handed him a root beer, refilled the water jug and, after changing again, hurried out the driveway.

When I returned, Frank's expression was grim. He rubbed his neck and shoulders, then slid backward once more onto the raft. Emitting a resigned sigh, he gave a halfhearted push against the wall with legs I could see were on the verge of mutiny. A small bow wave from the warship rippled across the Stygian sea.

This time as I waited, the shadows on the side of the house deepened, and I could feel the cool of evening approaching. I crossed my fingers and said a little prayer as I looked at my watch. Dusk would be on us in another hour—not that it much mattered to Frank, a captive in the underworld—but the day was moving on, and we had been fighting this battle since our long-dismissed breakfast date.

Not wanting to leave my post in case there were further orders from the commander, I sat in a tired stupor on the side of the access notch, my chin in the palm of my hand, awaiting results of the current foray. The longer I waited, the more depressed I became. What had gone wrong now, I wondered? What wretched problem was Frank struggling with this time? It was looking like the enemy forces had prevailed yet again. I knew they might win this skirmish, but Frank would ultimately win the war—I just hoped it would be today; the marines were battle-weary, far too tired for another round of combat. I shifted my position on the hard ground.

"I got it!" Frank's voice burst through the silence.

So prepared was I for bad news, I almost replied, "What now?" Catching myself in time, I whooped back.

Our cries echoed off the walls as the victorious ship sailed into view. I extended my hand and helped the exhausted captain struggle through the portal. Behind him, his trusty craft rocked in the choppy waves kicked up by thrashing feet. Abandoned, it drifted away from its mooring into the dark.

While I collected the tools, Frank propped the access panel against the house. "We'll have to wait until it dries out down there before fastening the panel back in place," he said. "That could be weeks."

We looked at each other. Frank was wet all over, and I, too, was splattered with black muck. Even though the receptors in our noses had long since been deadened to the stench, we were well aware that we carried with us aromas far removed from roses and lavender. I nodded toward the back porch.

With hardly a sideways glance toward our neighbor's house, we stripped off our clothes and dashed inside to the shower. Needless to say, our battle uniforms ended their days, not with some worthy charity or recycled for rags, but properly buried at the county landfill.

The basement eventually dried out and, for as long as we lived in the house, the Good Ship Muckaway sat aground, intact, and ready for the next call to arms.

Startling Truth

Harleen Gross

Tom's thick rubber boots covered him to the waist, and standing knee deep in the cold water of the Clackamas River, his toes freezing, he dreamed of fishing the river in a boat. He dreamed of having such freedom to find the fishing holes and land a giant salmon catch. He had pulled many Silver Salmon from the icy waters of the Clackamas River, there on the river's bend near his home. He watched the fishermen on the river, who seemed to maneuver the waters effortlessly, and he determined that he would buy his very own riverboat.

That's why Tom bought the wide, green, flat-bottom boat from a friend and spent days prepping, cleaning, and readying it for the river. She trusted him when Tom suggested they float the Clackamas River in his new boat, and she assumed he was knowledgeable of the river's fast channels and capable of keeping them safe. They'd have a wonderful warm day together, just the two of them, she thought.

"We can put in the river 15 miles up and float down to Carver."

The startling truth was that Tom shouldn't have been trusted, and her assumptions were the beginning of a dreadfully frightening day on the river. Her first clue was at the point where the river made a huge, wide swing to the left, and their boat drifted out of the main channel onto a large, rocky bed of shallow, slow-moving water.

"Hey, what are you doing?" she asked. She didn't think too much of it, however, as he guided the boat back into the main channel of the river.

"Isn't this wonderful?" Tom shouted to her. She leaned back in the seat and put her feet up, so she could more directly absorb the sun's glory. There wasn't a thing for her to do, since he was guiding the boat's direction with the only set of oars.

She agreed. "Yes, this is wonderful." The river was wide and running fast, but she remained cautious with her safety vest tightly strapped around her. The current pulled them along, and Tom released his grip and floated with the force of the great body of blue. She closed her eyes and remembered the times they had floated the Deschutes River. She loved the thrill of the rapids and the sun in her face. They had a guide on the Deschutes, and this time they were on their own. She had never floated this river, and she knew how dangerous some places were, but she relaxed completely, confident in her man, while the magic of the sun danced across her face like a sparkling jewel necklace.

The sound of the river and the cry of an osprey filled the air, and she opened her eyes to see the great bird, or perhaps spot its nest along the banks. She glanced along the river's shore, then at the steep wall on the river's right, and the channel narrowing as the water splashed and crashed around the bend.

She glanced again into the river ahead, full of rapids, bubbling over sharp river rocks, and was startled to see another fishing boat sitting in the middle of the current. Four men in the boat had their fishing lines launched in the water, obviously setting in a deep hole smack in the middle of the channel. The river guide screamed, "Get your lines in right now, boys. We are moving quickly." The guide was obviously experienced enough to realize they might be slammed by Tom's oncoming boat. Tom was helpless and unable to maneuver around them, but the power motor of the guide boat screamed as it kicked into gear and safely jetted the fishermen out of harm's way.

She gasped as she realized how close they had come to colliding with the fisherman. Scarcely did she have time to dwell on their near miss, when the river took another spin around into a white rock wall on the left. The river narrowed considerably, and the water ran deep and angry from being confined between the massive rock walls. There was no time to relax because, right in the middle of the next bend, sat another boat full of fishermen, anchored in a deep, promising fishing hole!

Immediately, Tom went into action, pulling, straining, and struggling with the oars, with no effect. Their boat raced in the current with horrific force towards the anchored fishermen. Terror painted lines of fear across their faces as the boats collided, Tom's boat slamming against the anchored boat once, twice, three times until the river's force finally let loose of its grip, their boat brushing past and back into the raging water.

Tom was visibly shaken as he intentionally banked the boat and pulled onto a rocky beach. Together, they dragged the boat out of the water, looking at each other without speaking, unable to escape the screaming and cursing voices that floated down the river's belly from the boat they had just slammed. She wanted to go back. She wanted to escape what seemed to be a prescription for disaster. The startling truth was there was no escape.

It wasn't enough that they had twice narrowly escaped potential disaster, but the river still held one more surprise. Perhaps Tom didn't watch closely, or perhaps he just didn't recognize the eddy until he was locked in the endless spinning, with the bow banging into the rock wall over and over. There was nothing she could do, so riddled with fear she reasoned that he might benefit from positive encouragement. "Go! Go! Harder, row harder. You're doing great!" she shouted, as if her verbal assistance might have an impact.

Tom threw his body weight into the rowing, while she shouted cheers of praise. Mustering up every ounce of power he possibly could, Tom brought the boat back up the powerful river, out of the eddy, while on-looking fishermen shouted from the river's shore. "Row back up the river. Get into the left channel on the river's side."

Finally, it was over. Both exhausted, they pulled the boat out of the water, loaded it onto the trailer and started home. There was not a word between them as the truck wound 'round the curves of black asphalt, almost finding its own way back home. The startling truth was that Tom wasn't knowledgeable of the river, and he didn't have the upper body strength to direct or guide the boat through the raging current. He'd been a foolish dreamer to think it didn't require experience and planning.

The two lovers rode home in silence. She realized how frightened she had been, and suddenly her fear turned to anger, radiating like Mount St. Helens, ready to erupt in a blast of steam and ash. Perhaps she'd never forgive him for putting them at such a risk. No, she thought, it was better to keep the anger inside. Hopefully, there would come a time when she would tell the story again, and laugh about the horrifying day they floated the Clackamas.

Like now.

There Was a Crooked Man

Judy Ray

The old man leaned on his stick as he paused to consider which avenue to take for the rest of his afternoon walk. From inside the north gate he could choose to follow the line of tall, symmetrical Norfolk Island pines that marked the widest roads, or he could stay under the shady eucalyptus trees. Ah, no, he must get closer to the jacarandas off to the side.

It seemed to the man on his walk that the jacarandas had come into bloom overnight, filling the late spring air with delicate clouds of purple or lilac or blue. No, not blue. That was the mistake in the oil painting that had just been hung in the hallway of the Home, a picture in which two women sat on a bench under a jacaranda, a blue canopy heaven above them and fallen petals strewn at their feet. But the blue was from the wrong palette, too much like the gown of a Madonna or a Renoir model. He remembered reading a description of jacarandas in which an author claimed they "were a color he had no name for, neither blue nor purple, but more beautiful than any color in the world."

The old man turned into the avenue at a sign marking the Anglican suburb. That's how he thought of the sections within this walled cemetery, with its acres neatly laid out and signposted. Presbyterian and Anglican encompassed the largest areas, but there were other enclaves marked by signs and distinctive architecture—Ukrainian Orthodox, Serbian, Roman Catholic, Baptist Christadelphian, Jewish Orthodox and Progressive, and many others.

When he had first moved into the Home, he had said, "I'll take my afternoon walk around the City," and the attendant in the dayroom said, "Fine, Mr. Watson," assuming he meant the streets that led to the little shopping mall. But shops seemed tedious now that he was not going to buy anything ever again. Everything was provided at the Home—meals and room-cleaning and television and library books and toothbrushes. So he preferred the grey, quiet symmetry of his chosen suburbs. When the staff discovered where he was headed every afternoon, they suggested alternatives, but he always replied, "I like to take my walk around the City."

"We didn't realize you meant the Cemetery."

"It's a City," the old man said. "But names don't bother me. The sign out front of this place says Green Hill Retirement Home, but you can still read the lettering underneath. Home For The Aged, it used to say. And the City could have other names. Town of Tombs. Garden of Graves."

The attendant raised her eyebrows with a sharp look, but then she shook her head and said, "Well, if you find it a good place to walk, I guess there's no harm. I don't think you should spend too much time there, though. By the way, what happened to your new walking stick?"

"I prefer this one."

His nephew had brought him a new, shiny walking stick. But after a short trip to test its pace and a few swings in imitation of a debonair Noel Coward character, he had gone back to using his old crooked stick. His daughter used to laugh, suggesting he might as well use the old-fashioned shepherd's crook that was propped beside the back door at home. The crook used to be brought out at Christmastime to hold up the lantern for a carol-singing group around the village. Its metal curlicue hook that could be wielded dexterously to catch a sheep's hind leg had been painted silver for its service as a lantern holder, making it look almost as grand as a bishop's staff. The old man's favorite walking stick wasn't a shepherd's crook like that one, but it did have an unusual curled handle and was itself crooked. When he leaned on it, he always appeared to be out of kilter.

He rarely went to the south gate, the main entrance to the City. The last time had been in a vehicle, and he had been astonished at the signs of development. There was an Information Office, a Florist's, a Gift Shop, as well as a new Tea Room and Public Conveniences. It reminded him of the entrance to a Zoo or a National Park in the High Holiday season. But the north end was almost always quiet, though not lonely. How could one be lonely in such a full field? The grey stone beds lay close together in rows, with open books of stone set like pillows at the end. "Their lives are open books—when they're gone," he said to himself. He could have wandered about reading the etched names and dates and verses all day long.

Not his wife's, though. He had kept their agreement not to have stone and had made the promised pilgrimage with ashes back to the hills of her childhood. They had taken walks together for many years, and in his ritual pause every afternoon to choose his path for the day there was a moment of connection as if he deferred to her wishes. Yes, she would have smiled toward the jacarandas on a spring day.

School children occasionally ran and skipped through the City. The younger ones chattered about their fights and adventures and discoveries, and didn't stay long. Sometimes, a small group of high school students would sit awhile and talk, leaning with their heads close together, intent on themselves. They, too, always managed to be somehow out of kilter, with a hangdog, untidy look, and they carried backpacks as if they were going camping instead of going home from a day at school. None of the children took any notice of the man as he made his slow way along the path.

On that spring day he breathed deeply in the blue air, and his bent back straightened a little as he left the north gate to walk the two long blocks to the Home. The street was empty except for a woman walking ahead of him, carrying a shopping bag in each hand. The bags must have been heavy, for her shoulders were pulled down, and she rolled a little from side to side with each step.

Then a figure in grey, a man, turned into the street and headed toward the slow walkers, the woman with the bags and the man with the stick. When he came level with the woman, the man in grey suddenly swiveled round with his arms jabbing out and pushed the woman down as he grabbed for a handbag hanging from her left shoulder, kicking at her to make her let go. The strap got caught in the shopping bags, and groceries spilled out with a sprawling crash on the sidewalk, apples and apricots rolling far.

The figure in grey pulled free and sprinted straight on down the street, changing direction close to the man as if only then noticing him. And the old man, his heart pounding, turned with surprising speed, too, and thrust out the handle end of his stick, jabbing hard so it tangled in the runner's legs and brought him sprawling down for a moment before he scrambled up and away. The thwack jerked the old man over, and then he yelled with a high-pitched scream that wasn't very loud, but was echoed by the woman's screams and dogs barking and another voice picking up the yell and other people racing after the thief

"Are you all right?" Someone helped the man up and handed him his stick.

"I think so," he said. "But what about her?"

The woman was still sitting on the sidewalk among her spilled groceries. "Nothing like this ever happened to me before," she kept saying. "Not in all my born days."

"He dropped the bag, he dropped the bag," a voice shouted down the street.

"Not in all my born days. You were there at the right time. Just think!" she went on when the man reached her. "Just think!"

A neighbor began gathering up the spilled groceries as the man moved on, shuffling down the street, thinking how different a sudden action was from the way a sickness crept in with its attack and wouldn't leave.

At the Home he did not mention his adventure to anyone, but sat quietly in his room until it was time to go to the dining hall. Gossip was buzzing around about the purse-snatching that had taken place so close by, though no one seemed to know any details. The director was urging the residents not to go out alone.

"That woman was lucky," he said. "She didn't get hurt. But one of you…" He looked around the room and went on, "…one of you would be an easy target. And no more Cemetery walks, Mr. Watson," he added. "You were lucky you didn't come along the street a bit sooner. You'd have been in the wrong place at the wrong time."

The old man's face twitched with a tiny smile, but he said nothing. He was thinking that tomorrow, if his knees weren't too bruised, he would walk all the way to the Memory Garden. His wife liked roses, and in that walled space they would be coming out early, filling the garden with a communal memory that pervaded the air like sweet perfume. One could sit a long time there, and it never felt like the wrong place or the wrong time.

Danger on Grove Street

Lucille Gang Shulklapper

A tattered poster covers the black suitcase strapped to the back of the motorcycle: HAVE YOU HUGGED YOUR CHILD TODAY? Once unusual, the saying is now as commonplace as pictures of missing children on milk cartons.

The motorcycle's metal glistens in the darkness of a cold North Carolina night as it passes our car over a deserted bridge on Grove Street. An icy wind sneaks through the closed windows. I look up. Gaslights, like flowers on a drooping stem, poles curving inward, cast a dim, yellowed light.

"It's ten o'clock," I tell my husband. In the back of my mind, a voice from an old television program chants...*Do you know where your children are?* I strain to see their faces...focus their blurred features...locate them in the distant places where they have moved.

"Pull over," a voice demands. The motorcycle rider blinks his lights, beeps his horn.

We slow down, pull to the side of the road. The motorcycle driver turns off his lights and jumps off. He's wearing leather boots, a police uniform, and a zippered ski mask that muffles his voice. "You made a left turn into the right lane of the bridge. Pull into that garage on your right. Follow me."

He drives his motorcycle into the blackened garage.

"I'm scared," I say. "How do we know he's a cop? In that dark place, he could rob...kill us."

The stranger waits, turns on his flashlight, waves it in circles, then points it toward the garage.

"I'm not going any farther." My husband drives forward until the rear of the car hangs halfway over the curb. He fumbles for his fishing knife in the glove compartment.

The flashlight goes out. Speaking through his ski mask, the stranger reaches inside his jacket. The leather holster gleams in the wintry moonlight. I think of my children. How often I hugged them when they were little.

"Why don't you drive in?" he asks. "You almost ran over me making that turn. Let me see your license."

My husband rolls his window down about an inch. "We're from New York, driving to Florida, looking for our motel. Sorry, I didn't see you. Could I see your badge?"

The man opens his jacket, flashes a gold badge. "I'm a police officer on my way to work. Never mind about the license. Your motel's a few blocks down on the left."

From the motel room, we speak to the Chief of Police. "No police officer is allowed to stop a car unless he's in full uniform. He must identify himself first."

That night, I dream I'm on television. White-haired. Alone. My arms, curved like the dimly lit streetlights on Grove Street, come right through the screen.

"It's ten o'clock," I say in a quavering voice. "Do you know where your children are?"

The gaslights flicker. In the dim light, the steel posts become milk cartons, and I hug the pictures of my missing children.

The Imperfect Character

Nik Grant

I tilted my hat to hide my head away from the neighbor and let the officer do the talking. The neighbor said the apartment was empty, so the officer keyed open the door and called inside.

"Police! Official business. Anyone home?" We waited, then, "Police! Coming in."

He switched on the light. The first thing I saw was the art—a lot of my favorite art on the walls.

"So, what are we looking for exactly?" I was excited by the art and scared of getting caught.

"Any clues to where he's gone, how long he'll be gone, when he'll be back."

"The neighbor said he'd not been back last night."

"Well, we want to know why. You're in a unique position to notice if anything's unusual or out of place here."

"Even though I've never been here or met him," I muttered to myself. We were all expecting a lot from me, yet I agreed that I had the best chance of helping find him. Bed was made, neatly, but no hospital corners. "Bed's made," I called. I slid open the closet door. The clothes were nice, not that many, and what I took to be "worn once" clothes were folded on a shelf. The bottom of the closet looked familiar: shoes shoved carelessly in a mild heap. I picked one up. My size.

I looked under the bed. Picture frames. I tugged at a few and realized that our collections overlapped here, too, with Parrish's Daybreak and a couple of others.

"You'll want to see this." The officer was peering at a computer screen.

"What's that?"

"His file on you. Extensive and current."

I looked and saw the doctor's appointment that had triggered our visit, and we both knew then that he was on the run.

I was disturbed. I'd been thinking about this, my coming to claim my clone for spare parts. I'd seen it as a living insurance policy, akin to a puppy mill.

"You know, I kinda thought he would be, well, like a cow. You know..." I trailed off. The cop laughed cynically. Yeah, I thought. Computer. Art. Books. Clothes. I could be living here. I suddenly wondered, does he drink milk, too? I looked in the fridge and nodded.

"So, how'd he get so...set up? I mean, I thought they'd be in some sort of institution or something."

"Hey—we were all fed the big lie. You remember cigarettes." His phone rang.

"Good news." He turned to me. "He's been spotted. Let's go." I stood, needing to drink in the whole place. "Listen," said the cop, "you probably want to hang around a bit. Lock up after you leave. You'll be getting your appointment scheduled in the next few days. Don't worry. So long."

I looked around. His collection of books was similar to my own. Science fiction, hard covers. I was glad to say my collection was much bigger. But, then, I'd been working on it a lot longer.

I was still reading when he came in, and he had a couple of friends with him. Clones—I could see their mandatory forehead tattoos. The door closed with an ominous thunk.

"Psycho, I see," he said pleasantly, but in a voice that I thought was overly high-pitched. I was still staring at his face, realizing that I had been so used to seeing myself in a mirror that I couldn't tell if we matched exactly. *Pyscho*, the book, I tried to assure myself.

"Is that how I sound to others?" I asked. He nodded his head. Then he took off his hat and turned slowly around. "Never seen the back, have you?" Still smiling, he sat down. The others remained standing.

"So, what do we do?" he said lightly.

"It's, uh..." I trailed off. I go to the store to buy my meat; I don't go into the meadow and look into the cow's eyes.

"You're curious, what's it do to you, the waiting? For you to claim some little health imperfection, and then have the doctors come take what's needed?" His clone friends blocked the door.

He laughed, then stopped. "What is the good that you have smelled linseed oil, and I have not? Or traveled places I have not? My eyes are sharper, my heart more stout. No childhood traumas to bow to. I'm the perfect You. Ironic, isn't it? You, the imperfect one, getting away with murder? Only it's not murder if it's a clone."

"Wait, let's—"

"Hold him!"

I struggled, but they were strong. "You can't get away with this. You can't kill me."

"Killing? No, my friend. Tattooing. Keep him still."

One of them fished some sort of band out of a briefcase, positioning the front over my forehead. Wires led back into the briefcase, where he clicked a few switches. I felt fear more than pain, and then moaned.

The band came off. "You want to look?" He hefted a small mirror off the kitchen wall. My horror-stricken face stared slackly back. The face of a clone. I looked at his forehead. His hand rose, tugged, a thin film came off, and I was looking at a clean forehead, his forehead, the forehead of a non-clone.

"I'm in perfect health, no damage to my liver. So your stinking body is safe. You...you can live out the rest of your cloned life. As I will live out the rest of your life."

They went to the door. Just before he left, he turned for one final look. "Nice place you've got."

The door closed.

The Mural

Natalie Gottlieb

I trace the painted birds
touch white wings and yellow beaks.
I soothe their feathered breasts.
So rare, these nameless birds
who seek to comfort me
cooing their song of love.

The mural stands above,
its painted cottage real.
I creep inside thick walls
to seek the warmth I need,
for I am six years old
and long to have a friend.

So, watch me as I blend
my body with the wall.
Watch me as I join
the cottage and birds
who send for me this day
and I obey their call.

Is love painted on the wall?
Is it simply just a game?
Embrace me with your wings
before I lose my way.

Hiding from the Enemy

Mike Ramsey

When the school had been built, things like cafeterias weren't part of the architectural plans. When the school had been built, kids went home for lunch.

But now, halfway through the morning, the custodian and his helpers would start setting up long folding tables in the gym. Near the main door, they would set two large trash cans and a smaller folding table for lukewarm pints of milk. Parent volunteers sold them for three cents apiece, while trying not to embarrass their offspring by acknowledging their existence. And on the outer edge of it all, a handful of bored teachers wandered aimlessly.

Davy sat by himself at the far end of the Outcast Table. He had an empty pint of milk near his right hand. His head was tilted down so all he saw was the fake wood surface of the table. Everyone seemed to be talking and laughing, while Davy worried about Cooper and Elgin.

When they'd first started terrorizing him, he'd quickly offered—"Here"—the only thing he had of value—"This is yours"—his lunch. Over the next few days, he was surprised at how easy it was to go without it, while being a little disappointed that no one seemed to notice. But, after awhile, handing over his lunch became dull routine. Until handing over his lunch wasn't enough.

Davy saw Cooper standing at his self-assigned place across the gym. He was chewing on a matchstick and making rude remarks about anyone wandering too close, then smiling at their discomfort and his wit. Elgin leaned against the wall next to him.

When handing over his lunch became boring to Cooper and Elgin, Cooper began talking in hints, raising an eyebrow to make a point, the master of silence between words. Davy finally understood what wasn't being said and volunteered—"I'll do your homework for you, Cooper"—his way out.

Elgin's arms were folded across his chest, his sleeves rolled just enough to show off his childish biceps. He also had his head lowered a little so his perfectly combed Brylcreemed hair looked like antlers, forcing his line of vision just under his eyebrows, his eyes locked on Davy, who was still watching Cooper.

Once Davy started doing Cooper's homework, he realized Cooper was turning it in without copying it over first. He tried to convince him of the trouble they'd get in. But Cooper sneered, and Davy trembled, sure it was only a matter of time before they were both called in to the office. And Cooper would blame him.

When Davy realized Elgin was looking at him, he blushed and looked down. After a few seconds, his eyes, like magnets, were drawn back across the gym. Cooper and Elgin were gone.

Davy froze. He'd only looked down for a few seconds. Rising up from his chair until he was half standing, Davy looked around. He saw kids in laughing, happy groups scattered around the gym. He saw teachers glancing at their watches. But he didn't see Cooper or Elgin.

He slowly turned his head to the right and looked down the Outcast Table. Maybe Cooper and Elgin had doubled back. But all he saw were the Outcasts, looking back in stunned silence. He finished standing up and headed for the double doors.

He passed a teacher who was busy yawning and started down the hall until he came to a door that opened on a corner of the teachers' parking lot and a slice of the playground. He opened the door and saw a brief flash of kids chasing each other. He started on through the door, then stopped. Cooper and Elgin could be waiting for him.

Davy closed the door and started down the hall again. He wanted to run, but had no idea where to go until he found himself in the first floor bathroom. With his back against the door, he looked around. Four urinals, four stalls. A paper towel dispenser at each end of a long mirror that hung over four sinks, and one lone trash can against the far wall, with the smell of disinfectant hanging over it all. There was nothing new here; nothing had changed in the thousands of times he'd been in this place. He relaxed and closed his eyes. Then he quickly opened them and looked at the stalls again.

Slowly, he slid down the door until he was squatting at its base with his shirttail pulled out. He carefully looked at the two feet of open space between the bottom of the metal walls around each toilet and the floor.

He didn't see legs or feet with or without pants down around the ankles. He was in the clear.

Davy got up and walked to the nearest sink. He'd wait until the end of lunch to leave, when he'd be invisible by mixing with the herd of kids going back to class.

If someone walked in now, it would seem strange for him to be standing at the sink, doing nothing. He turned the water on.

Then, back in class, Davy would do what he always did through the afternoon: figure a way past Cooper after school...

He looked at his dry hands and turned the water off.

...or how to keep the teacher from calling on him.

He went in a stall and closed the door.

Davy even made up a list once, trying to accomplish both.

For a few seconds, he stood in the stall facing the door. Then he glanced behind him and sat down.

In the end, Davy had come to the conclusion his teacher and Cooper were psychic and would always be waiting for him when he least expected it.

If someone walked in now, if they bothered to look, they'd see a pair of anonymous legs in faded black dress pants and feet in white socks and scruffy black dress shoes. They'd go about their business and leave him alone. And he wouldn't have to explain anything or face strange looks or laughter. And he wouldn't have to run the risk of being forced out to an empty hallway with Cooper at one end and Elgin at the other.

Protected, he leaned forward and rested his elbows on his knees.

He looked down at his hands, dangling between his legs, then at the floor between his feet. He thought how he'd like to stay where he was for the rest of the afternoon. That would solve both of his problems, because he was sure no one would notice or care. The only time the students paid attention to him was when they made casual insults while the teacher tried not to smile. So he didn't really think anyone would miss him if he wasn't in class.

The dull faraway sound of the gym seemed vaguely closer for a second, then retreated. He lifted his head. There was a minuscule drop in the air pressure around him. He licked his lips. A stray air current drifted like a feather across his left cheek. He strained to listen, but there were no footsteps, no whispers, no suppressed laughter, nothing.

Davy leaned to his right so he could see through the small vertical slot between the door and the stall. He saw a tiny piece of the opposite wall, a part of the mirror and sink. And beneath the sink, the floor, widening as it spread out beneath him—then nothing.

Relaxing a little, he started to look away, then quickly looked back. He was sure he'd seen a momentary flickering of the atmosphere caused by the swift movement of a body traveling in front of a light.

Davy carefully lifted his legs until he was able to hook the heels of his shoes on the front edge of the toilet. Then he wrapped his arms around his legs and rested his chin on his knees.

Safe

Natalie Gottlieb

My wounds have hardly healed
when the contents of the safe call to me again.
Mirror carpets the floor of my back room.
Sunlight slithers its way through tightly closed blinds.

A shot of light hits its target. While colors ignite,
shapes dance and bounce against decaying walls.

I enter slowly and lumber toward the safe,
the holder of secrets. As it opens,
lace and satin ribbons fly toward me.
Within, neatly packed baby buntings,
crocheted dresses, soft tee shirts.
Rainbows of pinks, purples and yellows
ironed and folded into small packets of love,
form a teetering towering sculpture.

Weekly, I guide my feet toward these hidden treasures,
unlock the safe, hold my baby jewels close
and smell their sweetness.

Lingering, I refold my gems
slam the door on yesterday and turn
when sharp pain surges through my body.
I bend in ecstasy. My long hair sweeps the floor
as I yank the fragment from my foot.

Dare I lie on this bed of glass?
I stare instead into the jagged shape.
One blue circle eye peers back
hooded by a purple powdered lid.

Too heavy, I confess as I place
the mirrored point against my cheek.
"Mirror, mirror," I chant and
clutching my instrument, carefully drag
the blade down the side of my face,
screaming with intense pleasure.

A Special Halloween

Manuel Torrez, Jr.

Mickey's sister, Evelyn, had been toying lazily with her bowl of oatmeal at breakfast, stirring her spoon about, when all of a sudden her mouth opened wide and out gushed words like water from a spigot turned on full blast.

"Gypsies are mysterious people! They keep to themselves. Did you know that, Mickey? Did you know they stick together like glue?"

Their mother was in the back yard, hanging wash. Evelyn leaned her lanky thirteen-year-old body across the kitchen table and clasped young Mickey's shoulders with her pale white hands. "Mickey, swear to me that what I tell you this morning you won't repeat to anyone." She squeezed tight. "Gypsy women have very dark hair and brilliant white teeth; they tell fortunes by reading palms." She let go and slid back into her chair. Her voice softened. "Josie is going to read palms tonight," she said. "Very appropriate... I'll tell you why later."

Mickey was eleven, and Evelyn's revelation confused him. "Where do Gypsies come from?" he said.

Evelyn's eyes narrowed, and she turned crimson. She jumped to her feet. "Europe, India! Don't ask questions, just listen, little brother. Haven't you ever read about Gypsies in the 'G' volume of our encyclopedia?"

"Okay! Okay! You don't have to bite my head off."

Evelyn took a deep breath, closed her eyes for a second, then leaned over, cupped her hand at the side of her mouth and whispered in his ear. "Josie is a Gypsy. She was left at her mom's doorstep in a basket as a baby—with a note from her Gypsy mom."

"What?" He gasped, his eyes bulging at her further revelation. But Evelyn had never lied to him.

Mickey was sitting on the top porch step of their three-room house, a small, wood-frame building flanked by large pecan trees. It was late afternoon on Halloween, and he'd been mulling over what Evelyn had said at breakfast while he tried to visualize what the evening would be like. They were invited to a party at Josie's, Evelyn's best friend. All his past Halloweens had been spent trick or treating in the neighborhood with his friends. This year, with Josie Valdez's party only a couple of hours away, he knew this Halloween was going to be special.

He pushed himself up till his backside was on the porch floor, then lay back on the cold wood planks, using his palms as a pillow. His eyes closed, and he tried to envision what the party was going to be like, now that he knew Josie was a real Gypsy. She did have very black, curly hair and brilliant white teeth. He'd thought she was pretty the first time he saw her, even though she was thirteen, like Evelyn.

The cool autumn breeze stroked his face and brought with it the fragrance of crimson roses from the full bush by the porch steps. Evelyn's voice carried from inside the house. She was discussing her costume with their mother. He opened his eyes. All day long, his mother had sat at her sewing machine, working on their outfits. Evelyn was going to the party as an angel. He was to be a pirate.

His mother cracked open the screen door. Her black-rimmed glasses were perched low on the bridge of her nose. He saw her strong, gray eyes look over them.

"Mick! Get up from that cold floor. Come inside. I want you and your sister to eat your supper before you go to the Valdez's."

After they ate, she led him into the living room, which also served as a bedroom for his sister and himself. Large pieces of black cotton cloth lay over the back of the worn, green sofa bed that he slept on at night. Smaller, leftover fabric scraps of many colors were scattered on the sewing machine cabinet and on the flower-patterned linoleum floor. She handed him a black vest. His face lit up, and he put it on in a hurry. Out of her apron pocket she produced a large, black and white patterned bandana.

"Remember to be polite to Mrs. Valdez. Greet her as soon as you see her," she said and wrapped the bandana around his forehead. She tied it in the back. From one of the drawers of the sewing machine cabinet, she produced a black eye patch that was threaded with an elastic string. She handed it to him. "Did you hear what I said, Mick?"

"Yes, ma'am," he said and covered his eye with the patch while he sprinted to his mother's bedroom. There was a dresser there with a large, round mirror. Evelyn was already in front of it in her angel costume.

"Wow!"

"Are you ready?" she said, turning sideways to show off her wings to him.

"You look like the angel in the calendar that's hanging on the kitchen wall."

"The guardian angel with the little boy and girl on the bridge?"

"Yeah, that one, but why an angel on Halloween?"

"I always wanted a costume like this one," she said and pranced around him. Her wings flapped with her movement while her auburn hair bounced on her bony shoulders.

"Are you ready?" she said again, and moved the curtain aside to peek out the window. "It's getting dark. Let's tell Mom we're leaving."

"Not yet."

"Why not?"

"I don't have a sword."

"Last night I saw Dad with a play sword…said he got it at the dollar store. Have you asked Mom?"

"Asked me what?" Their mother walked into the room. She had the shiny sword in her hand. The handle was a gold color, and the curved plastic blade was silver. "You can loosen your belt a notch and stick it between your belt and your pants."

"Yeah! Thanks, Mom." His uncovered eye gleamed with excitement.

"We'd better be going. It's already dark outside," Evelyn said.

"First, help me roll the sewing machine into the closet."

"Okay, Mom," Evelyn said and followed her. There was a hallway from the kitchen to the bathroom, but there was no closet there. His mom just called it that. It was a large space for the sewing machine, Evelyn's rollaway cot, and sheets and blankets stored on shelves against the wall. A curtain hung from a line that stretched the length of the hall. It hid everything.

Mickey straightened his eye patch and looked at himself in the round mirror. He twisted his mouth like his dad did when he knew something was missing in what he was wearing. There was a glass dish on the dresser top with his mom's cosmetic jewelry. He dug with his fingers till he found a hoop earring and attached it to the lobe of his left ear.

"Super!" he said, still looking at his mirrored image. He jumped on his mom's bed to wait for Evelyn.

"Let's go," Evelyn said, as they came back into the room. Mickey got off the bed and adjusted the sword in his belt.

"God bless you. Have a good time," their mother said and did the sign of the cross in the air in front of them. The springs on the screen door were new, and the door slammed shut with a loud bang. "Mick, stick with your sister," she said loudly through the screen. Mickey turned and waved.

The party was in the Valdez's back yard. An electric cord with orange Chinese lanterns sagged from above the back door to a storage shed that stood against the back fence. The lights cast tree branch shadows on the back wall of the white house. Mickey followed his sister's long strides toward a group of kids her age, who were hanging out by a makeshift tent.

Evelyn was quickly in their midst. Mickey stood outside the group, looking at a yellow paper sign pinned to one of the white sheets used to form the tent. "Palm Reading" was printed on it in bold, black marker letters. He could see Josie's shadow cast on the sheet by a flickering candle inside the tent.

"Go ahead, little brother. Get in there and get your palm read by the Gypsy," Evelyn said.

"Later," he said and walked away from them.

"Chicken!" Evelyn teased and laughed. Her friends quickly echoed her laughter. He glanced over his shoulder at them and glared. They cackled even louder when they saw his attempt at looking angry. He turned around and froze. The wind had increased, and the back wall of the house was a frenzy of whirling, bizarre tree branch shadows that gave him a start.

A few kids his age were bobbing for red apples in a metal washtub by the back door. Mrs. Valdez was there, supervising the game and handing out paper towels after they'd skimmed the cold water with their mouths in pursuit of an apple's stem. She caught sight of him and beckoned to him with a thick, red hand. Her round, shiny face grinned.

"Hello, Mrs. Valdez," he said quickly, remembering his mother's instructions.

"Come on, Mickey. Try your luck with the apples."

"Thank you—maybe later." The idea of dunking for apples held less appeal for him than getting his palm read by a real Gypsy as pretty as Josie. He turned and meandered toward the tent, where Evelyn and the other older kids were huddled. As he made his way back, he conjured up the picture in his mind he had of Josie with her curly black hair. He felt redness in his face.

"Whoa, little brother," Evelyn said and put an open hand to his chest.

"You said to get my palm read."

"Yes, I did, but you don't have to gallop in," she said and opened a flap of the tent entrance.

"Yeah," her friends parroted. Mickey gave Evelyn's friends another scornful look, then entered the tent.

It was dimly lit inside with only one candle. Josie, her long black hair pulled up in a bun and tied with a bright yellow ribbon, was seated on a wooden chair behind a small, square table. On the table was a tall, red stick candle secured to a red saucer. On the other side of the table was a wooden onion crate.

"Please, sit there, Mickey," she said and leaned to one side, exposing a long earring glittering with red translucent beads. She formed a perfect smile with her bright red lips. Mickey smiled back shyly, then struggled with the rough boards on the crate. They were uncomfortable to sit on, and he maneuvered side to side, trying to find a spot on the surface that was less hurtful to his backside.

"Please, could you stop moving, Mickey?"

He stopped shifting, but there was a wire around the crate that hunched upward, just enough to bother his right thigh.

Josie interlaced her hands on the tabletop and wriggled her fingers, showing off her long red fingernails. A black curl hung at the center of her milky forehead.

She is pretty, he thought. She's the prettiest girl I know.

"Let me see your right palm," she said, taking his right hand and drawing it gently to her. He opened it tentatively. The candle's light danced on his flushed palm. The wire embedding his thigh made him jerk to one side. "Mickey! Don't move. I'm trying to read the lines," she said and circled calmly, with a long fingernail, the part at the heel of his hand. "This is called the Mount of Venus. Yours is very round and firm. That means you're a very warm, sincere person." She had sparkling green eyes, and she winked at him. "This long deep line that you have going around Venus is your lifeline—you'll have a long life." She squeezed his hand gently. He felt his face get red again. "It also means you have great energy, but see this blank space that splits the line? Trouble," she said, then paused and gave him a long stare. He swallowed hard. The sweet aroma of the candle reminded him of his mother's rose bush by the porch steps at home. Josie softly pinched his cheek. "You shouldn't worry. It's nothing to lose sleep over."

"Are you a real Gypsy?"

She let go of his hand and made a sidelong glance to the entrance, then turned back to him.

"Do I look Gypsy, to you?"

"Well…you have very black hair, your teeth are brilliantly white, and Evelyn explained to me that Gypsy women have those traits. She also mentioned that, as a baby, you had been left in a basket on the doorstep of your mom's house with a Gypsy's note."

Josie's mouth opened wide, but no words materialized, then she reeled back and laughed so hard her whole body shook. "Evelyn told you this?"

"Yes."

"Well," she said, rolling her eyes upward and rubbing her chin with a fingernail. She locked her bulging eyes on his. "Your sister—being older than you, and thus wiser—you should believe. Right, Mick?" She said it as if her words were a medicine ball, and she'd just tossed it to him without warning.

"I guess," he said weakly.

Josie jumped up and banged hard on the table with her hands. She almost tipped over the candle, which now leaned precariously. Mickey rose and took backward steps.

"Now that you know my secret, there's no need to hold back. I feel exhilarated when I'm in this role. Sit down! I'm not through with you."

"What?" Mickey said, but slowly sat back down on the uncomfortable onion crate. Josie, still bug-eyed, slid back into her chair, too.

"It's not just a Halloween ritual with me," she bellowed. "I'm in my natural environment." She thrust her hand at his wrist like a snake striking at unsuspecting prey. She yanked it forcefully and twisted it around violently, so that she was looking at his palm once more.

"Oh, my—here they are." She shook her head and clicked her tongue.

"What?"

"This line that cuts across the top of your palm—your heart line." She stabbed with her long, red nail and slid it with great force along the line. "Those blank spots across it are more islands."

"More islands?"

"More islands. I didn't notice them before. Trouble. A sure sign."

"Are you sure?" His heart began to race, and his palm hurt where she'd dug in her nail.

"Gypsies don't lie on Halloween night!"

The candle remained lopsided, and the new angle of the flickering candlelight distorted the features on Josie's face. He saw red, wire-like streaks in the whites of her eyes that he hadn't seen before. Her thin eyebrows pointed cunningly to the bridge of her nose, which now appeared hooked and bony. Her hold on his wrist was too tight. What was she doing?

"Hey!" he said and pulled with all his strength to break her hold. She wouldn't let go. His lips quivered. "Let go of my hand. I want to go home!"

"Remember what I said about trouble. Halloween nights can be full of surprises."

"Let go!" He pulled again and finally broke her grip. Without saying another word, he dashed out. As he ran alongside the tent, he saw Josie's reflection and heard her laugh loudly.

Evelyn and her friends had moved. They were by the back door, listening to music from a portable radio. The younger kids had plucked all the apples from the tub and started playing Pin the Tail on the Donkey. Mrs. Valdez saw him and waved her hand to get his attention. He smiled at her, but his lips were trembling. He raced to Evelyn's side.

"Hey, Mickey, get your palm read?"

His whole body was a-jitter. "I'm going home."

"What? We just got here. It's Halloween."

"I don't feel good. Will you walk with me to our front yard?"

She put her hand on his forehead. "No fever," she said, "but you are shaking. What's wrong? Gypsy get you scared?" she teased and put her hand on his shoulder. He shook himself free and ran off. "Go ahead, go home if you like, but don't tell Mama we fought, 'cause we didn't. Hear me, Mick?" But he was away quickly, away from the orange Chinese lanterns and into the darkness of the empty street.

He was only minutes from home, but the street lamp was busted, and there was only the light from a full moon to illuminate the sidewalk. The wind continued to blow in unannounced gusts, sending a trash can tumbling in his direction from a driveway that separated two darkened houses. Mickey stopped, then jumped aside to get out of its way. He felt his heart banging in his chest. The can continued its noisy trek across the street, while the wind howled in the mostly bare crown branches of the trees, producing a verse and chorus appropriate for the night. He heard a familiar cough and turned in the direction of the sound. He could make out the porch of one of the darkened houses, and tiny red glows that would at times intensify and at times diminish. He recognized whose place it was. Old Mister Johnson, a house painter who drank too much, lived there with his wife. Cigarettes, he thought. The old couple must be smoking.

"Hey, you—pirate. Come over here!" It was Johnson, and he was spouting unintelligible beer blusters while he staggered toward him. Mickey's heart leaped again. "I said, come here!"

His first instinct was to run and get home quick, but he figured the old man deserved some respect, even though the whole neighborhood was aware of his weekday afternoon zigzagging trudges homeward from work. But he was a neighbor and, besides, he'd never bothered Mickey.

He felt the painter's callused hand grab his arm and squeeze tight. The contact made him instantly visualize the hall in his house and the space behind the curtain that his mother regarded as a closet. It was his hole to hide in whenever he felt threatened. He wished he were there now.

"I want to show you something," Old Johnson said and pulled on Mickey's arm as he led him to the porch steps. The old woman was sitting in her rocker in the dark. She was rocking leisurely and dragging on a rolled cigarette. Johnson grabbed Mickey by the back of the neck and pushed his head down.

"Look! Did you do this?"

With the light from the moon, Mickey could distinguish a broken clay pot on the ground and a red geranium strewn beside it. "No, sir."

The old man squeezed his neck again. "Don't lie, boy. You came here with your friends less than an hour ago for treat candy. When I told you there wasn't any, y'all did this. I ran after the whole lot of you, and I noticed one was wearing a pirate costume—exactly like yours."

"It wasn't me, sir," Mickey pleaded and broke away from the painter's grip. The old man tripped backwards and checked his fall by grabbing the porch step banister. "I was at a party at the Valdez's."

Johnson's wife got up and wobbled with a walking stick to get close to Mickey. Her long nose almost bumped his flushed cheek. "No, this isn't the same pirate," she said, her words whistling through a gap in her teeth.

"How do you know, Bess?"

"I'm sure. He's not one of them."

"Bah! You were inside."

"It wasn't me, sir," Mickey pleaded.

"I was looking through the window!" Bess thumped her walking stick against the wood porch floor several times.

"You can't see at night anymore."

"At night or in the daylight, I can see better than you, Johnson."

The old man scratched behind his ear and babbled to himself. "All right. Go home, boy. But don't bring your friends around here anymore. There's no treat candy here. Halloween is just another of the Lord's days. Unfortunately, it's being trampled on tonight by Satan's rowdies. Hear me, boy?"

"Goodnight, sir, ma'am," Mickey said, while making fast tracks to the sidewalk by the street. He dashed for home, losing the gold and silver sword somewhere along the way, but not stopping to retrieve it. When he got close to his house, he stopped. He was breathing hard and bent over to grab his knees. When he looked up, he saw Evelyn standing on the porch in the light. She was still in her angel costume and had her fists on her waist.

"Where were you?" she shrieked and jumped down, landing squarely in front of him. She grabbed his right ear lobe with her hand and pulled.

"Ouch," he howled and slapped hard at her wrist. "I was on my way home."

"That's nonsense, Mick. You weren't gone but a few minutes when I started after you. I never saw you on my way here."

"Why? Why did you follow me?"

"Because I wanted to see you home." She folded her arms and turned away, accidentally bumping him with a wing. She looked over her shoulder. "I'm going back as soon as you're inside the house, understand?"

"Why go back, Evelyn? Stay here. We can play Chinese Checkers with Mom."

Evelyn shook her head.

"Besides," he went on, "Mister Johnson is drunk again. He stopped me and asked if I had knocked a potted plant off his porch."

Like a pin bursting a balloon, Evelyn's confidence was gone and instantly replaced with an apprehensive tremor. "You're just saying that so I won't go back to the party. You know I'm scared to death of Mister Johnson when he's drunk. You're saying it to keep me home."

"Then go, but get across the street now and run till you get opposite the Valdez's house, then cross the street there."

"Mickey, go back with me," she pleaded softly and gripped his arm. "Please."

"No. Josie said something bad might happen tonight, and it already has…to me."

"What are you talking about? Not the silly palm reading? She can't really read palms."

He yanked his arm away from her grip. "Sure she can. She read mine. She's a Gypsy," he said and started up the stairs. "You said she was a Gypsy. She does have black hair and very white teeth. Besides, she didn't deny anything when I told her you said she was a Gypsy."

Evelyn pressed her ears with her hands and closed her eyes. "What did she say?"

"Something about me having to believe you, because you were older and smarter."

Evelyn opened her eyes and wrinkled her nose. "She's not really a Gypsy. I made it up. It's Halloween. I wanted to get you in the mood. Now, will you go back with me?" She grabbed at his hand, but he pulled away and got hold of the screen door handle.

"She is a Gypsy! She didn't deny it. I've already had bad luck. She is a Gypsy!" He opened the door and let it close slowly, so it wouldn't bang shut and make noise. His mother was by her bedroom window with her rosary beads in her hand. Her glasses were stuck in her hair above her forehead. Her lips moved quickly as she said a Hail Mary. He passed without a word, so as not to disturb her, and entered the living room. The large sofa bed was extended and his sheets and pillow were in place. Evelyn's rollaway was made up, too. He sat down on the edge of the sofa bed. He could hear his mother praying in the other room. Sometimes, her prayers were a faint whisper, other times louder, depending, he figured, on her reflection at the moment. He flipped himself up on to the sofa. His eyes grew heavy with her cadence. Just as he was dozing off, Evelyn stumped into the room with his sword, slung it on the floor, and it slid under the sofa. She flopped on the rollaway, still in her costume. He could hear her sniffling, then sobbing, then sniffling again. He turned on his side, away from her. His mother was still praying, but sometimes Evelyn cried out and drowned out her prayer.

Mickey dropped his hands and casually traced the flower patterns on the linoleum floor with his fingers, then pressed his hands together and prayed in a whisper, "Jesus, please forgive me for being afraid...please help me overcome my fear...and please let Evelyn be happy..."

"Trick or treat!"

Evelyn had forgotten to turn off the porch light. He got up and kicked her cot intentionally when he passed by her. He gave each kid a bag of pecans that his mother had prepared earlier and turned the light off.

The Birthday Shoes

Jackie Grant

As a kid, I always wanted to be a gypsy. It was only at Halloween that I could live out that fantasy. Yellow drapes became my skirt, beads and bangles and lipstick adorned my body. I felt at home.

I never dreamed that I actually would have the opportunity to meet real gypsies. But then it happened. We were staying with Uncle Clifford and Mean Aunt Martha in Spanaway, Washington. Mother was paralyzed from rheumatic fever, and I was put under the supervision of Mean Aunt Martha, who watched over me like a hawk.

When my eighth birthday came, Mother gave me the money to buy myself any pair of shoes I wanted. I was allowed to go shopping alone and chose the most beautiful pair of black, patent leather wedgies with ankle straps. I would prance in front of the mirror, admiring how glamorous the shoes made me look. I was so in love with them that I believed they brought me the luck that led to meeting the gypsies.

A few days after my birthday, Mean Aunt Martha said, "Make sure you do not cross the road to the empty lot, as the gypsies are camping there."

My eyes doubled in size, my heart beat loudly, and I could feel life roaring into my body. How could I slip away and see these real gypsies for myself? There must be some way I could just go and look for a minute without being caught. I had already learned the hard way that punishment in this house meant coming home from school to ten people's breakfast and lunch dishes with disgusting food dried on them. "Well, maybe you'll think twice about minding next time," Mean Aunt Martha would threaten. I came to hate washing and drying dishes.

It was almost sundown when I saw what I now call "a window of opportunity." I did not see anyone downstairs. As I quietly crept up the stairs, I could hear my mother and aunt talking. "Well," I told myself, "it is now or never." I didn't care if I had to wash a thousand dishes; I had to see the gypsies for myself. Running as fast as I could in my new wedgies—I'd only had flat shoes before my birthday—I tried not to fall as I ran across the road.

Sure enough, there they were—at least forty of them: women in colorful clothes, men with earrings in their ears, lots of children running around looking so free and happy. I bet they never had to do all the dishes. I was in heaven as I entered their camp. I tried to hide how nervous I felt as I said "Hi" to everyone. I tried to act very grownup, walking around in my wonderful black, patent leather wedgie shoes. It didn't seem to matter to them at all that a total stranger was peeking into their caravans. Unbelievably, one of the older boys—at least twelve years old—asked me if I wanted to ride one of their ponies. Not only had I never been in a gypsy camp before, I'd also never been on a horse before. "Sure," I said. There I was, parading around the camp with the gypsy children delightfully running beside the pony and me.

I didn't notice that the sun had set until I heard from a distance, "Jackie." The voice grew louder and louder. "Jackie, you come home this instant."

"I've got to go," I told my newfound friends, and I got off the pony and ran home as fast as possible. There she stood, Mean Aunt Martha, watching me as I crossed the road.

A family conference was held to determine my punishment. I sat on my mother's bed while she looked so sad, and Mean Aunt Martha looked so angry.

"We've got to do something really serious so she doesn't think she can run off and do what she wants again. She will do all the dishes for the entire next week—"

I didn't like the idea, but getting to meet the gypsies and ride on the pony was definitely worth doing dishes. I sighed with a sense of relief.

Then Mean Aunt Martha continued, "—and those ugly black shoes need to be thrown away."

I pleaded with Mother. "No, no, not my shoes." But Mom knew that Mean Aunt Martha was taking care of me while she was sick, and her gratitude for that blinded her to the worst punishment I could have been given. My birthday shoes were taken from me. I had lost the possession that I loved the most.

After that year, Mother improved rapidly, and we returned to our home in San Francisco. When Halloween came, I again wanted to be a gypsy, but

Mother demanded that I be a nurse. She spent hours making the costume and bought me the ugliest white oxford shoes to go with it.

Halloween was never the same. However, for years I dreamt about the gypsies and me in my beautiful shoes and knew, if I had it to do over again, I would still trade my shoes to get to meet the gypsies.

The Shoes

Kathy Hayduke

There they were, two little twin brothers, Ronnie and Donnie. They were about seven years old, with tiny frames, olive skin, dark hair and eyes, skinny little legs, and oh, so wiry. They were the total opposite of our tall, large-framed, blonde-haired, blue-eyed, sedate daughters.

I had taken my daughters along to get the boys' shoes. The girls sat on one side of me, the boys on the other side. The salesman made small talk while he would try a shoe or two on the boys, look up at the girls, then over to the boys. He'd try another shoe on, lace it up, gaze at the girls, and then the boys. This was repeated a few times; he would look at the girls first, and then the boys. All the while the kids were talking to me, it was "Mom" this or "Mom" that.

Finally, the salesman could contain his curiosity no longer. He stared one more time at the girls on one side and the boys on the other side, and then said to me, "Those boys must sure look like their father."

Without missing a beat, I replied, "I wouldn't know; I never saw his face."

Well, the poor man—his face turned beet red, the sweat poured from his brow, and his mouth slammed shut. I'm sure he was embarrassed down to his toes. He stammered, then shut his mouth again.

Finally, the boys yelled out in unison, "We're foster kids; she's not our real mom!"

The salesman sighed a big sigh, took a deep breath and said, "Lady, I'm a talker, and I have never been at a loss for words, but you really took the wind out of my sails on that one."

We both laughed together, and I told him he got what he deserved.

After that, we would see each other every now and then, when I was shopping. Once in a while, I would have a new kid with me, and he'd always say, with a smirk on his face, "That kid must sure look like his dad." And I would always respond, "I don't know; I never saw his face," and we'd both laugh.

In the end, we found that Ronnie and Donnie looked exactly like their mother: wiry, petite, dark eyes and hair, with olive skin.

Reminiscences of an English Village Girl

Margaret Francis

My parents divorced in 1938 when I was five, and I was sent to live with my Aunt Flo in Rickinghall. I was immediately enrolled in Mowbray House School, the only private school in the area. This was a wonderful school run by Miss Scates, and later she was joined by her friend, Miss Hall. Miss Muriel Warren taught the young children. They were all excellent teachers and very caring of their pupils. At the time I attended, there were rarely more than fifteen pupils. Miss Scates was the arty one and taught watercolors, *broderie anglaise* needlework, and French. Miss Hall taught science, geography, history, and her favorite subject, English.

Miss Hall had two interesting lessons she used when teaching us vocabulary. When I was young, she taught nursery rhymes in Johnsonese (erudite) English. An example of "Mary Had a Little Lamb" in Johnsonese English would read as follows:

> Mary was the proprietress of a small incipient sheep
> Whose outer covering was as devoid of color
> As congealed atmospheric vapor.
> To whatever vicinity Mary perambulated
> Her young Southdown was morally sure to follow.
> It pursued her to the dispensary of learning
> One diurnal section of time,
> Which was contrary to all precedent.
> Therefore the teacher expelled it from the interior,
> But it continued to remain in the immediate vicinity
> Until Mary once more became visible.
> "What makes this specimen of the Genus Ovus have such
>   an affection for Mary?"
> The irrepressible young progeny vociferated.
> "It is because Mary reciprocates its affection,"
> The perspicacious pedagogue promulgated.

When I was fourteen, I was the oldest child in the school, and Miss Hall used to take me in another room, where I would read aloud from "In the Steps of St. Paul" and "In the Steps of the Master." When I came to a hard word, she would ask me if I knew what it meant. If I did, we went on; if not, I had to write down the word. For homework, I had to look up the word and write three sentences using that word, so she could be sure I thoroughly understood its meaning.

Miss Hall was the practical one, and one day, while we were in the midst of doing our fancy *broderie anglaise*, she came in the classroom holding up a knitted glove with a hole in the thumb. She said, "I've got a glove and a very pretty glove, and who is the owner of this pretty glove?" I had to admit it was mine. Her comment was, "We must learn to darn our own gloves before going on to fancy needlework."

One morning we were told by Miss Hall that one of the pupils—a young boy—had passed her in the street and not raised his cap to her. So we all had to parade past her, the boys raising their caps and saying, "Good morning, Miss Hall," and the girls bowing their heads, smiling, and saying, "Good morning, Miss Hall."

At Mowbray House School there were not enough students for sports so we did calisthenics to the dates in history: "William 1st, 1066" and our arms would go up; "William 2nd, 1087" and our arms would go out; "William 3rd, 1100" and our arms would go down, and so on down the list.

Although I did a lot of cycling, I had no idea that I was at all athletic until we had the 25th Jubilee of King George and Queen Mary on the church school meadow. I won every race I entered. We all had a feast and were presented with a Jubilee mug.

I was thought to be a talented little actress. At school, we put on all kinds of performances, including Shakespeare's "The Merchant of Venice." I was Portia, but Miss Hall stole the show as Shylock. We even managed to do a French play, and many more. I had a photographic memory in those days and, just from rehearsals, I always knew everybody's part and could prompt on stage.

One year, when we were performing "Wind in the Willows," Mr. Rat came down with chickenpox, and I was asked to do his part as well as my own. I rose to the challenge with no problem. I was also asked to be in all the theatre activities in the village. When the village school put on a pageant for Empire Day, even though I didn't go to that school, I was asked to be Britannia. An adult group asked me to appear in their play entitled "The Little Factory Girl." I was the little factory girl.

When I was about twelve years old, I attended dancing classes. My friend, Enid, and I were always asked to dance at the local shows. We did the sailor's hornpipe, the tarantella, the Irish Jig, and the Dutch Clog dance. We always got whistled at, and encores were always requested. We thoroughly enjoyed the accolades.

Guy Fawkes day on November 5th was always an exciting time. The little ditty goes as follows:

> Please to remember the 5th of November
> Gunpowder treason and plot
> I see no reason why gunpowder treason
> Should ever be forgot

For days before the 5th we would go to the woods and collect deadwood for the bonfire. We always had a huge bonfire with a stuffed "guy" on top. A lot of families got together for this affair. We roasted chestnuts and potatoes in the fire, and set off fireworks.

I remember the Horkeys at harvest time. They were big social events put on by the farmers who had been blessed with a good crop: a big feast, followed by a "social evening" of dancing and singing and just having fun.

In my mind the summer days always seemed to be sunny. We took picnics to the fields by a river, lay down and listened to the flies and bees buzzing around. We vaulted the river with a pole. We collected tadpoles from a little river that ran beside the church, and put them in a glass bottle. I never knew what happened to them. I never saw them turn into frogs.

Mr. Smith, our big burly policeman, was gruff, but kind and fair. When he caught me riding my bicycle without a light, he gave me a long lecture, telling me how dangerous it was. He believed in prevention, not in citing you as a Juvenile Delinquent. He believed that the punishment should fit the crime, so when a group of young lads destroyed a farmer's haystack, he made them work for the farmer until the haystack was restored.

Christmases at Rickinghall were celebrated extensively. Aunt Flo always had a crowd, including my mother. I only saw her at Christmas and during the summer holidays, when I went to stay with her.

My Dad used to send a big box of "goodies" by rail in a big wooden box with presents for all the children, a Christmas pudding and iced cake that my Grandma Wilden had made, nuts and fruit, which were difficult to get in the village, and everything to make Christmas merry.

I left Rickinghall when I was fourteen to go to the Pitman's Business College in London and live with my mother, but I still return each year, and it is still one of my favorite places.

A Grandmother's Tale
...for Children Whose Parents Are Separating or Divorced

Adrienne Rogers

Once upon a time, there was a little girl a little older than Maggie (who is now four and a half) whose mother and father were very poor. The little girl's mother got sick, and then the little girl and her father went to live with her daddy's mother, Grandma Bessie, while her mother went back to her family, far away in Virginia. The little girl was very lonely and unhappy and missed her mother all the time.

Her father was away working during the day and did not come back until after she was asleep. He wasn't the kind of daddy who read stories or played games with her, so she didn't miss him as much as she missed her mother. Her mother had always been a stay-at-home mom, who spent all her time taking care of the little girl or cooking and cleaning until she got sick and had to go away for a while to rest.

Grandma Bessie's house had two floors. Grandma lived upstairs, while Uncle Norman, Aunt Tibbie, and their three sons lived downstairs. Uncle Norman seemed stern and mean, and the little girl didn't like to be around him. Aunt Tibbie was something like her mother, and Aunt Tibbie's house was nice and comfortable with pretty things, like a little porcelain cat and flowers in a vase with marbles on the bottom. The little girl didn't like baths too much, but when Aunt Tibbie let her use her bathroom and gave her great big fluffy towels to dry off with, she didn't mind taking baths as much. Aunt Tibbie cooked like her mother, too. Aunt Tibbie's sons were too old to play with the little girl, and they weren't interested in her at all. But there was one creature in Aunt Tibbie's house that the little girl really loved, and who came to love her and be her best friend on earth. His name was Jack, and he was a giant German Shepherd.

Grandma Bessie was a very old lady, small and bent over. She didn't speak English very well because she had come from far away in a place that now would probably be one of the Russian-speaking countries. She had strange habits the little girl couldn't understand. Every day, morning and evening, she would sit alone in a corner with a cloth on her head, muttering to herself. The little girl would fly to catch what she was saying, and sometimes, thinking she heard an English word that Grandma wasn't saying right, she would correct her pronunciation. After a while, she understood from Grandma's scowl that her interruption was not welcome, and she began to realize that Grandma was not speaking English. Grandma was praying in Hebrew, because Grandma was Jewish. On Friday nights, she always lit candles and said prayers, and that was the beginning of Shabbas, which lasted until sundown the next day, Saturday. That meant that, all day Saturday, no one could do anything that was work—no writing, no cooking, no cleaning, no playing the piano. It was very boring. But the little girl's father, who did not mind about Shabbas, would drive her to a movie and leave her there for the whole show. (This was before television was invented.) She spent most of the day in the movie, eating lunch from a paper bag she brought with her.

During the week, she went to school. The best part of the day was when she got out of school and got to play with Jack, the German Shepherd. After a while, Aunt Tibbie let Jack out around the time school let out, and he would be waiting at the school gate to meet the little girl and walk home with her and her friends. At night, he liked to sleep in her bed, but she had to teach him to wait until she got in and got settled before letting him get in, because he was as big as she was, and he would stretch out the whole length of the bed, just like a person, and even fight with her for a place on the pillow. But he was a great comfort to her—more than any stuffed toy.

When a school vacation came, the little girl and her father took a long trip by car to visit her mother in Virginia. Her mother was still not well enough to come back home and take care of her, and the little girl felt sad and angry, but she was so glad to be with her mother again for a little while that she didn't say she was angry. She just tried to be happy to be with her and hoped it would not be too long before she would be well enough to come home. There was another Grandma in Virginia, but she was such a very sick old lady that the little girl hardly saw her at all. She was in a dark room all the time, surrounded by medicine bottles. She was too sick to care that she had a grandchild. Although the little girl was very sad to leave her mother to go back to New York, she was not sorry to leave that house, where there was so much sickness and no fun at all.

One night, the little girl went to bed as usual. She went through the ritual with Jack, getting into bed herself, then letting him come up and settle first at her feet, then stretch out alongside her. When she felt very sad and lonely and unloved, she would imagine there was someone, somewhere, a special kind of person she didn't actually know, but who cared about her a lot and who looked after her because she didn't have a mother to look after her, and her father didn't really care that much about her, and she didn't have any sisters or brothers, and her cousins were all much older than she, and mostly boys. Before going to sleep, she would talk to her friend, whom she imagined to be like a perfect, good Daddy, and tell him whatever she was feeling—lonely, sad, angry—and ask for his help. After a while, she somehow got the idea that this friend she imagined was what other people called God, but since she had imagined him for herself, he was her own God. So this night, before going to sleep, she told her God how much she missed her mother and how unhappy she was not to be in her own home with her own mommy and daddy, and she asked God to please make her mother better soon. Then she fell asleep. She was asleep for a long time when she had a dream.

In the dream, she was sitting on a curb in the street, all alone, dirty and ragged, when an angel came up behind her. The angel was just like the ones she had seen in a children's Bible—very large, with gigantic wings. And the angel leaned over her and said, "Don't cry, little girl. Your mother will be back tomorrow." When the little girl awoke, she looked around, but her mother wasn't there. She was disappointed but, after all, it was only a dream. She went to school as usual. When she came home for lunch, Grandma Bessie said, "I have a surprise for you," and she pointed to the living room. And guess who was sitting in the living room? Mother had come back! The dream had come true. And, for a long time, the little girl was convinced that it was her God friend who had made it happen.

When the little girl grew up, she married and had children of her own. One of her sons had a little girl named Maggie, and another named Janet. And this story was written for them by their Grandma Adrienne.

The Cardinal

Sarah Wellen

The Cardinal came to lunch today
In stately robes of red.
He deigned to dine in my back yard
With other birds I fed.

His brown-plumed mate, two steps behind,
Trailed his Eminence.
She knew she must remain obscure,
Her role in life's events.

Although mere crumbs were left for her,
Her eating was restrained.
To serve her Lord she was intent,
His Grace must be sustained.

With kingly strut he did outshine
The reddest Maple tree.
He fed his fill, then, crown intact,
He flew away from me!

Daddy-O: A Father's Memoir

Michael Thal

I once considered visions the property of prophets or saints. I learned at an early age they are also for young men wishing for fatherhood. My vision wasn't a daydream formed by nights spent lying next to a pregnant wife. I was in my late twenties, unattached and without a prospect in sight. I sat in rush hour traffic, tired after a long day of teaching fifth grade. Through the windshield of my car, I looked out at Hondas, Nissans, Fords, Chryslers, and the setting sun. Magically, the glass filled with the face of a beautiful little girl. The dark-complexioned child beamed at me with a twinkle in her eye only duplicated by stars. Then she evaporated into traffic and cement. The car behind me honked. I rubbed my eyes and headed to my Santa Monica apartment, knowing I would someday be the daddy of this gorgeous child.

Four years later, July 9, 1983, my first daughter was born. Her mother and I had met while I was vacationing in Israel during the summer of 1980. After Daphna was in labor for thirty-four hours, Channie made her appearance. At 34, my dream of becoming a daddy had come to fruition.

The first years of fatherhood required patience and love—patience for the infant who woke me up with her wailing at 2 AM, and love for my wife who neglected me for the needs of the child. I was mother's aide, a job entailing trips to the market for diapers and food, and developing skills for cleaning dirty rumps.

I became a true practitioner of the fathering trade when Channie turned three. We were in an Italian restaurant with Daphna and friends. Channie sat in a highchair between her mother and me. As I took a bite of lasagna, my daughter tossed her spoon, spilled a glass of water, and wailed.

Clueless, Daphna shrugged.

I turned to Channie and said, "If you don't stop yelling, we're leaving."

She wasn't impressed. "Whaaaaaa!!"

My appetite for lasagna gone, I picked her up. To the relief of its patrons, we exited the restaurant with Channie's arms and legs flailing.

I took her to the car, placed her in the back seat of the Volvo, and said, "You are a wonderful daughter, but I don't like how you just acted. We do not scream and misbehave. Now sit there for the next three minutes and think about it."

I read a magazine. Through the rearview mirror, I caught a glimpse of her crying. My heart was broken, and all I wanted to do was comfort her, but I waited out the time. Then I invited Channie to the front seat to sit on my lap. That's when I fed her the "sandwich of love."

First, I served the compliment. "I admired how hard you worked this morning helping to plant the tomatoes." I praised her like a teacher flattering his 'A' student. I knew all those years educating other people's kids would reap personal rewards.

The middle of the sandwich was a question. "Why did we need to leave dinner?" The meat was hers, and I waited for an answer.

She shrugged, eyes downcast.

I asked, "Was Channie behaving like a big girl in the restaurant?"

She shook her head, rattling her long pigtails.

Satisfied she understood the reason for leaving our dinners, I added the top slice of the sandwich—a loving hug.

I said, "You know I love you very much."

"I wuv you, too."

"Now we'll go back into that restaurant, and you'll show me how well you can behave."

After that, I never had problems with her in restaurants. My dinner was cold, my appetite was ruined, but my first daddy victory made it all worthwhile.

My second triumph came under a cloud of fear. Daphna and I were hunting for a corner table at a local furniture store. On the way back to the Volvo, Channie darted across the street amid a din of horn blasts. I ran after her and grabbed her arm, turned her over my knee and smacked her bottom. She looked up in surprise and cried. I think she was more in shock from my hitting her than anything else. I don't believe in smacking children, for it teaches violence, and there are better ways to solve interpersonal problems without the back of a hand. However, when a life or death situation arises, extreme measures must be taken. Channie never ran across the street again.

A few years later, Channie returned from kindergarten with a picture. Tears filled my eyes and I stumbled into a chair, my mouth agape. In my trembling hand was a picture of the girl who had appeared in my vision those many years ago. A year later, my wife and I were blessed with a second daughter, Koren.

Koren wasted no time giving new meaning to "the terrible twos." Channie may have helped ease the transition by passing along her street crossing and restaurant lessons, but Koren developed her own creative forms of mischief. She threw things, failed to stay in her child's seat in the back of the car, and hit her sister. After I counted to three, in the corner she went. The time out plan: if she was two years old, she stayed for two minutes; at three she faced the wall for three minutes. I stood close by and watched her back, just so she would know she wasn't alone. Then I served "the sandwich of love"—something she needed, for her mother and I were newly divorced.

The children lived with me for the first two years, visiting their mother on weekends. After that I had them three to four days per week. Around that time, stories began floating around that Daphna was having an affair with one of our best friends. I confronted the man one day when my daughters were visiting his two girls. I said, "What's between you and Daphna is your business." I pointed to the children playing "Candyland" on the living room floor. "I don't want those kids to learn to hate." So we maintained a civil relationship. He eventually married Daphna, and over the years we have gotten together for Passover, birthdays, graduations, and other celebrations.

Three days a week, I picked up the children from school. They worked on their homework while I cooked dinner. Most of the time, I'd leave the food in the oven to help Channie read her social studies assignment or explain a science lesson. The tutoring paid off. She graduated from the University of California, Riverside with honors and is currently studying art therapy in graduate school.

Koren rarely asked for homework help. She preferred to do it herself. One day, however, she came home from school with her bottom lip extended. "What's the matter?" I asked.

"I got a 'D' in social studies."

"You want help?"

She shook her head. "No!"

"Fine, but anything less than a 'B' on your next test and you're grounded."

"Never happen," she said.

A good father practitioner must do what he says. Children respect honesty and can count on it like an anchored yacht. So, two weeks later, I grounded Koren—no TV, no phone. Every day we sat together with her social studies text, and she learned to study. This lasted for three weeks, until she came home with a clemency paper: 'A' on a Roman Civilization exam. I think those three weeks were hardest on me. I had to prepare lessons for my sixth graders and mark their papers late at night, not getting to sleep until past 1 AM, but the effort was worthwhile. The grounding prepared Koren for high school and college, where she's an honors student at the University of California, Santa Barbara.

I hit Channie once, and that was enough; the message was relayed to Koren by her sibling. I rarely yelled at my kids, because I grew up in a household where my father's temper was seldom dampened. I promised myself I wouldn't yell, though many times Koren tested me.

From years of teaching and fathering, I learned that effective men say little, but remain as supportive as an iron beam. One day, Koren was dismissed from school early. She asked if I would drive her friend home. Susan lived out of our way, but I agreed.

After we dropped Susan off, I said, "That was nice of you to help out your friend."

After the twenty-minute drive home, as I was unpacking the groceries, Koren asked me for the keys to the car. When she came back, I noticed her eyes were puffy, holding back a flood of tears.

"What's the matter?" I asked.

"I can't find my retainer. I think I left it in biology class. Can you take me to school to find it?"

Koren had lost her retainer before. She paid half the cost to the orthodontist. She knew she would have to pay the full $150 this time.

I said, "Sure, let's go."

While driving her to school, I noticed her furrowed brow and wringing hands. She was beating herself up better than any lecture I could give.

We found the retainer on the floor of her classroom and returned to the car. I said, "You know, you owe me one."

"Yeah? What is it?" she asked, her eyebrows jettisoning skyward.

"Do the same for your son or daughter one day. For the exact reason you helped Susan, I helped you. Each one of us is put here for the distinct purpose of making life easier for each other. I was given that opportunity today. I just hope you'll do the same for your kids."

"I will, Daddy-O, and thank you."

A father's words can be like a switch that causes either a short circuit of emotions, destructive and hurtful, or one that causes a series of lights to go on within the child, productive and helpful.

One Monday morning, after Channie started college, this theory was put to the test. It was 7:30 AM, and I had to prod Koren to wake up and get to school on time. While she showered, I walked Bear—Koren's responsibility. Given the urgency of the hour, I took him out.

Over a quick breakfast, I told Koren about my good deed. She said, "Thanks, Daddy-O, but I took him out at seven."

"You were up and didn't wake me?" I said. I seethed, but put my indignation in check. I wanted her to understand that she had acted irresponsibly. Unanswered questions rolled through my mind. Why did she go back to sleep? Why was she so thoughtless?

As we drove to school, I said, "It was very responsible of you to wake up early and walk Bear. However, you know you are a woman when you step outside your bubble and tend to the needs of your family."

I remained quiet during the ride to school. Koren left the ear mumbling her goodbyes and exited with a teen attitude, the demeanor that says, "I don't care." But I knew I had given her something to think about.

For the past twenty-five years, I've listened to my daughters. They come to me for advice and share their most intimate thoughts. Here's a note from Koren that shows how worthwhile those efforts were:

Dear Daddy-O: You make me cry and you make me laugh. I wouldn't be the person I am today without you teaching me that, with every step I take, there are different roads available to follow. If it weren't for you, my heart would be half full. You complete me. —Love, Koren

Last year Channie wrote this on Father's Day:

Dear Daddy-O,
   Happy Daddy's Day! I want to thank you for all the special moments and memories. I recall the time you invested in my childhood—the many hours you spent playing board games, cards, and taking Koren and I to the movies and playing miniature golf.

The dedication you put into our education—making flash cards with us when we were young to editing our college admissions papers. You were always the first to help. You always showed us love, even when we were not on our best behavior. Your unconditional love always shined through.

Thank you, Daddy, for the time, dedication, and love you put into raising me. —I love you, Channie.

Koren and Channie's words prove my point—fathering is more than being there. It's about fulfilling oneself as a man.

THE DAY AFTER MY FATHER DIED, I SAW ELVIS AT THE 7-ELEVEN

Sally Carper

As my father lay dying, I drove the 120 miles from his hometown back to my home to get the appropriate clothing for the imminent funeral service. The doctor had told us Dad might have a few days, but that he would not regain consciousness, so I said goodbye to this dear man whose voice I would never hear again.

I do not remember the drive home in the rain and the dark. My thoughts were filled with images and loving memories, and I had to fight to hold back the avalanche of tears that would make driving impossible.

I made it home and had just sat down when my big fat tabby cat jumped on my lap and snuggled up, trying to get re-acquainted with his owner, who had been gone for so many days and nights. As I held him close and listened to his comforting purr, the phone rang, bringing news that my dear father had died shortly after I left the hospital. I began to cry, and then to sob until I thought I could never shed another tear. Gathering all my resources, I began to get unpacked and re-packed for the return trip the following morning.

The day after my father died, I awoke after just a few short hours feeling surprisingly calm and rested. I quickly analyzed my feelings and decided that the stress and pain of watching my dad suffer were over, and we were both at peace. I could now move on to the next stage—whatever that might be—feeling strong and confident that I could go back and help care for my mom and see her through this, too.

I loaded my car and decided a cup of coffee was in order to start the day, so I stopped at the 7-Eleven. As I was pouring my coffee, I glimpsed a figure next to me, and then, as I turned toward the counter to pay, something made me look back. Standing at the coffeemaker with his back to me was a big man, wearing black pants and a black leather jacket with a large American flag on the back. The collar was turned up, and his longish hair seemed strangely familiar. Just then he turned—and there, looking straight at me through his sunglasses, was ELVIS!! I had a sense of the surreal as my mind registered his appearance, then I turned and left. For some reason, it did not seem all that strange.

I made it back to my parents' house in time to go to the funeral home to make some final arrangements. As we sat around a big table, listening to the funeral director, I found myself gazing out the window at a lovely pond with a fountain. Ducks were floating on the water, and geese were slowly strolling around on the cemetery grass. I found myself drifting away from my present surroundings, and I mentally floated and strolled with the ducks and geese, for how long, I do not know. It did not seem all that strange.

I am so proud of myself as I carry my father's burial clothes from the car to the funeral parlor. I do not shed a tear—I am OK! I can handle this.

That evening I again congratulate myself on how in control I am—how strong I am—and, as I prepare to retire, I do not find it strange that I have not packed any sleepwear, but I did pack my TV remote control.

All in all, this has been an interesting day. I can't wait to tell my dad that I saw Elvis at the 7-Eleven.

Dear Mr. Cosby

submitted by Sarah Bolek for her husband, Frank (1923 – 2004)

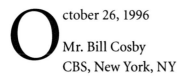

October 26, 1996
Mr. Bill Cosby
CBS, New York, NY

Dear Mr. Cosby:

When I saw you the other night on TV, I thought I would remind you of a little episode that took place way back in 1971, during one of your visits to Enrico Branducci's Coffee House in North Beach in San Francisco to play a game of chess with Enrico.

This particular night, my wife Sarah and I were sitting at a sidewalk table with a couple of friends, Mr. and Mrs. Jim O'Connell. Jim was an incorrigible name-dropper, and when I saw you coming in towards the back to meet Enrico, I thought of a devilish trick to play on him.

I went back and approached your table to talk to you. You were very friendly. I said to you, "Mr. Cosby, I have a friend outside, and I would like to teach him a lesson to cure him of his annoying name-dropping habit, but I need your cooperation."

You said, "What can I do for you?"

I said, "When I go back to my table, I will say to Jim that I have just run into my old friend, Bill Cosby. He will not believe I know you, and here is where you come in. You would walk up to the sidewalk table and, when you saw me, you would say, 'Why, if isn't my old friend, Frank Bolek.' That will impress the hell out of him."

You were such a good sport and agreed to do it. I went back to my table, very nervous, waiting for you to come by. Presently, you came by and said, "Why, if isn't my old friend, Frank Bolek." I fell apart, got all mixed up, and could hardly talk, but finally managed to say, "Bob Crosby, it is sure good to see you." You looked at me, and I am sure you must have thought I had played a dirty trick on you. You turned around and, without saying a word, went back to your table. At that point, my friend Jim said, "Frank, when you drop a name, you fracture it."

Mr. Cosby, I just wanted you to know, if you remember the episode, that I was not being a smart aleck. You gave me a perfect opportunity, and I screwed it up. Thank you for being a good sport.

Frank M. Bolek

A Universe of Stories

Albert J. Stumph

I'll never succeed as a scientist because, when I try to fathom the foundation of my universe, I don't look to atoms, molecules, quarks, protons, and other particles. The foundation of my universe is made up of stories. If I turn to theology and attempt to study the why of existence, I take what must be an heretical path, because I'm certain that it is the stories we share that hold us in existence and give our existence meaning.

One day several years ago, when I was working in my wife's antique store, a nicely dressed young woman, whom I quickly sized up as the spoiled daughter of a weekender, sauntered into the store. I was not surprised when she immediately demanded of me, "I need a small wooden box. Do you have any? My boyfriend likes boxes, and I want to get him one for Christmas."

My wife, Kathy, had a large collection of wooden boxes of all sizes in the store. I showed the woman a couple, and then suggested she continue looking around to see if any caught her eye. Less than a minute later, carrying a box about a foot square and eight inches deep, she came back to me. I saw that the box had four drawers, one set above the other on each side. Geometric designs were roughly carved on the face of each. Made from pine, oak, and one other wood I could not immediately identify, it broadcast character, but no artistic value.

"Can you tell me where this box came from? Do you know anything about it?"

I paused a moment to reflect before responding. Sometimes, if I did not know an item's history, I would invite potential customers to join me in creating a fictional story for the object that interested them.

I'd begin, "You know, this lamp was originally one of a pair that sat on..."

"...a dresser in the bedroom of..." the customer would continue.

"...one of the most crafty young women in the county." I might add. We'd continue to build our story in whatever direction our imaginations took us.

But I judged this young woman to be one who would not be interested in engaging that way, so I replied, "No, my wife picks most of her stock up at tag or estate sales and auctions. It's rare that we know the history of an item." I was hesitant to tell her that the box appeared poorly constructed, not a particularly fine piece. So I added, "It looks like one of a kind to me, obviously handmade."

"Well, I like it. Would you please set it aside for me while I look around to see if I can find anything else?"

After placing the box on the checkout counter, I turned to the computer and began typing.

This box was made by an old codger in 1979. He had not always been an old codger, of course. He lived most of his life in New York City, but also owned a hunting cabin near Chatham, New York. For years, he worked as the superintendent of Manhattan apartment buildings. On his time off, he often rode the Harlem Division of the New York Central railroad to Chatham, where he would spend a few days at his cabin. A year or two before train service to Chatham was terminated on the Harlem Line, he had saved enough money and was able to retire there.

One of his favorite activities was to walk along the newly abandoned railroad tracks, picking up scrap wood and other items. On rainy afternoons, he sat on his cabin porch, carving wood. Sometimes, he assembled the wood into boxes or other items for the cabin.

The man lived nearly twenty-five years in retirement, long enough to become known as an old codger. At his death, his money was dispersed to relatives. Many of his things went to auction. A box he made ended up at Welcome Home, an antique store in Chatham, where a young woman purchased it as a Christmas gift for her boyfriend. She knew he would like it.

The fact is that only that last sentence is true. But who is to say things really did not happen this way?

I printed the story on parchment paper and, when the young woman returned to the counter, I handed her those four paragraphs. As she read, a smile grew on her face. "I like it. Maybe the story is true. I'll take both the box and the story."

Customers who engaged with me in the creative process appeared to enjoy doing so. My personal attempts at writing fiction inevitably brought smiles to faces. Did creating stories sell more antiques? I have no idea. I do know that, today, my portion of the universe bulges with riches and meaning, in part because it has been molded by the stories we made up about some antiques found in a store in Chatham, New York.

My Imagination Takes No Holidays

Manuel Torrez, Jr.

We arrive early, to digest the cavernous dig,
while a cool breeze whispers long ago yarns,
and a hawk circles above, scouring and salivating.

Not far the black railroad bridge
leans against a turquoise, West Texas sky,
and my wife takes photos of yucca belles,
cactus yellows, and purple sage
that pepper Pecos Canyon in the spring.

Instinctively I lift binoculars to catch a glimpse
of Geronimo and his band of warriors
in one of the weathered caves—
my imagination takes no holidays.

Finally we devour a packed lunch of ribs,
with bottled water, and rev up the three hundred horses
in our Mercury Grand Marquis
and gallop on to Langtry and the Judge.

Chainsaws and Chinese Food

John Barbee

The year was 1972; it was spring, and I was in love. Iola and I were making plans. When and where to get married, how to find a home big enough for all of us, and I had to save up money for a ring. Just like love stories in books, we had obstacles to overcome. One of the biggest was finding time to spend together. When you are both single parents, with four children each, time alone together is hard to come by. One of the ways we found to achieve this sharing was to do our Saturday shopping together.

One Saturday morning, I arrived at her house early and eager, but she wasn't ready to go. She was trying to write a story about a man who carved wooden statues with a chainsaw. Her old Royal portable typewriter was fighting her, and I was underfoot until being told to "Pick out a book, sit down, and be quiet." I chose a book printed in 1933, titled *How to Build Your Own Home for $3,500 Dollars*.

The children, who kept dashing in to ask questions, were a worse distraction. The final interruption was when they all came in to tell Iola about the new Chinese restaurant that was opening on Whittier Boulevard. It was called the Five Lanterns and located in the old Nixon building. She sat them all down and made a deal. If they would go play and not interrupt again, when she received the check for the story she would take us all to the Five Lanterns for lunch. This was workable for them, and they disappeared into the kitchen to make cookies.

Now it was my turn to ask questions. "Didn't you say that the article was written in hopes that *Chainsaw Monthly* might buy it?"

Her answer was, "Yes, and there is only one chance in twenty that they will accept it."

My second question was, "And if it is accepted, don't they wait several months before printing it?"

She answered, "It's more like six to twelve months."

The last question was, "Don't they wait to pay until the story is printed?" Everyone knows this is true.

I told her she was sneaky, and she called it a talent that all mothers needed. She went back to her writing, and I returned to my book. After she finished the article and mailed it, we had lunch at a romantic Mexican restaurant and went shopping. Then, like all good stories, there was a twist.

Less than two weeks later, back came a letter of acceptance and a check for fifty dollars. Fair is fair, so off to the Five Lanterns went all ten of us for lunch. When we were finished, Iola gave me the fifty dollars to pay the bill. The problem with that was the lunch bill was over sixty-five dollars.

After paying, I started to tease her. "I don't know if I can afford for you to be a successful writer, if it costs me fifteen dollars every time you sell a story."

Iola smiled, patted me and said, "Don't worry about it. You don't have any money, anyway, and you probably never will have," and she was right.

The rest of the story:

I still have her book, *How to Build Your Own Home for $3,500 Dollars*. I recently found it while sorting a bookcase. After we were married, on our first anniversary, I got her an electric typewriter with interchangeable balls that had different styles of typefaces. This purchase may not seem like a romantic gift to someone else, but she loved it. And then, like all good love stories, we lived happily ever after. But that's a story for another day.

The Colman Touch

Richard O'Donnell

The Woodycrest Bar and Grill sat just east of Ogden Avenue and 167th Street, the geographic center of Highbridge. But if the Woodycrest was not quite the dead center of that Bronx community, it was certainly the social center for its patrons. One of the regulars, Hugh Caffrey, a certified intellectual with a master's degree in comparative literature, proclaimed it "the eccentric omphalos of our small universe," adding, for those who had not a clue what he was talking about, "We are but two streets removed from the bellybutton of Highbridge."

The layout of the Woodycrest was best described as traditional, meaning nondescript, as befits a neighborhood watering hole. The bar, a generous twenty feet of oak and brass rail, was immediately to the right as you entered. The bar turned at right angles at either end, adding stools for six more customers, mainly men. Women did not, as a rule, stop by for cocktails at five or nightcaps after the late show at the Crest movie theater, with one notable exception.

Loretta Crowley was the only woman who visited the Woodycrest with any regularity. But Loretta was not what you would call a regular. That term was reserved for the collection of young neighborhood men—a few married, most single—who collected there each evening to socialize, rag each other, and generally kill time. Loretta, on the other hand, kept to herself. She was young, closing on thirty, fairly attractive, wore little makeup, styled her own hair, and dressed tastefully, if inexpensively. Her signature piece was a tam o' shanter that her mother brought home from a trip to Ireland. Loretta worked full-time as a file clerk in the catalog card department of the H.W. Wilson Publishing Company down on University Avenue. Half the women in Highbridge worked at Wilson's, or so it seemed. Most were married, with older children, and looking for a second income or just something to get them out of the house. Loretta shared nothing in common with any of them. Lunchtime conversations mostly revolved around their kids, their husbands, or the physical problems that older women are heir to, leaving Loretta to her soup and sandwich. She would excuse herself early, though no one was paying attention, and return to her desk to finish her lunch hour reading or doing the Daily News crossword puzzle.

Loretta supplemented her income by working weeknights as a matron at the Crest Theater, a job she'd had since she was eighteen. Her work involved tending to the ladies' room and helping out at the candy counter. The job paid little, but it was easy work, and she got to see all the latest movies free. In time, Loretta became something of a movie buff. She saw so many movies, so many times, that she could lip-synch the dialog of her favorite scenes as they played out on the screen. I never saw her do it myself, but Caffrey said he'd caught her at it a few times, when she was supposed to be patrolling the aisles. That was the other part of her job.

On weekends, Loretta worked the day shift at the Crest. Her job then was not so much to tend the ladies' room as it was to keep the boys from running into it, setting the girls screaming and disrupting the movie in progress. This rarely happened during a John Ford western or a World War II epic, but it was fairly routine when the movie was dull, romantic, or one that required thoughtful analysis.

When the boys weren't raiding the ladies' room, they were usually raising hell in the orchestra. This involved crawling under the seats and grabbing some kid by the leg to make him jump and spill his soda, or inflating popcorn bags and punching them to explode during a kissing scene in a Joan Crawford flick. At other times, kids would just chase each other up and down the aisles and across the front of the theater, with Loretta in hot pursuit. Anyone who got caught got bounced. I was shown the door once, as were most of the guys, but Caffrey made it the focal point of the movie experience. He enjoyed baiting Loretta, then leading her a merry chase till he finally bolted out one of the fire exits. This infuriated Loretta, partly because she hated losing to the Little Blister, as she called him, but also because the sunlight streaming in from the open fire exit momentarily blinded everyone in the audience.

Loretta couldn't have been more than five or six years older than we were, but to kids that seemed like a lot. To us, "matron" described not just the job, but also the woman. Loretta Crowley seemed as if she were born to be middle-aged and still living at home with a widowed mother. We all knew she had no social life, working seven days a week at two jobs. The best she could manage was stopping by the Woodycrest after the Crest closed for the night. We reserved a stool for her nearest the door, just where the bar made its right-angle turn. Richie Berger occupied the next stool over and made it his business to see that no casual visitor dropping in for a drink appropriated Loretta's spot. Loretta would come in around midnight, take her place next to Berger, and wait while Dutch, a retired cop turned bartender, delivered her glass of port wine. Loretta leisurely drank two glasses and smoked two cigarettes over the next hour before sliding off her stool and saying good night. That was the extent of her conversation.

No one considered her stuck-up or antisocial, and everyone respected her privacy. I suppose it was partly because Loretta had thrown so many of us out of the Crest over the years that we still deferred to her. We might call her Loretta, but we thought of her as Miss Crowley. But, mostly, I think the cops, firemen, printers, electricians, and assorted blue-collars who met nightly at the Woodycrest recognized a lady in their midst. They welcomed Loretta into their company one hour a night, with the proprieties always observed. It continued like that for the better part of a year, so we were all surprised when, one evening, Caffrey violated protocol and addressed her directly from his customary spot at the center of the bar. Caffrey regularly arrived early, so he had a few in him by the time the rest of us turned up. Of all the guys who patronized the Woodycrest, he was the only one who drank enough to have it show. His condition on this evening was especially "fragile," as we chose to put it, when he opened up on Loretta.

"And what was featured at the Crest this evening, Loretta?" he asked.

Silence followed and heads were turned, first to Caffrey, then to Loretta. Loretta paused a moment, then answered, "'The Prisoner of Zenda.'"

"That's right," Caffrey said. "I completely forgot. They always show classic oldies on Wednesdays. Gives the blue-hair crowd something to wax nostalgic over. Douglas Fairbanks, Jr., playing the villainous Rupert of Hentzau with dash and panache, dueling it out with Ronald Colman. Delightful character. But Rupert wouldn't be your style," he continued. "Ronald Colman. Now, there's your man. Suave, mellifluous, delivered a mundane line as though it were a sonnet by Shakespeare."

Loretta was starting to look uneasy.

"I'll bet I know your favorite scene," Caffrey said. "The part where Colman delivers the famous 'If I were king' speech to Madeleine Carroll." With that, Caffrey raised his glass to Loretta and said, "If I were king and you my queen, you should wear a tiara instead of a tam, silk gowns in place of wool skirts, and seed pearls without a Woolworth's tag attached. And I should reach out and hand you the stars that shine instead of a glass of cheap port."

Caffrey's impersonation of Colman was dead on. If you closed your eyes, you might swear he was the actor incarnate. It was a brilliant performance, but also crude. Loretta turned red, but never budged from her stool. Ever the lady, she finished her second drink at her usual pace, stubbed out her cigarette, and said goodnight.

The tension broke the moment the door closed after her.

"Nice going, Caffrey," was all Dutch said, and he wasn't smiling when he said it. Richie Berger was more vocal.

"What the hell was that all about?" he demanded.

Caffrey shrugged his shoulders. "It was a joke," he said. "Something to brighten her otherwise drab day. I'd say she took it well."

If she had, she was the only one in the Woodycrest who did. Berger wouldn't look at Caffrey, and nobody spoke to him till closing. Caffrey smirked the whole time in that supercilious manner he often affected. I wanted to smack him right off the stool. Out on the street, after the Woodycrest closed, I put Berger's question to him again.

"Just what the hell was that all about? And don't give me that crap about brightening her day."

"She's got no business inflicting herself on us, Dan. She's older than we are—she babysat us for years in the Crest, for God's sake. She's a healthy young female who ought to be out dating instead of dangling at the end of the bar like a boil on the ass of the body politic."

"Where do you come up with this stuff?" I asked. "She's got as much right to be there as any of us. She doesn't stay long, she doesn't gab, she doesn't bother anyone."

"And she shouldn't be there," Caffrey said. "Let her find a life of her own."

"That's the first time I ever saw her angry," I said. "But at least she kept control."

Caffrey laughed. "She wasn't angry, Dan. She was embarrassed. About ten years ago, when we were maybe thirteen, the Crest once featured one of Colman's signature roles, Sidney Carton in 'A Tale of Two Cities.' Just before the end, I had to make an emergency run to the boys' room. Loretta was watching the movie from her usual place at the rear of the theater as I ran by.

"'Behave yourself, Caffrey,' she warned. I gave her my best smile and said, 'It's strictly business.' She was still there when I came out. I had made it just in time for the ending, where Sidney Carton is about to mount the guillotine, sacrificing himself to save Lucy Manet's husband. At that point, Colman delivers one of the classic lines in literature, as only Colman could do it, and I could hear Loretta whispering along with him: 'It is a far, far better thing that I do than I have ever done. It is a far, far better world that I go to than I have ever known.' Then she took out her hankie and dabbed her eyes and, so help me, I could hear her catching her breath. Would you believe it? Miss Crowley, the matron, was a romantic."

"And you waited ten years to throw that in her face," I said.

"Timing," said Caffrey. "It's all in the timing."

I left Caffrey at his apartment building and headed home. I'd known Hugh Caffrey practically my whole life, or at least I thought I had. He was always an imp who enjoyed putting his spurs into someone's flanks, but I never realized till now what a malicious little bastard he could be when he put his mind to it. It was sad, really, because he'd showed so much promise growing up. Caffrey was an only child, a small kid with weak lungs who couldn't keep up with the rest of us. He was always on the sidelines when we played stickball, kick-the-can, or touch football.

What Caffrey lacked in physical ability he made up for in brains. He was easily the smartest kid in the neighborhood—and I mean easily. While other kids learned things, Caffrey just seemed to know them. He absorbed knowledge without taking notes, could spell Czechoslovakia when he was nine, and claimed he never studied for a test. When asked how he did it, his stock answer was, "I read," and he wasn't being a smart-ass when he said it. When we graduated from grammar school, the principal handed out medals to students who excelled in English, history, math and the like. But Caffrey walked off with the big one, the medal for General Excellence, equivalent to winning the decathlon. It meant, quite simply, that Caffrey was the smartest kid in the graduating class. But we already knew that.

Caffrey also excelled in high school, where he won medals for excellence in Latin and English upon graduation. He graduated summa cum laude from college with a bachelor's degree in English, then topped that by getting his master's degree in comparative literature. A few of us went on to college, but nobody that I knew in Highbridge had a master's degree or had even heard of comparative literature. But that represented the apex of Caffrey's career. His biography from that point on could be subtitled "An Unfulfilled Life." For all his smarts, Caffrey had no goal, no sense of direction. What, after all, do you do with a degree in comparative literature? He tried to return to his alma mater to teach college-level English, but was told he lacked the requisite teaching credentials. He readjusted his sights, got himself certified, and began teaching sophomore English in one of the city's high schools. There he quickly lost patience with students who couldn't understand why books about sports didn't qualify as literature or why they should worry about their spelling when Shakespeare obviously never worried about his. That's when Caffrey decided that writing was his true calling. He took some meaningless daytime job so he might pursue his writing at night, except that most of his nights were spent at the Woodycrest, where he attributed his frequent presence to writer's block. "Nothing is moving," he once said. "I fear my muse is constipated." Even I knew better than that. One of my English teachers in college had said that successful writing was a craft infused with discipline. But discipline was alien to a man who had previously managed to distinguish himself without breaking a sweat. Caffrey finally gave up writing and took a job as a proofreader in the printing department of the H.W. Wilson Publishing Company, two floors below Loretta. A man who once read Virgil, Chaucer, Shakespeare, and Joyce for the sheer joy of their language now earned his bread scrutinizing catalogs for typos. It was no wonder he diluted his frustration nightly at the Woodycrest.

Caffrey's acerbity lay dormant for the next couple of weeks, so we all dismissed his ragging of Loretta as an isolated incident. Then another Wednesday came round. Loretta was halfway through her first drink when Caffrey asked her what was playing at the Crest. He already knew what was playing—a pair of classics, highlighting Errol Flynn at his best.

"'The Private Lives of Elizabeth and Essex' and 'They Died with Their Boots On,'" she answered.

"Again?" Caffrey said with feigned amazement. "They showed that same double bill years ago. You must remember, Loretta. You threw me out near the end of Elizabeth and Essex."

Dutch sensed something coming. "Don't start, Caffrey," he warned.

Caffrey ignored the hint. "It was right at the end of the movie," Caffrey said, addressing the bar in general. "Queen Elizabeth—Bette Davis, that is—pleads with her lover, Lord Essex—Errol Flynn, that is—to admit his treason and beg the Queen's mercy, else it's off with his head in the morning. It's the romantic highlight of the movie, with each professing love for the other. But, in the end, Essex must be his own man and take his medicine. When Essex turned to go back to his cell, tissues were flying like confetti among the girls in the audience. You could barely hear the dialogue for all the sniveling going on. Even Loretta, at the very rear of the theater, could be heard with a tear running down her nose. Isn't that right, Loretta? That's when I yelled, 'Lizzie took a headman's axe and gave Lord Essex forty whacks.' The guys got a great kick out of it, but Loretta threw me out for creating a disturbance."

"You ruined the ending," was all Loretta said.

"For the audience, Loretta, or for you?" Caffrey asked. "You always did like a teary goodbye. You gave a similar performance earlier, when Custer was taking leave of his wife before heading for the Little Big Horn. I thought that was a much better farewell than the one between Essex and Elizabeth—understated, but palpably emotional, almost erotic. I'd have cried myself, if I weren't already laughing."

"I should have thrown you out then," Loretta said.

Dutch leaned over till he was almost nose-to-nose with Caffrey. "Say what you want to anyone else here—they're used to you," he said. "But in my bar you'll treat a Lady with respect." Then he turned to me. "He's had enough, Dan. Take him home. There'll be a drink on the bar when you get back."

We walked for a full block in silence. Finally, I asked Caffrey, "Why are you suddenly so hard on Loretta? It's gone past your usual needling; it's downright cruel. I have to tell you, the guys don't like it. Keep it up, and you won't have a friend left."

"Does that include you?" he asked.

"I don't want it to come to that," I said. "Let it go. Put aside whatever's eating you and get off her case."

"She has no business there," he said. "Everyone has a reason for going to a bar. You go to socialize; I go to drink. I drink, therefore I am. Loretta has no reason. She doesn't drink—two glasses of port don't qualify—and she certainly doesn't socialize. So why is she there, five nights a week, like some stray that's lost its way home? If she needs something to give her life meaning, let her look elsewhere."

I realized then what he was up to.

"Don't do it, Caffrey. If you drive her out, the guys will never stand for it."

"Exactly," he said. "She's made herself the matron of the Woodycrest, babysitting the same bunch she used to throw out of the Crest on a Saturday afternoon, and they, poor fools, look forward to it. Enough! Let her be gone."

Talking to Caffrey was useless. I dropped him off, but I didn't go back to the Woodycrest for that drink. I hadn't the stomach for it.

The shoe dropped that same Friday. Mercifully, I had business elsewhere, but I heard the details later. Dutch said that Caffrey had come in earlier than usual and ordered old fashioneds instead of his customary short beers.

"I knew it wasn't good when he started on the hard stuff," Dutch said. "Beer does him damage enough; there was no telling what he'd be like on raw liquor. I tried stalling between rounds to slow him down, but it took only a few till he started going under. Then I cut him off. Beer or nothing, I told him."

Dutch said he had just served Loretta her first glass of port when Caffrey started.

"Loretta, I have a question that perhaps you can answer. What is it about the Woodycrest that could entice a nubile young woman to forgo the pleasures of the flesh on a Friday night for an evening with the likes of us?"

"I told him to knock it off," Dutch said, "or I'd show him the end of my nightstick."

Dutch was a man of even temper and slow to anger, as Caffrey could well attest, but it was folly to test the limits of his patience. The nightstick that Dutch kept under the bar was no idle threat.

"No need for that, my good man," Caffrey answered. "Just trying to engage the young lady in conversation." He returned to Loretta. "So what is it that brings you here on an evening when you should be in the back seat of a Chevy somewhere, defending your chastity from a sweaty male, like any respectable young girl?"

Loretta blushed, and Caffrey knew he had her. He paid no attention to the nightstick Dutch had quietly placed on the bar.

"Surely, you don't come here seeking companionship," Caffrey continued. "Ed and Denny are married, Harry's got a steady, and the rest of us eligible men might as well be eunuchs for all the interest we show in the fair sex. I ask you: When have you ever felt your virtue threatened by any of the men here? Berger's the only one who speaks to you, and with him it's like praying to a goddess. He worships the very stool you sit on. Did you know he sometimes places his hand on it to feel your lingering warmth after you've left for the night? I've caught him at it."

Loretta looked at Berger, who was now purple with rage and embarrassment. Dutch was livid. "That tears it," he said, as he gripped his nightstick.

"Let him finish," Loretta said. "Let's get it over with."

"As I was saying," said Caffrey, "you're wasting your time here, unless protection from the male sex is what you want. If that's it, may I suggest you'd be better off calling at the Temple of the Vestal Virgins on Nelson Avenue? Ring the convent bell and petition Sister Catherine for asylum. If you need a reference, mention my name. She well remembers me from grade school."

"Have you done?" Loretta asked quietly.

"One last bit of advice. If you look down the long corridor of time, you might catch a glimpse of yourself a few years hence, when two glasses of port no longer do the job, and you've graduated to four or five. By then, you'll be tossing back the first glass, the way the pros do it, and chain-smoking Chesterfields till your skin dries and your voice cracks. Then you'll be truly safe. Even poor Berger will have lost interest."

"Get out," Dutch said to Caffrey. "Get out while you still can."

"Excellent advice," said Caffrey.

With that, Caffrey picked his change off the bar and made his way out. He stopped briefly as he passed Loretta, leaned over, and whispered something, then left. An awkward moment ensued. Berger muttered something under his breath, someone belched, the toilet in the men's room flushed, but the bar was otherwise silent.

"You could hear a feather hit the floor, it was that uncomfortable," Dutch said. "It was Loretta who broke the tension. 'May I have another glass of port?' she asks, nice as you please. You had to hand it to her; the girl had class. Drank her port as if nothing had happened, finished her second cigarette, and said goodnight."

Loretta Crowley was never seen in the Woodycrest again, nor, for that matter, was Hugh Caffrey. He dropped from sight in a sort of self-imposed exile. The Woodycrest, he knew, was forever closed to him. It was the price he paid.

Whatever spell the Woodycrest had over me disappeared with Caffrey and Loretta. Eventually, I moved north to the Kingsbridge section of the Bronx, which was closer to my job. Still, I dropped by the Woodycrest from time to time to keep tabs on the old crowd. Most of them had moved on, as well. Ed Foley and Denny Cross, who were on the force, had moved to Orange County, a suburban haven for members of the NYPD looking for more living space for their growing families. Harry Lewis finally married his steady and migrated to Long Island. Berger also found a soul mate and married her, but stayed in the neighborhood.

Loretta was harder to track. Most of the news about her came from Berger, whose mother attended daily Mass with Mrs. Crowley. According to him, Loretta quit her job at the Crest on the heels of the incident with Caffrey. The reason, it was said, was that she was taking classes at night school. A few years later, she quit her job at Wilson's, and she and her mother moved out of the neighborhood. Mrs. Crowley had told Mrs. Berger they'd be staying in the city, but never mentioned where, only that it was near Van Cortlandt Park. It wasn't till sometime later that I ran into Loretta.

You know what they say about New York: If you stand on a busy street corner long enough, you'll meet someone you know. It's true. I was standing at one of the busiest intersections in the Bronx, where Fordham Road crosses the Grand Concourse, and at one of the busiest times of the day, noontime. I was waiting for the light to change when I happened to look over my shoulder and saw an attractive woman coming out of Alexander's department store. She was mature, well dressed, and carried herself with assurance. It wasn't till she stepped to the curb near me that I realized who it was. The features were sharper, the hair shorter, the clothes better tailored, but it was Loretta Crowley, no question. I called to her, even though I wasn't sure how she'd react, seeing I'd been a close friend of her worst enemy. But she smiled warmly. We barely had time to exchange greetings when the light changed, so I asked if she'd join me for lunch at Addie Vallins, which was where I'd been headed.

The restaurant was crowded, but as there were just the two of us we got a table by the window fairly quickly. Sitting across from her gave me a better opportunity to see what changes time had wrought. The shy, reserved Loretta, who rarely spoke to anyone, had been replaced by a vivacious woman, who conversed easily and articulately. Her face was leaner, with sharper definition, casting shadows that set her in relief like a finely etched cameo. She wore minimum makeup and jewelry and exuded only a trace of cologne. She was dressed in a beige jacket and skirt set off with a pale lilac blouse that revealed a stately throat circled by a strand of seed pearls.

We started lunch over iced tea as we caught up on the progress of our lives in the intervening years. I told Loretta that I ran my own business as a consulting investigator, mainly on retainer for a brace of prominent law firms that paid well and promptly. My office was nearby. Loretta's biography was much the more interesting.

"I quit the Crest years ago," she said, "but I guess you heard that. I enrolled at Pace College's night school down on Park Row and graduated with a bachelor's degree in business management. It took a long time, but I had plenty of that, with no distracting personal entanglements. After I graduated, I quit Wilson's and got a job as a clerk with a law firm in Lower Manhattan and worked my way up to office manager. For the first time in my life, I was earning real money, so I splurged on a nice apartment in Riverdale for mother and me. We have a grand view of the Hudson River and the Jersey Palisades across the way. On a good day, the apartment is filled with sunlight, and in the evening mother and I sit at the window and watch the sun go down. I'd never paid attention to sunsets before. I never realized how the colors change from moment to moment, with no two sunsets ever the same. Mother loves it."

Listening to her brought back something Caffrey had said years ago: "Miss Crowley, the matron, was a romantic." Perhaps, but I noticed there was no ring on her left hand, and that she'd never mentioned any man in her life.

"You never married?" I asked.

"No. Not that I haven't been asked, and by some very eligible men. It's just that I've worked too hard for my independence to share it with anyone yet. I have my own life. Caffrey gave me that."

The remark raised my eyebrows.

"Does that surprise you?" she asked.

"Well, yes, considering how he treated you."

"That night, on his way out, Caffrey whispered something to me that explained it all."

I waited as she sipped her tea, dabbed her lips with her napkin, and replaced her glass lightly on the table.

"Heed the man's advice," she said finally.

I shook my head.

"You don't remember Dutch's last words to Caffrey? Think about it."

I recalled the scene as it had been described to me—the nightstick lying ominously on the bar, with a glowering Dutch looming over it—and the words hit me: "Get out while you still can."

Loretta smiled. "The Little Blister actually cared about me, only it wouldn't have been in character to show it. It was a noble gesture, nonetheless, and one that cost him dearly—he sacrificed his seat at the Woodycrest."

I raised my glass and intoned, with a touch of Colman, "It was a far, far better thing that he did than he has ever done."

Loretta touched her glass to mine.

"And a far, far better life that he gave me than I have ever known."

Only in Washington

Richard Lampl

Thankfully, the cacophony of the benefit was over. Jake was relieved to be outside the hotel in the cool of the autumn evening. The crisp night air had begun to dry the perspiration trickling into the armpits of his starched shirt. Valet services were notoriously slow, and there was no way he could get his car any sooner. Though it was annoying, and he would have to wait, he was happy to be out of the stuffy reception and the impersonal hotel ballroom.

In contrast to the noise coming from the ballroom, the trio waiting behind him was silent. The wife wore a full-length blue evening gown heavily saturated with sparkling sequins, a white, fake fur cape covering her shoulders. The husband was in standard black tie, as was Jake. The daughter, a younger version of the mother, was weaving slightly, a strange, insipid smile on her face. She couldn't be more than twenty, thought Jake, as he watched her pace unsteadily near the curb. Too much to drink for someone just out of her teens. He could see she was anxious to relieve the interminable wait. She was slightly chubby and didn't really fit into the green taffeta evening gown with a deep décolletage. Without warning, she staggered close to Jake, circling her arms over him like a chunky halo. She stared into his eyes and swayed as she hummed the strains of "Moon River," the last song played by the six-piece orchestra. Her parents watched the inebriated antics of their daughter with amused indifference as she pranced around Jake. Seductively waggling her hips, the girl placed her index finger on the big dimple in his chin.

"You're cute," she said, slurring her words.

This seemed to amuse her parents, but not Jake. Why didn't people exercise more control over their children? He stood as still as a marble statue, hoping she would go away. Instead she got bolder.

She cupped his face in both of her hands. "I'm gonna take you home with me," she said, and moved to kiss his face. Her parents smiled at these shenanigans. Obviously, it was not the first time they had seen her like this, and they did not disapprove. Jake didn't think it was funny at all, and he moved to avoid a wet smooch. What a terrible, unlikely time and place for someone to come on to him. How could he get rid of this spoiled youngster without causing a scene? Maybe a mild, left-handed insult would do it.

"Sure, kid, let's get laid." The line came to him out of the proverbial blue. He knew it was not original. Maybe it was a misbegotten memory of a line from a long forgotten movie. He just could not place it, but he was hoping the shock of the sexual innuendo would stop the girl before the situation got out of hand.

The reaction surprised him. Mother and father almost doubled over with a burst of laughter. Daughter giggled and would have completely encircled him in her chunky arms if a black Lincoln had not drawn up and a mustachioed attendant swung the door open.

"Time to go," said the father, and jumped into the car with his wife and daughter as if nothing had happened.

Jake could not believe what he had just witnessed. The audacity of his offensive barb had only made them laugh. Was an indecent proposal funny? Were supposedly staid Washingtonians really fun-loving players at heart? Washington was a serious place, where serious decisions were made that affected the lives of the people and the direction of the country and the world. Could it have its flip side? This thought was interrupted by the arrival of his Mustang convertible, but the phrase he had uttered would not go away. "Let's get laid." He kept thinking about it while he drove home to his condo in the West End.

Jake hated going to benefit dinners, and he hated the people who attended them. What kind of meanie could hate noble causes, like support for inner-city children or finding a cure for cancer or any of dozens of other diseases? Jake could. He had a litany of reasons. He disliked the program from beginning to end. He disliked the institutional food, usually surf and turf, and getting dressed up in black tie. He disliked the crowded heat of the reception room, invariably too small for the size of the crowd jamming into it.

He disliked the people: the aging women trying to fit into gowns too youthful and too small for them. He disliked the posturing of their gray-haired and balding husbands, who tried to look important. He disliked the attempt at small talk that turned into loud talk as more and more people arrived and proceeded to get tanked-up at the open bar. He called it competitive conversation, though "shouting match" would be a better description. Where was the class, the dignity, the grace that, years ago, was synonymous with the wearing of black tie and elegant evening gowns?

He once asked a benefit official why they didn't use the money spent on the event for the cause instead of on the open bar at the reception, two kinds of wine at the dinner table, rental of the hall, the musicians. He got the answer he expected: people who did the work wanted to be recognized. But these weren't the people who did the work. The people who did the work, at least a carefully selected few of them, were given one ten-place table in a corner as far away from the speaker's stand as possible. Most of those in attendance were people like himself. They came because the higher officials in their organization didn't want to go, but had to send someone to show interest in the cause and justify the $10,000 table they had been coaxed into buying.

Most came hoping to be recognized and make a name for themselves. Some were nondescript lawyers and accountants, heads of small firms feasting off the government larder. When he had first been given the opportunity to go to these benefits, Jake was pleased. He thought these functions would be the springboard to a successful career. And, yes, he wanted to be recognized, too, but he was disappointed. The people at these benefits were no help.

Why was he still on a low rung of the corporate ladder after five years in Washington? He had the right assets: Yale graduate, late twenties, advanced degrees in political science and communication. Editor, *Yale Daily News*, ambitious, good-looking. Women liked his curly black hair, his dimpled chin, his thin, straight English nose. Good abs, nothing outlandish in dress. He followed the dress code in *Gentleman's Quarterly*. He was a self-starter. He had worked his way through school on scholarships and earned money as a reporter for a New Haven weekly. He had a good job as communications director for a Washington lobby firm, but where was the career path upward?

Liabilities? Aide to a professor in a failed campaign for senator. No Washington or family connections. What family? His father was in construction in Burlington, Vermont. Okay, he was a carpenter and didn't earn enough to make a meaningful political contribution. No help from Mother, either. Alcoholics need help, they don't give it. His parents couldn't even pay for his student loans. Those loans were his burden.

Lots of competition in Washington. He was not the only bright, young, ambitious face. There were all those eager young men and women who came to Washington as aide to a congressman or to further some cause, and some of them stayed after the congressman lost or the cause paled. Winners stayed, losers went back to Biloxi.

Someone at the lobbying firm must have thought he had potential. Otherwise, why hire him? It was a good job, but he didn't want to write press releases for others the rest of his life. He wanted accounts of his own. The road up was through contacts. It was easier for former congressmen and administration officials in the firm. They had the contacts that Jake didn't, but how to get them?

Benefit banquets were not the answer. Where were the congressmen? The administration secretaries? Where were the celebrities? They didn't attend these tiresome benefits. Oh, sure, aging actress Bo Derek showed up at a banquet one year. She was interested in keeping inner-city teenage girls from becoming pregnant. She lost interest after one year.

Some people tried to get noticed by buying something big at the inevitable live auction. Live auctions were another disgrace to dignity. A babbling auctioneer on a stepped-up mike would wheedle and cajole his trapped audience to bid on a series of villa vacations in France, Mercedes cars, or dinners for twelve at a famous restaurant. Was this a way to get noticed? Maybe for some. A lawyer once bid $8,000 for a lunch with the Washington Redskins quarterback. Jake couldn't do that. Too costly. He had to find a less expensive way to get noticed in the inner circles of Washington.

He needed a hook, something to arouse interest. It had to be something slightly provocative—not too inflammatory, but spicy enough to get attention.

"Let's get laid?" he mused. Could this phrase get him noticed? After all, most of the people in Washington originally came from someplace else. Maybe they would appreciate a little humor to break the stuffiness of this uptight town. He had to gamble on something different. His mother, when sober, had taught him that humor opened many doors. That's where Jake got the continuous half smile and the merry look in his eyes.

On impulse, when he arrived at the office on K Street that Monday, he tried it on Nancy, the good-looking-but-no-brains receptionist.

"Good morning, kid, let's get laid," he said as he walked in the door.

"Mr. Harris!" she reacted in mock horror. "You must have had a good weekend." She laughed. She was not offended. She knew he wasn't serious. Anything this outlandish had to be a joke. Within earshot, Bill Parker, the unofficial office womanizer, laughed too. "Nice try, but you'll never make out that way. You're lucky you didn't get arrested for breaking a cardinal harassment rule." Making out was the least of Jake's motivations.

At his desk, before he fired up his computer, Jake did some thinking. Was it dangerous? No. It was impudent, but harmless, and better than a real affair. His bosses frowned on negative notoriety. An affair might get him into real trouble. What would happen if he tried it at a benefit? It was worth a try.

He had gotten away with more outlandish patter at charity benefits. At his first benefit in Washington, he was abashed by what he considered to be a private and personal question about his occupation. In Vermont, it was considered a social no-no at a party to ask what someone did for a living. Not so in Washington. Invariably, it was the first question asked after the initial introduction.

"What do you do?" Underlying this was the real question: what can you do for me? This was Washington, where contacts reigned supreme.

Before he became accustomed to this effrontery, before he started to play the "Who do you know" game himself, he had devised some atrocious answers.

"Do? Oh, I don't do, I did. I did five years for embezzlement." Or, "I'm a sex therapist." This usually stopped the questioner cold.

He decided to try his new line in one more place, a singles bar on 19th Street. He spied a perfect victim, Miss Lonely Hearts, a rotund redhead with a crooked nose and bad teeth. Instead of a variation on the "Do you come here often" line, Jake opened with, "Hiya, kid, let's get laid."

She laughed, not the least bit galled by his impudence. "That's funny." She squirmed on her stool. "Not very subtle, and not very seductive, but funny." Her smile turned to a frown. "You're supposed to lead up to it," she said, as she left her seat and waddled away to another stool farther down the bar.

Jake was encouraged. "Even Miss Loser gets the joke, and she's not offended. I'll try it at a benefit."

The next charity affair for some unpronounceable disease was at the Wardman Park Hotel with its giant ballroom that could easily seat a thousand people and its outlandishly small reception area, where the same thousand people were jammed tightly into a room suitable for five hundred. After acquiring a white wine at the open bar, Jake was eager to try his line. He approached a bare-shouldered, bare-armed, well-dieted, well-coiffed woman standing alone on the fringe of the mob.

He took a quick sip of wine and a deep breath, exhaled and walked up to the woman. She looked slightly agitated, probably peeved at not being part of the general conversation. Her face broke into a smile as Jake stopped in front of her. The last thing anyone wanted at these events was to be ignored.

Jake wasted no time. "Hiya, kid. My name is Jake. Let's get laid."

There was a pause. Her face froze. She stood motionless for three ticks of the clock, four ticks, five. Had he made a mistake? Maybe he had picked the wrong woman. This was no receptionist. This was no Miss Lonely Hearts. Maybe he should not have tried this line at all, he thought, but then the moment passed. She broke out in a hearty, open-mouthed laugh that showed a magnificent set of commercially whitened teeth.

"Oh, that's rich. Wait till I tell the girls." She turned away without a second glance at Jake and melted into the tightly interlaced crowd.

"Well," reasoned Jake as he watched her go. "She's not offended. She gets the humor. So far, so good."

He watched her move through the compact mass of partygoers and approach a flock of women on the other side of the room. They looked like a bevy of multicolored, chirping flamingos in their Claire Dratch gowns with plunging necklines and low-dipped backs. She held up her hand to put a stop to whatever inane twittering was going on. He knew he was the subject of conversation from the animated way she talked and the blatant way she pointed at him. After a mild scene of pushing and shoving to decide who should go first, the ball-gown procession began. One after the other, three women came up to him and said, "I'm Ann," or Betty or Linda, "Who are you?"

Jake did not disappoint. To each he said. "Hi, I'm Jake. Let's get laid." Nor was he let down. Their reaction was immediate and somewhat similar. They responded to the absurd suggestion with raucous laughter, ranging from a high squeal to a low snort.

One played along with a cheerful, "Not tonight, dearie," and immediately went off like the others to tell her experience to whoever would listen.

One more test. Would the stiff-necked husbands in their rigid tuxedos appreciate the comedy? Would they want to punch him? No problem. As Jake watched, when Ann, Betty, or Linda related what had happened, there was the now standard awkward moment of disbelief. One husband looked like he had just been stung by a bee. He eyeballed Jake, then broke into a shrug and a smile in appreciation of the daring joke. One husband gave his wife a pat on the bum and gently pushed her in Jake's direction.

The next day, the Washington Post's gossip column, The Reliable Source, had the item complete with his picture and pet phrase. He didn't know how they got his name. Maybe they looked it up on the guest roster.

His boss, a former long-time congressman and longer-time lobbyist, was both cautiously optimistic and pragmatic in the office next day.

"Nice going. Daring, but nice." His bent-over frame tilted forward in a Groucho Marx walk. Thirty years of verbal combat had taken its toll. "I wouldn't have tried it. If asked, I would have said don't do it, but I see it works. You now have name recognition, but watch out you don't get a bad reputation moniker attached to it. If this goes wrong, there'll be a one-way ticket back to Burlington, Vermont, and you'll have to pay for it."

Jake was on his way. Invitations cascaded in. People invited him to parties just to witness his routine. He had cracked Washington's uptight, formal attitude. You weren't an insider Washingtonian unless your wife had been verbally accosted by Jake. His host or hostess would introduce him to an unsuspecting newcomer, while others in the know gathered around to watch the unsuspecting guest's reaction. Jake didn't mind being the purveyor of the game as long as he was recognized. He was now a minor celebrity. He had the luxury of selecting which parties he would attend and made sure some Washington insider from the administration or Congress would be present at those he picked.

He discovered he had to be careful from another perspective. At a senator's house, a desperate woman took him seriously. He had a ready answer for the prominent, but unsuspecting Washington dowager who wanted to complete the assignation.

"Meet me tonight at the Willard Hotel, Suite 1616," he told her. The Willard has fifteen floors.

He had another arrow ready in his verbal quiver, which he used at a colonial mansion, one of the many that lined River Road in Montgomery

County. It was owned by a former administration official, who was now a power broker for the party in the White House.

When a more serious woman ventured, "You must get your face slapped a lot," he replied quickly, "I do. But I get laid a lot, too."

His boss rewarded Jake with two accounts based on his dubious success: a diesel association that wanted certain restrictions on the odiferous fuel removed and a Green association that wanted to save a forest in Oregon from being clear-cut. Sitting on different sides of the environmental fence didn't bother Jake. He had made the transition from Vermont and its down-to-earth principles to unprincipled Washington. In the nation's capitol, he had learned, you needed to stay objective. There was no room for sentiment. A lobbyist could not be saddled with belief in any one cause. If you wanted to succeed, you had to play tough hardball. Now he could play ball with the best of them.

Jake was giddy with his newfound success. *The Washingtonian* magazine called him one of ten rising young notables in Washington. He compared his success to the Peter Sellers character in the fantasy movie, "Being There," in which a simpleton Washington gardener, who can neither read nor write, becomes president of the United States.

After weeks of anxiously sorting through invitations, it finally came, the apogee of his success: a tasseled, gold-encrusted invitation for dinner at the White House.

On the Sidewalks of Cedar Falls

Bill Alewyn

"I like your hat!" Uncle Sam shouted between the passing cars from the opposite side of First and Main.

"It's not a hat." I pointed to the spongy six-point halo that emanated from my green forehead. "These are beams of light." I had a torch, too, just like the real Lady Liberty, but it wasn't much, just some papier-mâché piece of crap with a triple-A battery flashlight inside.

"Far out!" Personally, I always hated it when a guy shouted "Far out!" just because he probably didn't have anything intelligent to say. And, of course, it's worse when the boy is wearing stilts under his shiny red and white striped pants. Aside from that, Kent wasn't bad looking: a lot of hair, kinda tall and stringy, the perfect size and shape to play a sidewalk Uncle Sam to hustle fireworks in the middle of Iowa. Cedar Falls to be exact. It was the summer of 1967 and, corny as all this now sounds, we were all so much more innocent back then. I had just turned eighteen.

I jumped at the gig because I had recently graduated from high school and wanted to do something challenging that would build up my self-confidence. I also wanted some money and security and a little independence to call my own. That's the way it's supposed to work, right? The market pays you for your time and talents, and maybe the inconvenience of doing something you wouldn't otherwise do. That way, everyone, both labor and management, gets a little something in the bargain; it's not demeaning, and it's not exploitation—at least, that's what everyone tells you.

So, anyway, this is what happened. There were these two competing fireworks concessions in town, Liberty and Uncle Sam. For reasons beyond my marketing skills, these two competitors had set up their stands practically next door to each other on Main and First, on account of the traffic. I was paid to dress up as Lady Liberty. Kent Drummand, a boy I'd known casually since the eighth grade, shilled for the competition across the street.

Kent could see for himself I really wasn't into the whole Statue of Liberty thing, being that I was so self-conscious and all. "Come on!" he told me on my first day of work. "Get into it, Jeannie!"

"What do you want me to do?" I asked.

"You're Lady Liberty! Hold up your torch! Wave to the cars! Let's see some enthusiasm!" Kent's own enthusiasm, genuine though it was, wasn't exactly contagious.

It is embarrassing at eighteen, knowing in advance and with all your heart that you're not the Statue of Liberty type. But I needed that summer job, and it wasn't hard work, just a little more humiliating than I'd expected. That year I was 5 feet 11 inches in flats and very self-aware about my appearance in general. Being big in places didn't help matters much. You see, I was what some people might charitably refer to as "stately." Believe me, the last thing a girl at eighteen and practically still a virgin wants to be called is stately. It sounds too much like being a young Ethel Merman.

I'd had the job for a couple of days now, against my better judgment, and there were other disadvantages. Believe me, after an hour or two on your feet, those sidewalks really started to heat up. There were still more disadvantages, too. I was draped in a couple of lime-green bed sheets over my leotards and bikini, which was slightly better than being out there in your underwear. Usually, the same hecklers drove by five or six times and honked their horns. Once, a potty-mouth creep shouted, "Show us your tits!"

On the other side of the street, Uncle Sam was getting flipped off left and right by unknown political extremists, maybe libertarians who didn't believe in paying taxes, or maybe anarchists on general principle. He even had to dodge a couple of water balloons, not an easy stunt on three-foot stilts, and Kent wasn't much of an athlete to begin with. What Kent was, you might say, was outspoken and political. And this was 1967, back when everyone was, in one way or another, political: Vietnam, draft boards, civil rights, campus unrest. We hadn't gotten much campus unrest in Cedar Falls, but we did have our share of the draft. Boys my age were getting their induction notices, compliments of the real Uncle Sam. And because my father worked on the local draft board, I knew that Kent was one of them.

"That was close!" Kent shouted when a third water balloon burst between his feet. There was an attitude to his voice, the seasoned street veteran maybe, as if his life somehow remained more dangerous than mine, and I told him as much.

"At least you're not getting heckled because of your sex."

"Wanna bet?" he shouted right back.

"Occupational hazard," I said. It was true: Americans in general were angry because of the war, or someone's opposition to the war, or someone else's opposition to the opposition, and that year Uncle Sam and I were just easy targets for everyone's misplaced aggression. "You're a victim of the times!" I shouted. "Don't take it so personally."

"What do you mean?" he asked.

"You know—it's the whole Uncle Sam thing. Some people are going to react negatively to it. Besides, your character's all wrong for the image."

"What's wrong with my character?" Now it was Kent's turn to get defensive. "At least, I'm not the one getting called a slut!"

"Who's a slut?" Looking back now, I know he didn't mean anything personal by it.

"Lady 'flash us your tits' Liberty! Who do you think?"

"It's a better image than Uncle 'I Want You for Cannon Fodder' Sam!" I retaliated.

"You got that right!" he shouted right back. "Talk about your negative advertising. I'm against the war myself." That much I already knew. In fact, Kent made sure everyone in school knew he opposed the war. Like I said, he was very outspoken. Personally—if push came to shove, I mean—I guess you could say I opposed the war, too, but mostly I just wanted to avoid the subject altogether, especially out there in public.

"Here we are out on the street," I said, "getting blamed for everyone's problems."

Uncle Sam shrugged his skinny padded shoulders in a big helpless "it's beyond me" kind of gesture, which, considering our situation, certainly left a lot up to individual interpretation. I mean, if you couldn't dump your problems, both foreign and domestic, on Uncle Sam, who could you? I also knew, having been out there on the street for a couple of days, that it wasn't Kent's fault so much as the image he projected. Meanwhile, Lady Liberty, I decided, didn't symbolize American military aggression; she was all about individual freedom, and what American in his or her right mind would have a grudge against that? That's the way I figured it, anyway. But with the times being what they were, maybe I figured it wrong.

So there we were, everyone's targets, shilling fireworks in our patriotic finest, Kent all glittered up in a red, white, and blue stovepipe hat and Old

Glory tails, and me dressed up like a seasick Statue of Liberty. No, it wasn't much. Kinda pathetic, actually, if you thought about it, which I tried not to do. You see, by then, most of the girls in my class were either engaged to be married or going off to college in the next couple months. Not me. I was stuck on the sidewalks of my hometown, waving to the cars and dodging insults as they drove past.

"What's with the green?" Kent asked on my third day.

"It's supposed to be verdigris," I said.

"You mean, like a fungus?"

"Yeah, something like that." I waited for the traffic light at the corner to turn green and the cars to thin out before I asked, "So, what are you up to these days, Uncle?"

"I'm signed up for community college in the fall. Theatre Art," he said. "But there's a good chance I won't make it."

Being a Theatre Art major didn't surprise me about Kent. He was always a little too melodramatic about everything back in high school, and a lot of the girls thought he might be gay. It also explained why he was just so much more enthusiastic and career-oriented about his work. Kent liked playing to the crowd, especially the little kids. He also overdid it with the waving and the enthusiasm, in my opinion, and that's why he got the occasional water balloon and middle finger. As for me, Lady Liberty was strictly a one-time gig.

"What time do you get off work?" he asked.

"Five o'clock. You?"

"Same. Wanna go to McDonald's and get something to eat?"

"Yeah, sure."

Kent took us to the drive-up window on account of our costumes, and I just didn't want to be seen in public any more than I had to. Fries and shakes. Neither of us was much into hamburgers, which was really quite unusual back then. Afterward, he drove us back to the little strip mall where my car was parked. We stayed in his truck and slurped our shakes. This was practically dinner for me. My dad was a chamber of commerce salesman type who drove out of state a lot, and my mom worked the evening shift at a local diner outside of town. I didn't know what Kent's family was doing for dinner, but he didn't seem to be too concerned about it.

Kent was still in his Uncle Sam suit, but barefoot now that he'd taken off his shoes and stilts so he could drive. I couldn't help but notice that his feet were big and skinny, and his big toes were covered with little black hairs.

"So how was your day, Lady Liberty?" he asked.

"I've had better," I said. "I'll be glad when the Fourth of July is finally over."

"Not me," he said between hits of his chocolate shake. "Aside from the water balloons, it beats workin' at McDonald's, don't you think?"

"Anything beats workin' at McDonald's," I said. "Except maybe workin' at Jack-In-The-Box."

"American employment," he said. Then we both cracked up because it was funny and because he was still dressed up in his Uncle Sam monkey suit. Okay, maybe not that funny, but we both still laughed, out of the irony or our nerves or something that was in the air between us.

We talked a little more about work and school and our futures—mostly, *que sera, sera*—and then, before I knew it, he leaned over and kissed me. It was a pretty good kiss, actually. No, actually, it was better than just pretty good, and if you really want to know what Uncle Sam's lips tasted like, I'll tell you: chocolate shake with just the right pinch of salt. But for Kent it was just another kiss, I think, even though it took me far away from Cedar Falls to a place I hadn't been before, but desperately wanted to go. That kiss made me forget for a moment that I was just another awkward 5-foot 11-inch Iowa girl. It made me think, if just for a moment, that I was someone special and destined for a lifetime of Audrey Hepburn-type romantic adventures. But when one of my foam rubber points of light poked Uncle Sam in the eye, we both decided it was time to call it quits.

"We probably shouldn't be doing this," he said.

"Why not?" I asked. I was just beginning to get used to the idea myself.

"On account we each work for the competition," Kent said. "You know, conflict of interest." I thought for a moment he was going to mention something about the local draft board and my father being on it, but thankfully he didn't. Then he changed his voice to make it sound like Humphrey Bogart or something. "You and me, kid, we work different sides of the street." That was Kent; I guess he thought it was supposed to be funny or something.

"You really take your job seriously, don't you?" I said. Now that the kissing was over, I felt worse than before.

Then he made that same Uncle Sam shrug he'd made a couple days earlier. "It's what I do," he said. "You know, as a Theatre Art major—it's all show business to me."

"You mean it doesn't matter to you whether they make you dress up as Uncle Sam or Lady Liberty or Daffy Duck?"

"I'm an actor, Jeannie, and these jobs are like commercials to me. As an actor, you hafta do everything you can to bring in the money between Shakespeare in the park and the movies."

I hadn't seen any of Kent's movies because of the simple fact he hadn't made any yet. As for playing Shakespeare, he made a pretty hammy Mercutio back when we were juniors, and that was about it.

"I've been watching you out there on the sidewalk," he said. "You don't look like you're having much fun."

I told him I wasn't, but I didn't go into any big detail about it, either.

"You were cast against type," he said. "That isn't your fault but, as an actor, you should use that to your favor."

"Like what?" I asked.

"Tomorrow I'll bring you some greasepaint and we can paint our faces in Stars and Stripes. Everyone will love it."

"I feel so awkward out there. Almost naked."

"You just need to loosen up a little. Trust me, you have great physical presence. You remind me of—"

"Don't say Ethel Merman."

"I was going to say Marilyn Monroe."

He was playing to his new audience now, doing what he did best and trying to make me feel good about myself. Strangely enough, I liked him for that, and sometimes, when you're looking for any kind of reassurance, that's more than enough. "So what else should I do to feel more comfortable out there?" I asked.

"Listen," my know-it-all thespian friend said, "all you really have to remember is be brave and honest with yourself and at the same time stay unpredictable. That's my keynote advice to you."

"Brave and honest," I repeated, his dutiful student. "Thanks, Uncle, I think it'll help." Then, when the conversation suddenly came to a grinding halt, we started kissing each other again, and that was more than okay by me. You see, that's another thing I learned about Uncle Sam that evening: he wasn't gay.

The next day, we were back on the sidewalks outside First and Main in our Stars and Stripes greasepaint, working both sides of the street. It was different now, less competitive, and I was actually having a little fun. Kent's little theatrical tips helped. When I smiled and waved at the passing cars, I meant it, because I was smiling and waving with a real purpose now, because I was really smiling and waving at Kent. It was good for business, too. It didn't matter to either of us who sold the most fireworks; we were just having a good time playing to the crowd and each other, and the people in the cars loved us. Kent came over once and worked my side of the sidewalk for a while. What did it matter, he said, if everyone saw us together? They could just decide for themselves what brand of fireworks to buy.

Then my mom showed up around lunchtime to see how I was doing and wanted to know who was my "new best friend." More important, she wanted to know what he was doing on my side of the street. I was so embarrassed, I just wanted to quit.

"Mom, this is Kent. Kent, this is my mom."

"Well," Kent said, "I really should get back to my side of the street." And he did. And for the rest of the afternoon, the waving and the smiling wasn't nearly so much fun. After five, however, back in Kent's truck, things really started to heat up. "You were having fun out there today," he said, when we finally called it quits. "I could tell."

When I got home later that evening, my father had just driven back from a business trip to Chicago, and he was waiting for me, which was usually not a good sign. Mom had told him everything about my friend, Kent Drummand, not that there was all that much to tell.

"I don't think it's such a good idea to see that boy, Jeannie," my dad said. "Not even after work."

"I'm eighteen now," I said. "I'm an adult. Besides, he's just an old friend. Kent's not as bad as you think. He's just a little…theatrical, that's all."

My father seemed to weigh this for a few seconds. "Theatrical, huh? Is that what you two have in common?"

"Honestly, Dad, he's just a drama type, so it's really not as serious as you might think."

Calling Kent Drummand a "drama type" didn't exactly alleviate my father's concerns. And knowing what I know now, I couldn't blame my father much for being a little overly protective on top of everything else. You see, I'd gotten into a little trouble with another boy, Vernon, a hog farmer's son, back in my junior year. But that was over, and it had ended badly, and now my parents were making sure to keep me on a pretty short leash.

"The thing is, Jeannie, your mother and I just don't want to see you get hurt," he said with a weight that went far beyond a concerned father's usual responsibility.

"What do you mean by that?" I asked.

"I know for a fact that your friend, Kent Drummand, will be leaving for the Army soon, that's all," he said, his voice full of warning and apprehension.

The next day was Saturday and just about the Fourth of July. There was business enough for everyone that day. Kent and I were competitors again, at least during the hours of nine to five with thirty minutes off for lunch. In the afternoon, it got up to almost ninety degrees and, with the humidity and all, the streets really started to cook. That day I got bombarded by two red water balloons, both of them near misses that landed at my feet. Across the street, Uncle Sam got called "Murderer!" by a couple of anti-war protesters, which was really kinda funny—ironic, I mean—considering how opposed to the war he was himself.

"Take it easy, Uncle!" I shouted across the street. "Everybody's got a right to his or her opinion."

"I'm just doing my job, Lady Liberty," he said. As a performer, Kent took himself pretty seriously, a regular Brando, maybe, or maybe it was that cheesy Uncle Sam costume he wore that day, or the whole Stanislavski number he had going for himself as an actor.

"For someone who's supposed to be against the war, you can be a bit of a fascist!" I shouted, pointing at him with my torch. What I didn't expect was the emotional reaction I got out of Kent. Maybe my father was right; outside of a couple of classes together, I didn't have much in common with him. Who was Kent kidding, anyway? I had no business out here on the street. I was a big, gawky redhead who didn't look a thing like Marilyn Monroe.

"Whore!" a voice I thought I recognized shouted from a passing car. Honestly, it could have been almost anyone yelling at almost anyone. A second later, another red water balloon exploded against the sidewalk, splashing my puke-green liberty dress. When the car turned around and made a second pass, I saw that it was Vernon, my ex-boyfriend, no doubt about it this time. He tossed something with a wisp of a fuse out the passenger window at the fireworks stand behind me. It turned out to be a cherry bomb or an M-80, maybe, something illegal and dangerous. But aside from making a lot of noise, Vernon's big bang didn't amount to much, except to scare a couple of old ladies and get on my nerves with all the unwanted attention, which he was always pretty good at. Like I said, the romantic thing I had with Vernon didn't exactly end on a high note. Aside from everything else going wrong that day, it was like he was never going to let me forget it.

"I hate this stupid job and this stupid costume and this stupid town!" I screamed. By now, I could have been yelling at almost anyone, too.

"Why don't you quit?" Kent shouted. Maybe dressed up as Lady Liberty, like I was at the time, his question sounded more like an ideological challenge than it probably was.

"I don't know," I said. "Why don't you quit?"

"I need the money," he said. "Didn't I tell you? I'm leaving town. I'm going to New York at the end of the summer."

I was stunned. How could someone forget not telling someone something as important as they were leaving town? "Why?" I asked. "What's in New York?"

"Broadway! Then, I dunno, Canada maybe, if it comes down to that."

"Why? What's in Canada?"

"I got my induction notice last month. I'm 1-A, Jeannie, and it's time for me to split."

I felt sorry for Kent for just being Kent, and I felt sorry for my father just for being on the draft board, but most of all I felt sorry for me just for being me. After that, I didn't know what else to say, so I shouted, "American imperialism sucks!" at the top of my voice.

"Don't tread on me!"

"That's right!" Lady Liberty responded. "Don't tread on me!" I wasn't in love with Kent or anything serious like that, but I didn't want him to leave town, either.

Our anger really started to escalate back and forth after that. We walked off our jobs together about fifteen minutes early and talked out our troubles over a couple of chocolate shakes.

"What's wrong?" Kent asked. I guess he could tell I was really upset.

"I guess this job turned out to be less fun than I thought," I said.

"No, it's more than that," he said, taking off his rinky-dink Stars and Stripes hat. "I can see the disappointment in your eyes. What is it, Jeannie?"

It was a lot of things really, so I told him, most of it, anyway. "It's the war, and you leaving, and Cedar Falls being such a pukey little town, and me being eighteen with no place left to go."

"Come with me, Jeannie," he said. No big dramatization on his part, but I could see that he really meant it.

"Where?" I asked.

"New York City," he said. "And, afterward, Canada, if it comes down to it."

"You're crazy," I said. But I was eighteen, and I lived at home, and I was sorely tempted.

"We can do it," he said. "Together, we'll support each other through the hard times—that's what best friends are supposed to do, right?"

Best friends? I knew in my heart that my own expectations were a little beyond friendship at this point, and I was still kinda holding out for something more. Then again, why should I? Maybe Kent had heard about my reputation, undeserved though it was, thanks to that stupid Vernon. Or maybe, somewhere deep inside, a new and vulnerable part of me was beginning to hurt more than I thought it had a right to hurt. And maybe that same part of me now wanted to convince myself that Kent really was gay, because that would be the easiest solution to my latest disappointments and doubts. Looking back, it's still hard to gauge the depth of my fears and insecurities that day. All I knew for certain, from that moment forward, was that I wouldn't be going to New York City or Canada or anywhere else with my new best friend, Kent. Maybe, I remember thinking, I'll just start classes at community college in the fall, like everyone else.

"It's a dangerous world out there, sweetheart, and you gotta look out for number one." He was back to doing his stupid Humphrey Bogart.

"You keep forgetting," I said. "I've already been out there with you, Uncle, and the front lines scare me to death."

"That's funny," he said, his sad blue eyes fixed on the bottom of his empty shake. "You would have thought the experience would bring us closer together—like Uncle Sam and Lady Liberty in the trenches, or something."

"I can't go with you, Kent," I said. "What would I do in a place like New York? I can't even sell fireworks in Iowa on the Fourth of July without getting all weird about it."

"But, don't you see, Lady Liberty? It would be the brave and honest thing to do."

"That's the thing you keep forgetting about this Lady Liberty," I said, readjusting my foam rubber points of light. "I mean, it's one thing to talk about honesty and bravery, but on the inside I'm just as scared and dishonest as everyone else."

"Jeannie. I—"

"And don't preach to me about bravery, Kent, when you're the one running away."

"If I don't run away now, your father, or someone just like him, will see to it that I go to jail."

So that was it: a silly little romance that ended before it began back in the year 1967, when all eligible eighteen-year-old males were legally obligated to serve in a war many of them did not believe in. Yeah, I know, they say freedom comes with a price for every generation, and maybe it does, but at the time I didn't quite see it that way. And I didn't see much of Kent after our jobs abruptly ended on the Fourth of July, either.

We went out for shakes a couple more times that summer, but that was about it. By the end of Labor Day weekend, Kent was gone and out of my life for good. I didn't go with him, of course, for reasons I've previously mentioned. I'm a grandmother in Aimes, Iowa now. I never heard from Kent, whether he became a professional actor, or if he went to Canada, or got married, or what. The funny thing is I rarely think of him after all these years, except maybe around the Fourth of July, when I pass a fireworks stand with my husband, Vernon, on our way to Wal-Mart or the bank.

All My Courthouses Have Burned

Anita Curran Guenin

The courthouses,
the churches
have all burned;
my ancestors
elude my grasp.

Their gravestones
have blurred letters,
the unlisted occupants
spared from callers
at eventide.

Come now into daylight,
be praised for your courage,
sailing to this soil of pain,
your stoicism
in mortal winter tests.

Come now into daylight,
be praised for your fortitude
to birth a new nation,
despite interests
as narrow as a Bible,
a tax ledger.

Come out of the ashes,
Boneyards, musty pages,
let your story be heard.
Upend New England rocks
and sing your psalms,
harmonizing with the wind

Rebuilding the Divided House
—November, 2008

Joan T. Doran

We tried to build the house with solid stuff
that would withstand the ages,
forgetting that the alabaster facade
we erected to the sun need proudly rest
on trunks and limbs of ebony, as well,
and though the house grew wings
and soared to stories reaching heaven,
still, the fissures starred early,
and the beams were never thick enough
to fully bear the weight of dreams,
till finally the house began to fracture
and the people in the upper rooms
locked out those whom they had pushed below,
and those inside soon lost their sight
and hearing so they didn't see
the outstretched arms or hear
the songs and sighs outside,
so only when the wind blew strong enough
was desperation carried through
closed windows where it shattered
into unswept shards.
But then one day when those inside
despaired of shoring up the cracks
and fissures, wondering how long
before the ceiling and the walls
would tumble, too, they saw outside
a growing crowd of upturned faces
and they heard outside another voice
whose song, borne on a soaring wind,
carried keys to unlock doors
and swung a bridge where all the people,
lonely for each other for so long,
could meet and take each other
by the hand and lift each other up,
and say at last, *My brother, come:
together let us build this house
the way it should have been.*

CONTRIBUTOR'S NOTES

HELEN BENSON: How "Market Prices" was born: To those of us who grew up in the Depression, it seemed that a few dollars more would have solved all of our problems. Times were tough, but even though those too young to have lived then may picture lines of unemployed standing in the rain or a gaunt-eyed woman holding a baby as typical of the time, we were really quite happy. A dishpan filled with popped corn would be a party, and ice cream twice a summer was living *la dolce vita*. If someone had an apple tree, everyone had apples. In retrospect, "those were the days"—we just didn't realize it. [100]

MARY H. BER is a writer who has spent fifty years in classroom teaching. Currently, she teaches at Pima Community College Northwest and in writing workshops. Her most popular workshop is called "Writing from the Deep Heart," a combination of writing with Sufi meditation practices. She has been the founding editor of Moon Journal Press for the past fifteen years. Contact her at Maryhber@aol.com. [55]

BETTY P. BIRKEMARK: Born in Kansas, I've lived in Japan, Australia, and, most recently, for sixteen years in Sweden. Returning to California three years ago, I joined a small, creative writing group and started writing again. My first poem was published in high school. Later, I had poems accepted by *California Crossroads, Desert Magazine*, Ace Publications (two in *Gaze Magazine*), and *Popular Dogs*. I also sold articles to *United Church Herald* (reprinted in *Catholic Digest*) and *Fate Magazine*. At one time, I wrote weekly book reviews and humorous, short verses for two newspapers in San Diego County: *The Poway News Chieftain* and *The Escondido Times Advocate*. I once covered a waste basket with rejection slips, but emotions kept coming out in poetry. [179]

JANE BORUSZEWSKI was born in Eastern Poland and deported to Siberia in 1940. After amnesty, her family left the place of their imprisonment. While traveling by train, she and her sister and brother were put in hospital somewhere near Bukhara. They survived typhoid, but were left alone and homeless. Jane crossed the Caspian Sea in 1942 and was brought to East Africa, where she attended school in Tengeru, near Arusha, and graduated from high school. After WWII ended she refused to go back to Poland and went to work in a textile factory in England, where she met and married her husband, Walt. They emigrated to America in 1950. Their three daughters were born here. Jane went back to school and graduated from Onondaga Community College with highest honors. Jane's novel, *Escape from Russia*, based on her childhood experiences, is due to be published in 2010 by Pennywyse Press. [207]

ESTHER BRUDO: My autobiographical poem, "Oh Joy!", marks a period in adolescence of pure self-absorption and romantic excitement. The year following, the sudden death of my father and the plunge into World War II changed everything. My brother shares my intense interest in our childhood growing up in Washington, D.C., and he and I recently decided to put together poetry, prose, and photos in some kind of book form for our own satisfaction and as a valentine for the family. *OASIS Journal* has recognized and encouraged my poetry for many years. Thanks to my OASIS-sponsored poetry class and instructor, and to the *Journal*. [218]

JOHN BARBEE was born in Nebraska, raised in Wyoming, finished his education in California, then studied under Julian Haight at the Institute of Photography. His first adult work was taking wedding pictures. He served as a Navy Photographer during the Korean war. A devoted family man, he helped raise eight children, and has sixteen grandchildren and seven great-grandchildren. After retiring, he moved to a small farming community in the desert. At the age of eighty, he decided to learn to write, to leave a record of the many stories about his family. He has been writing about life, thoughts, and feelings for one year and discovered that, for an old man living alone, expressing himself in stories that he shares with others can be therapeutic. [295]

SARAH BOLEK's work has been accepted by *OASIS Journal* in 2003 and 2006. She writes: "Thank you for accepting 'Dear Mr. Cosby' for publication in *OASIS Journal 2009*. I do not know whether my husband, Frank, ever sent this letter. I do know we never received an answer. When I found it among his writings in the Creative Writing Class at OASIS, I thought it deserved a wider audience. Every word of it is true. Call it a memoir. Our children have been very impressed by their Mom breaking into print, and now to see their Dad (even though posthumously) enjoy public acclaim will be very gratifying to all of us." [289]

EVELYN BURETTA returned from California to her Midwestern roots after completing careers in technical writing and the U.S. Army Reserve. She finds retirement enjoyment in learning new writing genres. Some poetry inspirations come from her early experiences in rural southern Illinois in the 40s and 50s. "Rising From Ruins," one of her first poems, was published in the anthology, *Tree Magic: Nature's Antennas*, SunShine Press Publications, 2005; "Delayed Delight" and "Journey to Contentment" were featured in *OASIS Journal 2007* and *2008*, respectively. "Jane Pelczynski's Wedding Gift" is loosely based on a description of a Polish wedding custom from the early 1900s, as told to her by her father. Evelyn resides in St. Louis, Missouri. [168]

JACK CAMPBELL: Through the years of a satisfying career, I would occasionally write poetry for special days, a letter or a paper as a favor for a friend. When retirement loomed, my "well to go to" was overflowing, and I have not stopped writing poetry, short stories, memoirs, and an occasional song lyric. I have been published by a few insignificant outlets, but my joy still remains in the fulfillment I get from birthing a new effort. Selling my work would probably be a high, but I don't dwell on it, or need the money, which leaves me free to please myself, and not an editor. I enjoy distributing my work to shut-ins, mostly as a sounding board—their feedback can be priceless! [185]

SALLY CARPER: I have been attending a creative writing class at a local senior center for about three years. I value the writing experience, but the fellowship with my classmates and our instructor is priceless. I could not sleep after returning to my father's house the day after he died. I felt an urgent desire to put on paper the strange happenings of the day. After putting my thoughts on paper, I was able to go to bed and sleep soundly. The next morning, I found my brother at the kitchen counter, drinking coffee and reading the newspaper. He began reading a small article about a holiday parade held the day before that included marching bands, floats, and several Elvis impersonators strutting to "old geezer music." [287]

ANITA CLAY: In defiance of F. Scott Fitzgerald's pronouncement that there are no second acts in life, I am bravely and proudly embracing a third act. My first act was teaching school for 35 years while a wife and mother. At 58 I began my second act as Senior National Language Arts Consultant for Prentice Hall textbook publisher, moving from Wal-Mart and debit card to corporate America and American Express. I was awed by the respect the corporate world has for common sense and surprised by my own abilities. My second act was cut short by my husband's illness and a 24/7 caregiver role I had never imagined. Now I am a widow, finding myself through writing. World take note. I've found the OASIS—Act 3 begins! [155]

DENI COMPERE: 1924: Born. 24 moves in 18 years seeking greener pastures. Impermanence bred independence. 1942-1948: WWII, miscellaneous, a career in air cargo. 1948-1972: Married, 3 children, 7 handicap, 7 hours to solo. 1973-1983: Mexico! In fractured idioma reconstructed casa antigua and established "The Tequila Tree," a tourism business of apparel, jewelry, and crafts, quickly taking over a small mall in the Zona Dorada of Mazatlan, Sinaloa. 1983: Banks nationalized. Reaccessed, cashed in and came home. Reestablished "TTT" on 3 floors in Market Square, San Antonio. 1992: 3 months solo around the world on a freighter. Wonderful! 1996: Closed business and retired. 1996-2009. Spending most time outdoors and enjoying new challenges from OASIS. The 85 years weren't always a ball, but they sure have been interesting! [216]

ANNABELLE DEUTSCHER writes short stories, memoir, and poetry. When writing memoir, she refers to herself as "Margaret," as that name change releases any inhibitions she might have in telling the story. She also supports Willa Cather's premise that "most of the basic material a writer works with is acquired before the age of 15." [60, 61]

Now a delighted great-grandmother, JOAN T. DORAN continues to find great pleasure in writing. A poem, "Scarlet Woman," won a top prize in a recent Seacoast Writers' Association contest. Her poetry has appeared this year in *The Poets' Touchstone*, and will also be included in *The Poets' Guide to New Hampshire, 2010*. One of her memoirs appears in a collection of family stories, *Cupcakes on the Cupboard*. Her current contributions to *OASIS Journal 2009* reflect both her continuing fascination with the natural beauty of New Hampshire and her daily excitement about living in this era of amazing social change. [50, 329]

ELISA DRACHENBERG: As a former filmmaker, I am accustomed to thinking in pictures. As a perpetual foreigner, I am used to paying close attention to detail and nuance of languages not my own. As a writer, I mainly sit, despite the herniated disc that implores me to do otherwise. My repayment is manifold: I entertain myself—and hopefully others—with the characters and situations I create. By the time the movie in my head starts rolling and the soundtrack begins, I cease to exist. My actors are ruthless in their demand for truth and consequences. And though they wear me out during the day and wake me at night with bedside stories of their own, I only blame myself for letting them get away with it. [21]

MARY ROSE DURFEE, born in 1916, has lived her entire life in Central New York State. She began writing short stories eight years ago, after a grandchild asked her what life was like when she was young. Since then, she has written numerous articles and stories about her life and those around her. Some have been published in local newspapers, and she deems it a special honor to be included in *OASIS Journal* again. The idea for "Under the Full Moon" came from an old letter she found among her deceased sister's memorabilia. Her hobbies include gardening, playing cards and Bingo, cooking, and collecting antiques. At 93, Mary Rose continues to live a happy, independent life and loves keeping in touch through email. [85]

JOANNE ELLIS: Twenty-five years ago I joined a journaling group where I've struggled with writing, helped with the publication of two books relative to those struggles, and have continued to find the variety of mentors and assignments very rewarding. Writing memoirs in essay, poetry, and story form has challenged me to deal with the problems and joys of the past. Good friends made it all possible. After graduating from the University of Arizona, I taught reading to many children, both in the public schools and in our home. Today, my husband, Bob, and I live in the middle of Tucson with Maxwell, our long-haired companion. [140]

JAMES FOY is a physician poet, a retired Professor of Psychiatry from Georgetown University School of Medicine in Washington, D.C. His work has been published in medical journals and periodicals: *Pharos, Commonweal, Pulpsmith, Cistercian Studies, The Journal of Poetry Therapy*, and others. His poetry appears in the anthology, *Blood and Bone: Poems by Physicians*, University of Iowa Press, 1998. He is the author of research papers on the creative process and the creative person. In 2008 he read his poetry at the Library of Congress. His poem, "Autumn Meditations," exhibits some influence of Chinese poetry, which he has studied in translation, and frequent retreats to mountain hideaways with his adult children. [82]

MARGARET FRANCIS was a wren in the W.R.N.S. British Navy during the war and worked on the Turing Bombe, which broke the German codes. It was kept a secret for thirty years, but is now being much publicized. She has had a chapter in a book printed in England telling of her experiences in Enigma. The book, *They Kept the Secret*, is only available in Britain. Margaret has also had an article published in "A Millennium Miscellany," published by the historical society of Rickinghall, Botesdale, Hinderclay, and Redgrave. Last year, at a W.R.N.S reunion, she had an article about her work in Enigma published in a pamphlet, which was for sale. While in a writing class at OASIS, she became very interested in writing Haiku poetry. [273]

FRANK FROST: I entered the Navy four days after graduating from high school. War was raging. A year later my ship was returning from the kamikaze fury at Okinawa when the bombs were dropped on Hiroshima and Nagasaki. Within days the war was over. There was no longer a war but I had been accepted into the V12 (officer training) program, so I had my freshman year of college in uniform before being discharged. Some time around Thanksgiving I began dating a pretty, endlessly curious young woman. An attraction grew and before I could start my sophomore year we were married. Now, 63 years later, we are still married, and she is still pretty and endlessly curious…and I count myself blessed. [181]

GINGER GALLOWAY "grew up" on a small farm in northern Kentucky. She wasn't always a passionate writer; she was mostly a dreamer. Her short story, "Prince of the Night," was born of dreams, based on life experiences with her real pony, a beautiful, red Tennessee trotter. Ginger's writing includes many short stories and poems, and a delightful children's book, *Jasper*. She is currently publishing two more books for young readers, to be available in October 2009. Her goal is to encourage children to read for fun! Ginger presently resides in west Tucson with her three adorable cats. She received her Master's degree in Language, Reading, and Culture from the University of Arizona, and she invites readers to contact her at her email address: gingerkgalloway@yahoo.com [51]

KATHLEEN ELLIOTT GILROY: My eldest son, T. R. Gilroy of Casper, Wyoming, got me seriously involved in our genealogy. He, his sister, Erin, and I traveled to Missouri this June and were able to visit the farm that my great-grandfather—who came from Ireland—purchased over one hundred fifty years ago. That trip brought forth new friends, many new poems, but still too few answers about my father, who is mentioned in the memoir. [67]

CELIA GLASGOW: After years of teaching, I am trying to part with material and books I acquired over the years. There are also mounds of photos in boxes, slides in carousels, costume jewelry sadly out of date, hangers of 'thin clothes' unworn for years…I'm sure many seniors could finish this list. I thought writing about my struggles with clutter might help me and others! Ever since being introduced to Dick, Jane, and Sally, I have always loved reading. After retirement from the Defense Language Institute at Lackland AFB, I enrolled in various OASIS writing classes to explore the flipside of reading. San Antonio poets Mary Ann Haddad and Jenny Browne were two of my instructors, as well as local writer Robbie Snow and OASIS' own Gloria Jennings. [104]

HENRIETTE GOLDSMITH came to write "His Name Should Have Been Houdini" because, in looking through her files, she happened upon a delightful photo of her son, Neal, with the dog's paws on his shoulders, and thought what a wonderful story this would make. Her prior publication credit is "The Tiger in the Picture," *OASIS Journal 2007*. [109]

NATALIE GOTTLIEB is a retired Psychotherapist and a practicing fine artist. Recently, writing has been added to her pool of creative expression.

Counseling people, painting them, or writing about their struggles all seem to mirror one another. She strives to extract the hidden emotional kernel that stirs just beneath the surface and to translate that feeling into a painting, poem, or story. It is her constant search for the unseen that motivates her. Natalie is deeply concerned with the human condition and how people's desires, disappointments, and triumphs affect their lives. [250, 255]

JACKIE GRANT, 71, is a retired California Community College Counselor and Instructor. In order to encourage her husband, Nik Grant, who she believes is a wonderful writer, she signed them both up for an OASIS Creative Writing class in Escondido, CA. To her amazement, she enjoyed the challenges and rewards of writing. Limiting herself to her memoirs, she entertains her reader with an open and honest account of a life fully lived. [268]

NIK GRANT wonders if *he's* the Imperfect Character: half-writing for years without seeking publication, during which he traded a perfectly good set of green eyes for a narrow peek at the computer screen through trifocals. Getting older, yes, but no less contrarian. Give Nik lemons, you'll get apple juice. Luckily, Nik's wonderful wife dragged him into the Escondido OASIS writing class, where he was plied with writing assignment after writing assignment. It was only a matter of time before an exercise in character study caused Nik to write about an imperfect character. No lemons were harmed, but that's another story. [247]

HARLEEN GROSS has been happily married to a wonderful man, Tom, for 19 years, with whom she shares five children and six grandchildren. After she retired, she started a small home-based business of long-arm quilting. With the long-arm she completes the surface design that also makes the sandwich of the backing, the batting, and the quilt top. She loves the creativity of the design and has enjoyed the challenges of quilting for customers for over five years now. A year ago, she needed to stimulate her creativity in a different way, so joined a creative writing group. She loves writing and sharing her thoughts through the magic of words. Besides quilting, she enjoys her grandchildren, church work, gardening, family history, and writing. [238]

ANITA CURRAN GUENIN: I was born and raised in Providence, Rhode Island and now live in San Diego with my husband, Bruce. The poetry workshop at OASIS, under the guidance of Mary Harker, gave me the opportunity to try writing poetry. The poem, "All My Courthouses Have Burned," exhorts my pilgrim ancestors to reveal themselves to me directly. My genealogical research has often been stymied by missing, blurred, lost, and burned records. "The Pieta of Abruzzi" came out of seeing graphic television footage of the earthquake in Italy. The sight of this one man's suffering struck me as universal. We all try to maintain our balance on the same slippery, precarious earth. We could easily be him. [40, 328]

KATHY HAYDUKE is a native of Detroit, Michigan. During her school years, her teachers often remarked that she was a gifted writer and should pursue a career in writing. However, nearly fifty years ago, while stationed at Fort McPherson, Georgia, she met her husband, a Ukrainian immigrant. Fascinated by the story of his family's journey during WWII, she wanted to get the story down. Unfortunately, life took over, and the writing was shelved. In 2006 she joined the Cicero, New York Senior Center Journalism group. Through lots of encouragement from the other members, she started recording the life stories of people she has known. These two pieces were assignments for the group. Kathy hopes to eventually publish the saga of her husband's family. [204, 271]

ANDREW HOGAN received his doctorate in development studies from the University of Wisconsin-Madison. Before retirement, he was a faculty member at the State University of New York at Stony Brook, the University of Michigan, and Michigan State University, where he taught medical ethics, health policy, and the social organization of medicine in the College of Human Medicine. Dr. Hogan has published more than five dozen professional articles on health services research and health policy. The story included in this volume is his fifth published work of fiction and was prepared for the Advanced Fiction Workshop at Pima Community College, where he is a student of creative writing. [191]

RUTH WEISS HOHBERG: A graduate of the Cooper Union School of Art and Architecture in New York City, she holds a BA from the College of the City of New York, MA from the College of New Rochelle, and MSW from the Wurzweiler School of Social Work of Yeshiva University. "Getting Here, Ruth's Story 1935-1949" is her tale of surviving World War II. She has written a continuation of the autobiography in "The Girl from Bielsko," currently in the publication process. Accepted as a contributor to *OASIS Journal* in 2007, 2008, and 2009, she is a member of the Press Club of North San Diego County, dividing her time between writing, visual art, and travel. She is a former member of the National Association of American Pen Women. [89]

UNA NICHOLS HYNUM, a transplanted New Englander, published this year in *Poppyseed Kolache, A Year in Ink*, and *San Diego Poetry Annual*. In recent years, a finalist in James Hearst Poetry Contest, *Margie*, and *The Writers Digest*. [66]

HELEN JONES-SHEPHERD, born in New York, received her BA and MA in English Composition and Literature from California State University in San Bernardino. Retired from teaching 4 years ago, she continues to write poetry, memoirs of her world travels, essays, and some short stories. She attends Writers' Workshops, does volunteer work at church as an Advocate on Canon Law, and enjoys reading, especially the classics and Shakespeare, nature hiking, square dancing, tennis, and listening to some opera and classical music. She has been published locally, as well as in other editions of *Oasis Journal*. Her poem, "White Exultation," was written after spending a month in the "frozen tundra" of Minnesota while visiting her son, Tom, and his family last winter during the Holidays. [53]

WILL INMAN's most recent book is *I Read You Green, Mother* from Howling Dog Press, which also published *Surfings: Selected Poems*. Throughout his long career, Will Inman has produced many chapbooks of poetry, including *Leaps of Hope and Fury* (Pudding House Publications), and has conducted many poetry workshops. He lives in Devon Gables Health Center in Tucson, and can also be reached via his editors, David and Judy Ray: djray@gainbroadband.com. [39]

RUTH MOON KEMPHER has lived in St. Augustine, Florida since 1960, first at the beach, and now out in the woods. Retired from teaching at the local community college, she still owns and operates Kings Estate Press, which this summer brought out her latest collection, *The Chronicles of Madam X*. Her two dogs, Sadie and Mr. Frost, are not impressed with her work, but delight in interrupting, bringing assorted small creatures, geckos and beetles, as live gifts. [128]

Born and raised in Berlin, HELGA Kollar moved with her husband and their two children first to Michigan, then to California, where she opened Kollar Center for Health, Well Being and Education. Her MA in Psychology from Pepperdine grew out of her interest and love for people; the BFA reflects her passion for color and beauty. "As an intrepid bookworm, words come alive for me; I play with them and make up new ones. They are like music, like splashes of color, and I feel my way into a word's meaning and origins. Writing came naturally after consistently earning 'A's in essays." Living alone now in Pacific Palisades provides space for observing nature at the beach and in the mountains: for thinking, feeling, and writing. [45]

JANET KREITZ: My uncle, Bill Maddox, climbed into a B-29 "Twenty Nine Times" and sparred with death. He was a hero. Unfortunately, he died two years ago and will never know of my tribute to him. One of my life missions, documenting the family story, prompted conversations with Bill about his military service during WWII. The conversations peeled away his wrinkles, arthritic knuckles, and declining body to reveal a young man who willingly left the safe environs of home to defend America. Currently, I'm working on turning one woman's journal, begun 1908, into a book. She lived in five different houses, making each into a home for her family. My home was one of those houses. Her story is a timeless tribute to every woman. [184]

RICHARD LAMPL's story, "Only in Washington," is his second successful submission to *Oasis Journal* and reflects a frivolous look at some of the background activities of the would-be power people in our nation's capitol. Lampl, a veteran of the political wars in Washington, wrote testimony, speeches, press releases, and newsletters for an aviation advocacy group. This job of tangling with bureaucracies and congress was followed by a more benign position as author and editor of books on aviation for the McGraw-Hill Aviation Week Group. [309]

KAY LESH: I work as a professional counselor in Tucson and teach Psychology for Pima Community College. I enjoy working, so I have no plans to retire at this point. When work is no longer a pleasure, I will know it is time to stop. I have written some professional articles in the past and co-authored books on self-esteem and dealing with the psychological aspects of money. My writing is changing as I age, and I am moving into doing more personal essays and fiction. "Getting Older" grew out of taking a look at my own aging process and seeing how my ideas about aging have changed. [143]

ELEANOR LITTLE was born in Detroit, Michigan during the depression. She began piano lessons when she was four and studied classical piano until she was 14. She attended Albion College in Michigan and is a graduate of Wayne State University. She taught high school, then came to San Diego in 1958. Eleanor taught piano for 10 years, worked at the UCSD Department of Music, and began to write poetry in 1998, after she retired. She has studied in the OASIS Poetry Workshop of Mary Harker. Eleanor plays piano and is the leader of a traditional jazz ensemble called *Senior Moments Jazz Ensemble*. She takes classes, writes, gardens, and spends time with her family and Scooter, a beloved mini-poodle. [54]

ELLARAINE LOCKIE has authored seven chapbook collections of poetry. She has received eleven nominations for the Pushcart Prize, the Lois Beebe Hayna Award from *The Eleventh Muse*, the One Page Poem Prize from the Missouri Writers' Guild, the Writecorner Press Poetry Award, the Skysaje Poetry Prize, the Dean Wagner Poetry Prize, the Elizabeth R. Curry Prize from *SLAB*. Curry Prize and First Place in the 2009 Summer Shark Poetry Contest from the Aquarium of the Pacific. Ellaraine teaches poetry workshops for schools, libraries, and special interest groups, and she serves as Poetry Editor for the lifestyles magazine, *Lilipoh*. Her home page is at http://literati.net/ellaraine-lockie. [178]

ANNA MAE LOEBIG was born and raised in Pittsburgh, Pennsylvania to Irish immigrant parents who settled in a predominantly Irish area of the city. Many of Anna Mae's stories reflect the memories she and her four siblings had of her childhood days and Irish roots. She joined the Scribes OASIS Memory Writing group as a way to pass on her stories to her children and grandchildren. Her main focus is writing about her experience growing up in a loving family dominated by a strict policeman father and a gentle, soft-spoken mother. Anna Mae was surprised and delighted to have "Back Porch Callers" accepted for this year's *OASIS Journal* and again extends a very special "thank you" to Bea Hicks and Joan Zekas of the Scribes writing group for their encouragement and support. [103]

VERA MARTIGNETTI was born in New York City, raised in Jersey City and has lived the past thirty-five years of her life in Tucson, where she was a businesswoman for ten years before retiring. She has four children and six grandchildren. Her first published work, an essay in *OASIS Journal 2008*, was named Winner: Best Non-Fiction 2008. Her book, *The Widow Business—a survival guide*, will be published before the end of this year. [159]

SERETTA MARTIN, author, artist of *Foreign Dust Familiar Rain*, finalist in *Atlanta Review* and *Margie*, hosts the Barnes and Noble Poetry Series, La Mesa, California and is a regional editor of *San Diego Poetry Annual*. Her life is enriched by teaching elementary adult workshops through Border Voices Poetry Project and California Poets in the School at libraries, schools, and symposiums. Seretta's award-winning poems and art have appeared in U.S. and international publications: Best Poem, *OASIS Journal 2007*, *Margie: The American Journal of Poetry*, *The Best Of Border Voices*, *Poppyseed Kilache*, *San Diego Poetry Annual*, *A Year in Ink*, California State Poetry Society, *Tidepools*, Magee Park, St. Marks Art Festival, and on-line journals. Her book review of Anna Swir is forthcoming on Web Del Sol. [41, 154] [web.mac.com/serettamartin] [wordsoup@juno.com]

MARILYN L. KISH MASON: My love of poetry came from my father. I enjoy writing about my South Dakota prairie farm roots. I have also traveled extensively throughout the United States. While living in Concord, Massachusetts, I visited homes and graves of several great writers and poets. Attending Middlesex College, I took creative writing courses that sparked a desire to write short stories and, later, poetry. When I first signed up for Mary Harker's motivating poetry class, I was determined to develop my writing skills. Some of my poetry appears on Internet sites and in a book authored by a friend. Survivors of the Witch Creek fire inspired me to write this poem. I am pleased when people identify with the feelings expressed through my words. [42]

MELFORD P. MCLAIN: I was born in 1938 in Coolidge, Arizona, the sixth of ten children. We grew up poor, following the harvest. Our education was limited. At age forty, I was told, "You have an unusual way of expressing yourself. Why don't you try writing?" My writing teacher said, "Get your thoughts on paper. You should write fiction based on fact, because no one will believe you, anyway." The lady that put my material on the computer said, "You're sick, and I love you for it. Keep up the good work." The rooster story was written for a family letter. Now I attend a class each week and enjoy their support. [229]

LOLENE MCFALL: At an early age I knew I wanted to write, act, and be an artist. I've dabbled in each with a measure of success and great experiences. In 2002 I stumbled into the world of poetry—and my niche in the universe. Discovering a dormant talent is a thrill and being able to share is a gift to me. Thank you, Leila Joiner, for these opportunities, and to my teachers, friends, and fellow poets, who encourage and counsel me. I was recently introduced to Villanelle form poetry; "Trust in the Magic" resulted. "The Parting" is recall of a place in time, years prior to my Mom's eventual departure. At age ninety-eight, she journeyed on to other possibilities. [148, 170]

ANNE MCKENRICK: "Little Girls" is about my 11-year-old granddaughter, Cheyanne, and her friends, Payten and Kona, with whom I spend a great deal of time, and who fascinate me. I have had a lifetime love affair with words and have always written. In most every organization to which I belonged, I became editor of its newsletter. My only other personal publication was about first becoming a grandmother at 38. Those feelings have changed dramatically since then. I belong to a small weekly writing group led by Pat Arnold, who teaches creative writing at the Milwaukie, Oregon Senior Center. She and my fellow students are encouraging and critical and have everything to do with any success I achieve. Thanks to OASIS for my "15 minutes of fame." [58]

MARGARET S. MCKERROW: Born in Ireland, raised in England, and immigrated to Canada, where I met and married my English husband. Work brought us to California, where we have raised our family. I am now retired and enjoying time to write. My poem, "Leaving," is about my husband's mother, Norah, who came from England to live in our guest house. Her two passions were her grandchildren and knitting. I went to her door to invite her to join us for tea and found her exactly as my poem states. Norah died many years ago, but it was in a recent poetry class, where the assignment was to write a poem about "leaving," that I found my emotions from that moment returning and was finally able to put them into words. [136]

Tucson writer/geologist SUSAN CUMMINS MILLER, a research affiliate of the University of Arizona's Southwest Institute for Research on Women, edited *A*

Sweet, Separate Intimacy: Women Writers of the American Frontier, 1800-1922 and penned the award-winning Frankie MacFarlane mystery novels, *Death Assemblage, Detachment Fault, Quarry, Hoodoo,* and *Fracture* (in press). Her poems have appeared in regional journals and anthologies, including, among others, *OASIS Journal, What Wildness Is This: Women Write about the Southwest, SandScript 2009,* and the forthcoming *New Texas 2009* and *Western Writers of America Anthology 2009.* Observing the flowering cycle of saguaros in the Tucson Mountains inspired "One Night and a Quarter of Tomorrow." [139]

CAROLE ANN MOLETI is a midwife and nurse practitioner in New York City. She lectures and writes on all aspects of women's health with a focus on feminist and political issues. In addition to professional publications, her work has also appeared or is forthcoming in *This Path, Noneuclidean Café, The Fix, Tangent Online Review of Short Fiction,* and *The Internet Review of Science Fiction.* "Everything Must Go" is an excerpt from Carole's memoir, *Someday I'm Going To Write a Book,* which chronicles her experiences as a public health nurse in the inner city. She is at work on her second memoir *Karma, Kickbacks and Kids,* the title of which is self-explanatory. [71]

MIMI MORIARTY lives on an escarpment overlooking Albany, New York. It is there she can watch the hawks spiral over the fields. One summer, she noticed a juvenile goshawk learning to fly. She took a picture of the hawk perched on the railing of her deck. Shortly after that the hawk disappeared. Mimi is convinced the hawk had come to say goodbye. Among other interests are her three grandchildren, her poetry and short stories, and in summer spending time in the Adirondack Mountains. She has been published in many journals and magazines. Her book of poetry about the aftermath of war, *War Psalm,* was published by Finishing Line Press in 2007. [116]

ELEANOR WHITNEY NELSON has enjoyed a career as an exploration geologist traveling worldwide with her geologist husband, Frank. A longtime Tucson resident, she holds degrees in English (BA) and Geology (MS). For years, she has kept journals of her wide-ranging experiences, and often draws on them for her short stories, memoirs, poetry, and novels. With more than a dozen short works in print, she can be read in literary journals and anthologies, including *The Story Teller; Chicken Soup for the Dog Lover's Soul; Chicken Soup for the Soul: Loving Our Dogs; A Way with Murder;* and four previous *OASIS Journals.* She credits Saint Philip's Writers' Workshop for helping her develop as a writer and extends her thanks to the members for their support. [231]

JAN RIDER NEWMAN: The day Lee Roy dropped out the sky—literally— proved to be a life-changing experience. It's strange to find that learning to love an animal who will never love you back shows how much love you already have every day, for and from the human beings in your life. Lee Roy was a focal point at a pivotal time of my life. "The Party" sprang from an incident at my first major writers' conference in Santa Fe, New Mexico. I have published short stories, nonfiction, and poetry in *The New Orleans Review*, *The Denver Quarterly*, *Louisiana Literature*, and *OASIS Journal*. A story that appeared in *OASIS Journal 2008* was reprinted in *Sweet Tea and Afternoon Tales*, Gulf Coast Writers' Association, May 2009. [129, 180]

KATHLEEN A. O'BRIEN: I began writing in 2002, two years after the death of my husband. I was walking around a small lake and my first poem, "Permission" (to be happy), came to me. I've written over 500 poems now and can't stop. I wrote "You Should Have" on a cold winter day when warm stew and company were appealing. I attended Summer Writing Institute at Marist College for the third summer and Women's Writing Retreat in the Adirondacks for the first summer this year. I was a teacher. I'm now an LPN, working two days a week in a dermatologist's office. I love reading, writing poetry, dancing, gardening, and volunteering for hospice. I'm the mother of four grown children and "Nanny" to four grandsons. [93]

RICHARD O'DONNELL, a native New Yorker, says he has been a committed writer since a high school English teacher encouraged him to consider it as a career. He eventually did just that, as a business writer producing news and feature stories, annual reports, science and technology articles, and executive speeches, as well as editing several corporate newspapers and magazines. He now works freelance, writing marketing studies, editorials, and science articles for professional journals. He recently turned to writing short fiction and has since published three stories in *OASIS Journal*. Many of his stories, like the one in this issue, are set in the Bronx neighborhood where he grew up, but the characters, he states, are wholly fictional. "They exist nowhere," he says, "but on the printed page." [297]

RON PORTER lives with his wife, Erika, in the rural community of Valley Center in San Diego County, California. His writing includes short stories, spiritual essays, and poetry. In his words: "I try to write daily, just putting down on paper what comes to me. I really don't control what comes out. Also, credit must be given to the wonderful inspiration and support of others during our weekly writing class at OASIS." He is currently writing a spiritually based monthly editorial column for the Philosophical Library of Escondido, California. [165]

MIKE RAMSEY: I have written two book length manuscripts (who hasn't?) and am working on a third (who isn't?). All three are about Davy (surprise), and I hope to write one more to finish the story. Though I have sent the first novel out, and I do get some nice comments, no one seems interested. Yet. [251]

DAVID RAY lives in Tucson, where he pursues literature and activism. His books have varied themes; *The Endless Search: A Memoir*, was praised by Robert Coles as a story of childhood vulnerability become, in the hands of a gifted, knowing poet and essayist, the stirring reason for a lyrically expressive memoir. He has received the William Carlos Williams Award twice from the Poetry Society of America, an N.E.A. fellowship in fiction, the Nuclear Age Peace Foundation Poetry Award, among others. He has taught at universities in the U.S. and abroad, and was founding editor of *New Letters* magazine and *New Letters on the Air* radio program. David has also edited several anthologies and often presents readings and workshops. He lives in Tucson, and is available at www.davidraypoet.com. [36, 222]

JUDY RAY's recent book of poems is *To Fly Without Wings* (Helicon Nine Editions), and recent chapbooks are *Fishing in Green Waters, Judy Ray: Greatest Hits 1974-2008*, and *Sleeping in the Larder: Poems of a Sussex Childhood*. Of the story here, Judy writes: "In the early 1990s my husband, poet David Ray, and I spent several months in Australia, mostly in Perth in the far West. One of my favorite places to ride a bicycle there was the huge Karrakatta Cemetery, the setting for 'There Was a Crooked Man.' I imagined this man's story, but it has become so identified in my mind with the reality of the place that I have almost convinced myself it is true." [241]

CONSTANCE RICHARDSON worked in film and video for 25 years before retiring to Tucson, AZ in 2001. *Falling*, a feature she produced, was nominated for a national award in Cinematography by the American Society of Cinematographers. Her documentary, *Finest Kind*, about life on a small island in Maine, was shown at the Museum of Modern Art (MOMA) and on PBS. As a Director Fellow at the American Film institute in 1981, she directed three screenplays, two of which she also wrote. Publishing credits include "A Work in Progress" in *Art, Rage, Us & Writing by Women with Breast Cancer*, Chronicle Publishing, 1998; "Circles" in *OASIS Journal 2005*; "The Path" in *The Storyteller*, the Society of Southwestern Authors, October 2006. She has just completed her first book, *Swimming Upstream*. [171]

LENA ROACH: "Midday's Sunset" celebrates an elderly neighbor of years past who spent eight-hour days working in her yard. Under her beloved sycamore tree, she welcomed friends to sit on plastic lawn chairs and served them iced tea or hot coffee. Her corner lot, perhaps the most colorful on our street, changed with the special beauty of every season. When I thought of a submission to *OASIS Journal*, a poem I felt compelled to write in her memory was my first choice. I am grateful the judges thought it worthy of inclusion in this publication. [146]

ADRIENNE ROGERS: "A Grandmother's Tale" is dedicated to two granddaughters, now teenagers, who gave no indication of being particularly impressed with it when they read it some years ago. Maybe when they see it in print, and with "older" eyes, they will have a different reaction to it. In any case, I found satisfaction in telling the tale, and hope "outside" readers may enjoy it as well. [277]

KATHRYN ROMEY: Retiring early from elementary school teaching, I intended to immerse myself in my hobbies, one of which was writing, so I joined an OASIS group in Pittsburgh, Pennsylvania called "Scribes." Even when teaching, believing I had some original thoughts, I would often jot down my ideas, on occasion completing short poems, letters, or stories. Now, I am finding these written bits and pieces of my life experiences, often not legible, sometimes humorous, but always windows into my almost forgotten past. "A Letter to Rita" was written to a dear friend. We were hired by the Penn Hills School District in 1960 and shared many teaching and life experiences. With this letter, Rita was to know she would be forever Rita, my friend. [135]

GLORIA SALAS-JENNINGS teaches Creative Writing classes at San Antonio OASIS and has been previously published in *OASIS Journal*. "I wrote 'In Honor of My Mother' for the children and grandchildren who never knew my mother, in hopes they will see a little of the person who formed the woman I am today." [99]

NANCY STEIN SANDWEISS receives inspiration from the sights and sounds of daily life and tries to capture the ironies and complexities of relationships. Her three grandsons are a source of endless fascination and provide a rich source of ideas for her poems. She thanks teacher Mary Harker and her fellow classmates at San Diego OASIS for their ongoing encouragement and helpful critiques. [108, 228]

IRMA SHEPPARD: After twenty-some years living in Tucson, I have become water-hungry. My longing for rain has given rise to remembrance of other longings. The richness of the Sonoran Desert has underlined the richness of what is not here, of what I have yet to long for. "It Rains" arose during a walk in a mid-town neighborhood, after a vigorous thunderstorm. My short stories and poems have been published in *SandScript, OASIS Journal, Facets Magazine,* Portrait, Freshwater, *July Literary Press,* and *HeartLodge*. [107]

LUCILLE SHULKLAPPER: A workshop Leader for The Florida Center for the Book and the Palm Beach Poetry Festival, I write fiction and poetry. My work has been anthologized and appears in many publications, including *Jerry Jazz Musician*, *Slant*, and *Poetic Voices Without Borders 1 and 2*, as well as in four poetry chapbooks: *What You Cannot Have*, *The Substance of Sunlight*, *Godd*, *It's Not Hollywood*, and *In The Tunnel*. [245]

STEVE SNYDER, a native Tucsonan, has had a short story and many poems published in *The Laughing Dog*, *Erete's Bloom*, *The Tucson Poet*, *The Black Hammock Review*, and *Poetry at the River Annual Review*. He won second place in a local poetry contest in 1995 and an honorable mention in a national contest in 1990. "'Before the Kiss' is based on an event that occured during a reunion with a former girlfriend I'd not seen in 28 years." [167]

ZOLA STOLTZ is a 76-year-old widow living alone in the little hamlet of Portal, Arizona in the Chiricahua Mountains. There is plenty to write about in these environs, be it truth or fiction. She has traveled Europe and lived in Libya and Spain with her military husband. They reared three children in several states in the twenty-six years of his enlistment. As they were always far from extended family, Zola wrote constantly. Her credits include an honorable mention in the 2007 *Writers Digest* contest. She is studying with Long Ridge Writers Group, and has been encouraged to submit two different styles of her tales to magazines. Her instructor thinks she is ready. [95]

MARDY STOTSKY writes poetry and memoir (previously published in *OASIS Journal 2007*). She finds the vast changes in the ways we live fascinating, compared with early Tuscon of her childhood in the 20's and 30's. "About poetry, I'll always be learning. Sometimes, the writing is hard work; other times, it arrives almost without me." [94, 115]

ANNETTE STOVALL: I started writing poetry around 1973 in St. Louis, Missouri. Now living in Winnetka, California, I decided to write this enjambment style poem (as you can see, it groups a lot of short sentences). The loneliness is exactly what I felt as a young child. The only thing different concerning the poem is that my daughter never broached the subject of why no sister, but I could see the longing in her eyes sometimes. And she did have neighborhood girlfriends to play with, which I didn't. There were no young children on my block that I knew of. So the story poem is virtually true. [133]

ALBERT STUMPH was born near Indianapolis and attended schools in several States and Hong Kong. After joining with Kathy Kinyon in a marriage agreement nearly forty years ago, he took up a career in social services work. When Kathy opened an antique store in Chatham, New York in 2001, Albert left the world of employment to work with her and to free himself for new ventures. By that time, their four children were grown, and today he and

Kathy enjoy six grandchildren. Albert has written for foster care journals and other professional publications. He drafted "A Universe of Stories" in Kathy's store on a day when business was slow, a few weeks after the event it depicts. [291]

MICHAEL L. THAL is an accomplished freelance writer. He has written and published over sixty articles for magazines and newspapers, including *Highlights for Children, The Los Angeles Times,* and *San Diego Family Magazine.* He won First Place in Writers Digest 73rd Annual Writing Competition, Inspirational, for his story, "The Lip Reader." He also came in first place in Stepping Stones 2006 Childrens Writing Competition. His novel, *Between Two Worlds,* is currently being prepared for publication by Royal Fireworks Publishing Co. You can visit him at his website at http://www.authorsden.com/michaellthal. Michael lives in Sherman Oaks, California. You can reach him at michaelthal@sbcglobal.net. [281]

MANUEL TORREZ, JR.: "A Special Halloween" comes from experiences when I was young. The characters are from the neighborhood. "My Imagination Takes No Holidays" originated from a trip my wife and I took to see where Judge Roy Bean delt out his Law, West of the Pecos. The scene at Pecos Canyon stayed in my head, and I felt I had to share it in a poem. My work requires a lot of revision. I enjoy research. I learn more than I need, usually, and that's not a bad thing. Recent poems to be published in the anthology, *Voices Along the River,* are: "Flat as Flat Can Be," "It's Who You Think You Are," "I Wished It Were Fall," and "Isn't It Ever Going to End?" [257, 294]

SHERRIE VALITUS: Born in Iowa and transplanted to California as a teenager. Attended high school, Valley Junior College, and Skadron Business College in San Bernardino. Married, 71-year-old legal secretary, with five children, six grandchildren, and five great-grandchildren. When I was a child, my Scottish Great Grandmother, Cora Campbell, related a story to me about how she had journeyed as a teenager from Pennsylvania to Iowa in a covered wagon. I was too young to ask all the many questions to which I now wish I knew the answers. I decided to write my memoirs five years ago. I write in the hope that my stories will be read and told for posterity. "Attitude Adjustment" is the first work I have ever submitted for publication. [223]

JOANNA WANDERMAN, a native of Los Angeles, grew up in the shadows of Desilu Studios, where she made a career in TV and film production. She began writing after her retirement and now spends time attending classes at Emeritus College in Santa Monica, going to doctor's offices, and being thankful for a good life with her husband, Stanley. [101]

PHYLIS WARADY's most recent credits for her short fiction are *The Creative Writer, Fresh! Literary Magazine, Dan River Anthology, Manorborn, Fresh Ink,* and *The Magnolia Quarterly.* In addition, *Shattered Image* was awarded first place in Foster City's 2008 International Competition. To ward off hunger pangs, she also writes historical novels set in Regency England. Her latest release is *Virtue and Vice,* published by Cerridwen Press. [137]

TINA WEAVER's stories have been printed in an ezine publication. She won a short story contest and is in the process of submitting a book for publication. In response to a "Dialogue Only" contest prompt, she wrote "The Unguarded Truth" based on Alzheimer patient conversations she has heard recounted from her sister's employment. She loves to write for contests and is revising her first novel and working on a paranormal novel she hopes to have finished and ready for editing next spring. [149]

TILLIE WEBB was engaged in teaching for 56 years in elementary, middle, high school, university, and adult programs. Along the way, she earned a doctorate in Child and Youth Studies, and now enjoys writing and listening to her classmates' stories at the OASIS creative writing class in Escondido, California. When the one-word theme, Extraordinary, was suggested, she remembered an experience she had while traveling in Latin America. Those breathtaking moments at the Falls of Iguazu on the border of Argentina and Brazil were never forgotten. Another unforgettable experience on the same journey was previously published in *OASIS Journal*. She is pleased to be able to share some of her life's most meaningful moments and other creative efforts with the wider readership of *OASIS Journal*. [37]

SARAH WELLEN: Living in suburbia, raising four children, I became a back yard birdwatcher. One day, when a cardinal and his mate came to our feeder, I observed their behavior and wrote "The Cardinal." Poetry has been my passion for many years, helping me to express my feelings about the world I occupy. Previous publications include *OASIS Journal* 2004 and 2007, along with various newspapers, newsletters, and anthologies. I won first prize for unrhymed work in a statewide contest sponsored by The American Association of University Women in Florida and have won prizes in poetry contests in New York. I do poetry readings and belong to a Poet's group in my town. "The Cardinal" appears in my first self-published book, *Reflections,* August 2007. [280]

ANNE WHITLOCK, a retired teacher, shares her canyon home with two cats, Baby and Fuzzy. She began her teaching career as a Catholic nun in the 50's, when religious vocations were popular. In the 60's, as the Church adopted reforms, many young women left the convent. Today, communities are faced with the burden of caring for those who remained. In her poem, "The Old Nuns," Anne revisits the site of her earlier life in recurring dreams. [152]

NEAL WILGUS was married to the late educator, artist, and poet, Ramona Puhuyesva Wilgus, for almost thirty years. Ramona's father was a member of the Hopi Tribe in northern Arizona, and her mother was from the Isleta Pueblo, south of Albuquerque, New Mexico. Neal lives in the village of Corrales, just north of Albuquerque, and continues to write poetry, fiction, and nonfiction. His son, Warren Asa Wilgus, is active in drama and musical theatre. "Song and Dance" is based on a true incident. [220]

ORDER INFORMATION

Copies of *OASIS Journal 2008* and *2009* are available at:

www.amazon.com
www.barnesandnoble.com

Copies of *OASIS Journal* from previous years (2002-2007) may be ordered at a discount from the publisher at the address below as availability allows. Please enclose $10.00 for each book ordered, plus $3.00 shipping & handling for each order to be sent to one address.

Please make checks payable to Imago Press. Arizona residents add $0.81 sales tax for each book ordered.

Proceeds from the sale of this book go toward the production of next year's *OASIS Journal*. Ten per cent of the net proceeds are donated every year to The OASIS Institute. Your purchase will help us further the creative efforts of older adults. Thank you for your support.

Imago Press
3710 East Edison
Tucson AZ 85716

www.imagobooks.com

Breinigsville, PA USA
20 November 2009

227881BV00002B/2/P